30TH ANNIVERSARY EDITION

MINISTER'S

TAX & FINANCIAL GUIDE

2021

FOR 2020 TAX RETURNS

Your clear step-by-step guide to making minister's taxes easy.

MICHAEL MARTIN

Appreciation

This guide is a successor edition of a guide originally authored by Dan Busby. The availability of this guide today would not be possible were it not for Dan's original authorship of it and his improvements to it over the years. ECFA is most grateful for Dan's vision in creating this resource and for his contribution of its content to ECFA for publication of subsequent editions.

ECFA expresses our sincere appreciation to Mr. Michael Batts, CPA, and managing partner, Batts Morrison Wales & Lee, P.A., Orlando, Florida, and the staff of the firm for their valued assistance in reviewing the two sample tax returns included in this guide.

2021 Minister's Tax and Financial Guide

Requests for information should be addressed to:
ECFA, 440 West Jubal Early Drive, Suite 100, Winchester, VA 22601

ISBN 978-1-949365-27-6

Publisher's note: This guide is published in recognition of the need for clarification of the income tax laws for ministers. Every effort has been made to publish a timely, accurate, and authoritative guide. The publisher, author, and reviewers do not assume any legal responsibility for the accuracy of the text or any other contents.

Taxpayers are cautioned that this book is sold with the understanding that the publisher is not engaged in rendering legal, accounting, or other professional service. Readers should seek the professional advice of a tax accountant, lawyer, or preparer for specific tax questions.

References to IRS forms and tax rates are derived from preliminary proofs of the 2020 forms or 2019 forms, and some adaptation for changes may be necessary. These materials should be used solely as a guide in filling out your 2020 tax return. To obtain the final forms, schedules, and tables for filing your return, contact the IRS or a public library.

Any internet addresses (websites, blogs, etc.) and telephone numbers in this book are offered as a resource. They are not intended in any way to be or imply an endorsement by ECFA, nor does ECFA vouch for the content of these sites and numbers for the life of this book.

Printed in the United States of America

Contents

How to Use this Minister's Tax and Financial Guide

This is the 30th anniversary edition of the *Minister's Tax & Financial Guide*! As with earlier editions, this Guide, now published by ECFAPress, includes the latest tax forms from the IRS, the impact of Capitol Hill legislation, the effect of court decisions, and more.

But this 30th anniversary edition of the Guide is not just another book—it is your gateway to ECFA's incredible and FREE online resources for ministers.

- You may have a printed copy of the book in your hands. Or you may have accessed our webpage for the book (*www.ecfa.church/TaxBooks/MinistersGuide.aspx*), and you are viewing the book online.
- If you are viewing the book online, you may have already clicked on some of the links embedded in the book which open the world of ECFA's online catalog of 50 eBooks and over 700 Knowledge Center documents.
- Listening and watching may be your preferred learning style. If so, there are a series of short videos on our website that highlight the key takeaways from the guide.

You get the picture—here at ECFA, we want to serve you. We do this by helping you understand the basics of minister's taxes and finance through a variety of learning formats.

Our prayer is that God will use these resources to help you to be the best possible steward of your God-given resources and free you to focus on ministry!

Michael Martin, JD, CPA
ECFA President

New Bonus Videos for Ministers

From author: Michael Martin, ECFA President

- **Introduction**

  Video: Welcome to the World of Minister's Taxes and Finances

- **Chapter 1 – Taxes for Ministers**

  Video: Should I File My Taxes as Minister?

- **Chapter 2 – Compensation Planning**

  Video: Compensation Planning – Step-by-Step

- **Chapter 3 – The Pay Package**

  Video: Creative AND Compliant Compensation Strategies

- **Chapter 4 – Housing Exclusion**

  Video: How to Maximize the Housing Exclusion

- **Chapter 5 – Business Expenses**

  Video: Business Expense Basics

- **Chapter 6 – Retirement and Social Security**

  Video: Minister's Social Security and Medicare Tax—Avoiding the Common Confusion

- **Chapter 7 – Paying Taxes**

  Video: Paying Your Taxes: 7 Key Principles

ECFA.church/TaxGuideVideos

The **ECFA 2021** ***Church and Nonprofit Tax and Financial Guide*** continues to be one of the few resources offering tax and financial advice to churches and nonprofit organizations. Issues of financial accountability, receiving and maintaining tax-exempt status, accounting for charitable gifts, and other crucial topics receive careful and full discussion. The 2021 edition also contains a thorough description of tax laws affecting churches and other nonprofit organizations, ensuring compliance with all regulations. The book includes CARES Act updates, expert advice on handling charitable gifts, sample policies and procedures, easy techniques for simplifying financial policies and procedures, insights on expense reimbursements, key steps in sound compensation planning, and examples of required IRS filings.

Recent Developments

Special universal charitable giving deduction for 2020. In response to the Covid-19 global pandemic, Congress passed the CARES Act, including a limited above-the-line charitable deduction. Taxpayers will be able to claim up to $300 in cash contributions made to a church or nonprofit charity in 2020 as a deduction from their gross income if they take the standard deduction on their 2020 tax return (see Form 1040, Line 10b). This deduction will reduce the amount of a minister's taxable income for gifts within the limits.

Two laws change some of the rules for retirement accounts. The CARES Act also included a one-year suspension in 2020 for retirees to take required minimum distributions (RMDs). This one-year waiver applies to any retirement account subject to RMDs, such as IRAs, 401(k)s, Roth 401(k)s, and inherited accounts.

Additionally, the SECURE Act changed the age that a minister must start taking withdrawals (RMDs) from all employer-sponsored retirement plans from 70½ to 72 years of age. This change was effective for distributions required to be made after December 31, 2019.

Legislation introduced to allow ministers to opt back in to Social Security. In February 2020, Congressman Kevin McCarthy introduced a bill, the Clergy Act, that would allow ministers a two-year "open season" to effectively opt-in to Social Security.

Under the bill, an application must be filed by a minister no later than the due date of the Federal income tax return (including any extension thereof) for the minister's second taxable year beginning after December 31, 2020. This proposed legislation does not require the payment of retroactive social security taxes for years before the opt-in is effective. As this guide goes to press, this legislation has not passed Congress. ECFA will continue to monitor this and similar legislation that might alter the Social Security tax status of ministers in the future.

Key federal tax limits, rates, and other data. The IRS makes adjustments annually for certain tax items that are required to be inflation-adjusted. The tables on the next two pages provide the latest inflation-adjusted amounts, plus certain rates, and other data that are available as this guide goes to press.

Key Federal Tax Limits, Rates, and Other Data

	2019	2020	2021
Standard deductions, exemptions, and exclusions:			
Standard Deductions	Married Joint Return $24,400 Head of Household 18,350 Single 12,200 Married Separate Returns 12,200	Married Joint Return $24,800 Head of Household 18,650 Single 12,400 Married Separate Returns 12,400	Married Joint Return $25,100 Head of Household 18,800 Single 12,550 Married Separate Returns 12,550
Foreign earned income exclusion	$105,900	$107,600	$108,700
Social Security:			
SECA (OASDI & Medicare) rate	15.3% on wages up to $250,000 married-joint, $125,000 married-separate, and $200,000 all others	15.3% on wages up to $250,000 married-joint, $125,000 married-separate, and $200,000 all others	15.3% on wages up to $250,000 married-joint, $125,000 married-separate, and $200,000 all others
OASDI maximum compensation base	$132,900	$137,700	$142,800
Social Security cost of living benefit increase	2.8%	1.6%	1.3%
Medicare Part B premiums - Basic	$135.50	$144.60	$148.50
Earnings ceiling for Social Security (for employment before FRA; special formula in FRA year)	Below FRA: $17,650 Over FRA: None	Below FRA: $18,240 Over FRA: None	Below FRA: $18,960 Over FRA: None
Earnings limit in year FRA attained	$46,920	$48,600	$50,520
Benefits and contributions:			
Maximum annual contribution to defined contribution plan	$56,000	$57,000	$58,000
Maximum salary deduction for 401(k)/403(b)	$19,000	$19,500	$19,500
401(k) & 403(b) over 50 "catch up" limit	$6,000	$6,500	$6,500
Maximum income exclusion for nonqualified plans in 501(c)(3) organizations (IRC 457)	$19,000	$19,500	$19,500
IRA contribution limit – age 49 and below – age 50 and above	$6,000 $7,000	$6,000 $7,000	$6,000 $7,000
Highly compensated employee limit	$125,000	$130,000	$130,000
Maximum annual contribution to health flexible spending arrangements	$2,700	$2,750	$2,750
Other:			
Gift tax annual exclusion	$15,000	$15,000	$15,000
Estate tax annual exclusion	$11,400,000	$11,580,000	$11,700,000

	2019	2020	2021
Per diem and mileage rates and other transportation:			
Standard per diem: Lowest rates in continental USA	Lodging $94 Meals & incidentals $55	Lodging $96 Meals & incidentals $55	Lodging $96 Meals & incidentals $55
Business auto mileage rate	58 cents per mile	57.5 cents per mile	
Moving & medical auto mileage rate	20 cents per mile	17 cents per mile	17 cents per mile
Charitable auto mileage rate	14 cents per mile	14 cents per mile	14 cents per mile
Airplane mileage rate (1)	$1.21 per mile	$1.27 per mile	$1.27 per mile
Motorcycle mileage rate (1)	51.5 cents per mile	57.5 cents per mile	54.5 cents per mile
Maximum value of reimbursement of business expenses (other than lodging) without receipt	$75	$75	$75
Qualified parking monthly tax-free limit	$265	$270	$270
Transit passes/tokens-monthly tax-free limit	$265	$270	$270
Health savings accounts:			
Contribution limit: Individual Family	 $3,500 $7,000	 $3,550 $7,100	 $3,600 $7,200
Maximum annual out-of-pocket expense: Individual Family	 $6,750 $13,500	 $6,900 $13,800	 $7,000 $14,000
Maximum deductible: Individual Family	 $1,350 $2,700	 $1,400 $2,800	 $1,400 $2,800
Increase in annual contribution limit – 55 and older	$1,000	$1,000	$1,000
Earned income credit:			
Taxable and nontaxable earned income of less than (to qualify for the earned income credit):	Single/Married Filing Joint	Single/Married Filing Joint	Single/Married Filing Joint
No qualifying child	$15,570/$21,370	$15,820/$21,710	$15,980/$21,920
One qualifying child	$41,094/$46,884	$41,756/$47,646	$42,158/$48,108
Two qualifying children	$46,703/$52,493	$47,440/$53,330	$47,915/$53,865
Three or more qualifying children	$50,162/$55,952	$50,954/$56,844	$51,464/$57,414
Long-term care insurance:			
Premiums deductible as medical expense based on the insured's age before close of tax year:			
40 or less	$420	$430	$450
41 to 50	$790	$810	$850
51 to 60	$1,580	$1,630	$1,690
61 to 70	$4,220	$4,350	$4,520
More than 70	$5,270	$5,430	$5,650

(1) Privately owned vehicle mileage rates set by the U.S. General Services Administration

Note: In some instances, the rate for a particular year may apply to a tax return filed in a subsequent year.

Court affirms churches are exempt from withholding FICA tax from ministers. Individuals who qualify as ministers for tax purposes are never subject to FICA-type (Federal Insurance Contributions Act) Social Security. Therefore, churches (and other employers) should never withhold FICA-type Social Security from a minister's compensation. This is because qualified ministers are always subject to SECA-type (Self-Employment Contributions Act Social Security, calculated on Schedule SE).

These principles of the tax law are illustrated in a recent court decision. During a pastor's over 20-year tenure, the church classified him as an employee for income tax purposes and reported his compensation on Form W-2. The church did not withhold FICA Social Security from his compensation. The pastor did not pay SECA Social Security taxes with his annual Form 1040s. Neither did he opt out of paying SECA taxes.

Upon retiring from pastoral service, the pastor learned that he did not have any Social Security coverage relating to when he served the church. The pastor sued his former employer for negligence because they did not withhold FICA from his compensation. The court dismissed the lawsuit because withholding FICA tax on ministerial compensation is not required under the tax law. See *Kuma v. Greater N.Y. Conference of Seventh-Day Adventist Church, District Court Southern District of New York*, August 28, 2020.

Author's note: While a church has no *obligation* to withhold FICA-type Social Security tax from the compensation of individuals qualifying as ministers under the tax law, neither should a church *voluntarily* withhold FICA tax from a minister's pay. To do so results in a minister underpaying income and Social Security taxes because the church's FICA match (7.65%) would be categorized as tax-free compensation when it is actually fully taxable.

For more information on the proper handling of Social Security for ministers (including the alternative of a permissible SECA tax allowance), read Chapter 6 of this guide and ECFA's eBook, *10 Essentials of Social Security for Ministers.*

IRS considers change in treatment of healthcare sharing arrangements. The IRS has proposed expanding the definition of medical expenses to include payments to healthcare sharing arrangements (REG-109755-19). The intent of the IRS was to provide relief for individuals who reach or surpass the threshold for claiming medical expenses as itemized deductions on Schedule A.

The proposed regulations also raise the issue of the inclusion of payments to a healthcare sharing plan. This is important for employers. If an employer makes healthcare sharing payments on behalf of an employee and the payments constitute medical insurance in the future, they could qualify for tax-free treatment under a qualified small employer health reimbursement arrangement (QSEHRA) or an individual coverage health reimbursement arrangement (ICHRA).

Taxes for Ministers

In This Chapter

- Ordaining, licensing, or commissioning ministers
- Performing ministerial services
- Individuals not qualifying for ministerial tax treatment
- Income tax status of ministers
- Importance of the employee vs. self-employed decision on income taxes
- Social Security tax status of ministers

Taxes for ministers may seem like a maze at first, but it does not have to be overwhelming! With practical pointers and easy-to-understand explanations, this guide is here to help ministers each step of the way. Another excellent resource is ECFA's eBook, *10 Essentials of Taxes for Ministers*.

In determining who should be considered a minister for tax purposes, the opinion of the IRS, based on tax law, is the only one that counts.

It all begins with a proper understanding of the special tax provisions available to ministers and who qualifies as a "minister" for tax purposes, which is the focus of this first chapter.

There are six special tax provisions for ministers who, under federal tax rules, qualify as ministers of the gospel and are performing services that qualify in the exercise of ministry:

- For income tax purposes, exclusion of the housing allowance and the fair rental value of a church-owned parsonage provided rent-free to clergy

Remember

There is some flexibility in applying certain ministerial tax provisions. For example, a minister is exempt from mandatory income tax withholding but can enter into a voluntary income tax withholding arrangement. However, if a minister qualifies for the housing allowance, he or she is subject to self-employment Social Security tax (using Schedule SE), not FICA—this is not optional.

- For Social Security tax purposes, treatment of all ministers as self-employed as it relates to income from ministerial services
- Exemption of ministers from self-employment Social Security tax under *very limited circumstances*
- Exemption of ministerial compensation from mandatory income tax withholding
- Eligibility for a voluntary income tax withholding arrangement between the minister and the church

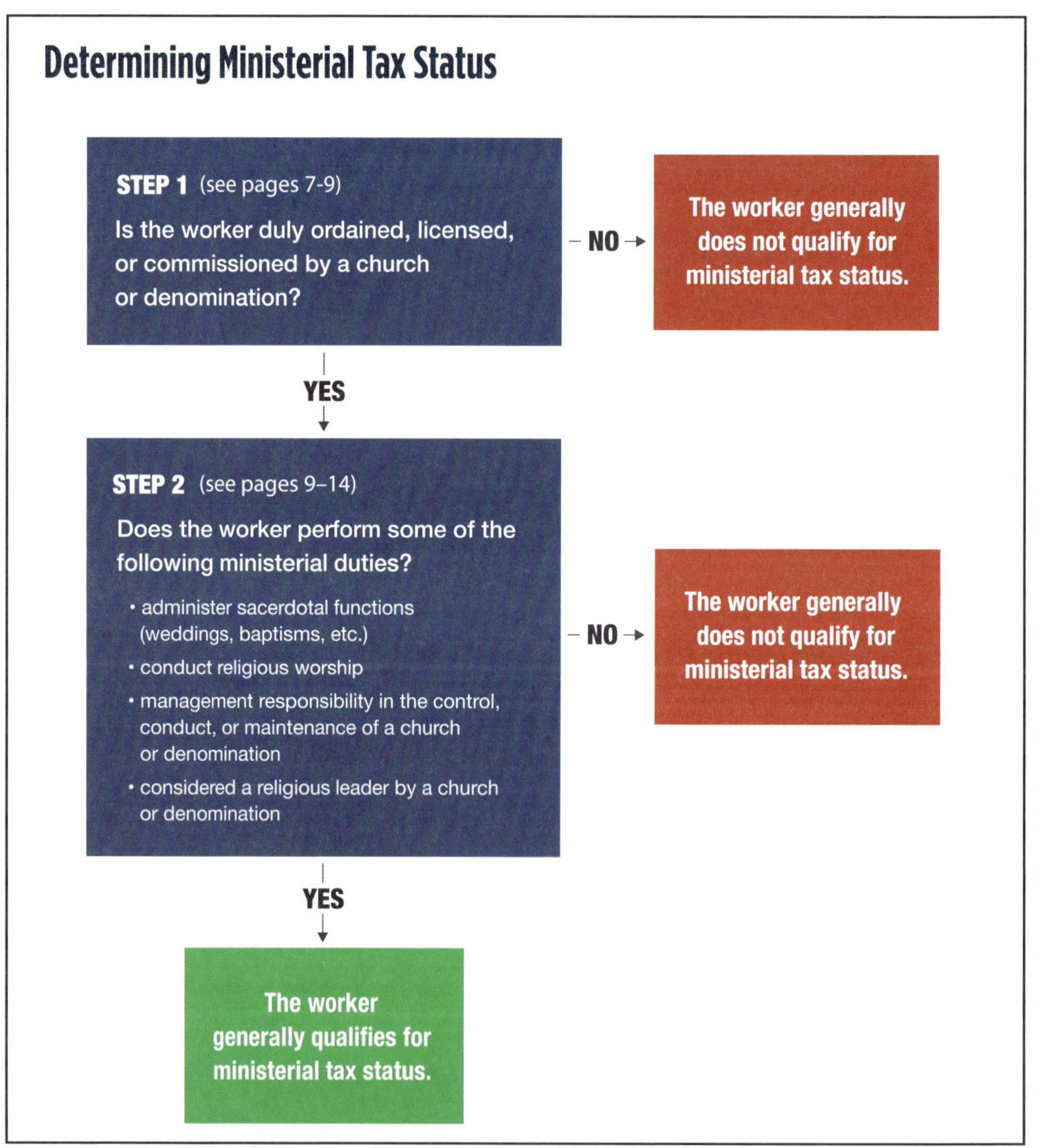

- Potential double benefit of mortgage interest and real estate taxes as itemized deductions *and* as excludable housing expenses for housing allowance purposes for ministers living in minister-provided housing

Classification as a minister for tax purposes is very important. It determines how a minister prepares federal tax returns for income and Social Security tax purposes. For example, a qualified minister is eligible for the housing allowance. This alone may be the basis to exclude thousands of dollars from income taxation. Also, ministers are subject to Social Security tax as a self-employed person and calculate self-employed Social Security tax (SECA) on Schedule SE, which is then included with other taxes on Form 1040. Conversely, nonministers are subject to Social Security tax as an employe and are responsible for paying one-half of their Social Security tax (FICA) through withholding from salary payments, while their employer pays the other half.

According to tax law, there is a two-step process for determining whether the special tax provisions available to ministers apply to a particular worker (see flowchart on page 6). The first is whether the individual qualifies as a minister. The second is whether the minister is performing ministerial services.

Related to the first step, whether an individual qualifies as a minister generally begins with determining whether he or she has been ordained, licensed, or commissioned.

Ordaining, Licensing, or Commissioning Ministers

Denominations generally have a process for ordaining, licensing, or commissioning ministers. An individual serving in a denominational church must meet the denomination's guidelines, if they exist, to obtain and retain status as an ordained, licensed, or commissioned minister. The question of whether an individual who is ordained, licensed, or commissioned by a local church will be recognized as a minister for federal tax purposes has not been directly addressed by the IRS or the courts. Still, the following steps should be considered by a local church that is considering ordaining, licensing, or commissioning individuals:

- **Appropriate bylaw provisions.** The church's bylaws (if the church is incorporated) should provide specific authority to ordain, license, or commission individuals as ministers of the gospel. This is essential to develop the proper chain of authority for ordination, licensure, or commissioning. The bylaw provision could be as simple as the following:

Caution

Ordination, licensing, or commissioning by parachurch organizations is generally not recognized by the IRS.

> *An individual may be ordained, licensed, or commissioned as a minister of the gospel by ABC church after the candidate has met the qualifications for ordination, licensure, or commissioning. These qualifications may include, but are not limited to, certain education, experience, and training. The qualifications will be determined by the governing board of the church.*

The bylaw language should not reference the tax benefits or provisions afforded to those who qualify for ordination, licensure, or commissioning. Doing so could appear to indicate to the IRS that the church is only ordaining, licensing, or commissioning individuals for the tax benefits.

- ➢ **Development of ordination, licensure, or commissioning guidelines and procedures.** If the church wishes to ordain, license, or commission individuals as ministers of the gospel, the church governing board should adopt written guidelines and procedures for ordination, licensure, or commissioning.

  In developing these guidelines, it may be important to consider requirements of formal theological training prior to being ordained, licensed, or commissioned. Another guideline for consideration might be pastoral experience in a local church.

- ➢ **Revocation of ordination, licensure, or commissioning status.** Ordination, licensure, or commissioning guidelines should include a provision that gives authority to the governing board to revoke the status, absent termination of employment *(e.g.*, in a "revocation for cause" provision). Otherwise, lifetime ordination, licensure, or commissioning status might be implied.

- ➢ **Privileges granted by ordination, licensure, or commissioning.** Additional duties and responsibilities generally come with ordination, licensure, or commissioning. The procedures and guidelines should stipulate what privileges and duties are conveyed to an individual upon ordination, licensure, or commissioning (*i.e.*, those that changed *after* the individual is ordained, licensed, or commissioned, such as conducting weddings and funerals). Detailed job descriptions would supplement the general description of the additional privileges granted.

While the process of ordaining, licensing, or commissioning varies depending on church belief and tradition, it is clear that individuals cannot be self-appointed as ministers in order to qualify for special tax treatment.

What about ministers who are licensed or commissioned but not ordained?

Some churches or denominations ordain, license, and commission ministers. Others only ordain, only commission, or only license ministers, or provide some other combination of the three types of special recognition of ministers.

Will an individual be treated as a minister by the IRS if he or she is only licensed or commissioned? It depends. Ministerial status with the IRS will depend on all the facts and circumstances, *e.g.*, the validity of the licensing or commissioning process and the extent to which the worker administers the sacraments; conducts religious worship services; has management responsibilities in the control, conduct, and maintenance of the church; and is considered to be a religious leader by the church.

> ***Example 1:*** Pastor Smith is an ordained minister who serves as a minister of counseling at his church. He does not preach or conduct worship services and never administers sacraments. He has management responsibility for the operation of a counseling center in the local church. He occasionally makes hospital visits. While he qualifies under the "control, conduct, and maintenance of the church" test, he does not administer sacraments or conduct worship services. With professional advice, the church must decide whether he qualifies as a minister for tax purposes.

> ***Example 2:*** Pastor Gomez is commissioned under guidelines established by the denomination. However, the denomination specifies that commissioning does not qualify an individual as a minister for federal income tax purposes. Therefore, Pastor Gomez does not qualify for the housing exclusion and is subject to FICA-type Social Security tax.

Not all individuals who are ordained, licensed, or commissioned qualify for ministerial tax status (see pages 14-16). The duties performed are critical to the determination of whether an individual is a duly ordained, commissioned, or licensed minister.

Performing Ministerial Services

The second step in determining whether an individual qualifies for the special tax treatment available to ministers is evaluating whether the minister is performing ministerial services.

Ministers may perform ministerial services in various settings: preaching or teaching in a local church, as evangelists and missionaries, or in denominational or other service.

Warning

Individuals serving local churches must meet certain factors to qualify as a minister in the eyes of the IRS. An individual who is not ordained, licensed, or commissioned generally does not qualify for ministerial tax status.

Ministers serving local churches

If an individual is employed by a local church and is an ordained, commissioned, or licensed minister, four factors are generally applied by the IRS to determine whether ministerial status applies under the tax law. The individual must qualify in some or all of the following areas:

Caution

Determination of ministerial status is far from a precise matter. There has been considerable inconsistency in the position of the IRS and Tax Court on this issue across the years. Only a review of all the pertinent facts and circumstances for a particular minister will assist in determining whether an individual qualifies for ministerial tax status.

- ➢ administer sacerdotal functions, such as, but not limited to, performing marriage and funeral services, dedicating infants, baptizing, and serving holy communion (The sacerdotal functions performed will often vary depending on the tenets and practices of the denomination or church to which the minister relates.)
- ➢ conduct religious worship as part of the minister's regular duties
- ➢ have management responsibility in the control, conduct, or maintenance of a church or religious denomination
- ➢ be considered a religious leader by a church or religious denomination

The IRS and the courts generally use a balancing approach in applying the four above factors; *i.e.*, some, but not necessarily all, must be met in determining ministerial status. This flexible approach is beneficial to many ministers because some ministers of music, education, youth, or administration will not meet all four factors.

There is no requirement that one must be *qualified* to perform and *actually* perform *every* sacrament or rite of his or her religion. If one is qualified to perform certain sacraments and actually performs or could perform some of the sacraments on occasion, he or she will generally meet this test. A similar test applies to conducting religious worship and providing management services. If one currently conducts religious worship and provides management services, has done so in the past, or could do so in the future, the test will generally be met.

Job titles have little significance for tax purposes. A licensed, commissioned, or ordained minister may have a job title that implies a ministry function. However, the actual responsibilities of the position will determine if the four-factor balancing test is met. Individuals performing services of a routine nature, such as those performed by secretaries, clerks, and janitors, generally do not qualify as ministers for tax purposes, even if they are ordained, licensed, or commissioned.

Missionaries

The qualifications needed for missionaries to enjoy the special ministerial tax provisions are generally the same as for ministers serving local churches.

Qualifying for benefits such as a housing allowance is often less important for a minister-missionary because of the foreign-earned income exclusion. However, the issue of ministerial tax status is vitally important to determine if the minister is subject to Social Security as an employee or as a self-employed person.

A missionary may qualify for the foreign-earned income exclusion (Form 2555) whether or not he or she qualifies for ministerial tax treatment. The foreign-earned income exclusion affects income tax but not Social Security tax.

Ministers in denominational service, on church assignment, and in other service

Denominational service

This category applies to ministers performing services in the administration of religious denominations and their integral agencies, including teaching or administration in religious schools, colleges, or universities that are under the authority of a church or denomination.

The IRS uses the following criteria to determine if an institution is an integral agency of a denomination:

- ➢ Did the denomination incorporate the institution?
- ➢ Does the corporate name of the institution suggest a denominational relationship?
- ➢ Does the denomination continuously control, manage, and maintain the institution?
- ➢ If dissolved, will the assets be turned over to the denomination?
- ➢ Are the trustees or directors of the institution appointed by or must they be approved by the denomination, and may they be removed by the denomination?
- ➢ Does the denomination require annual reports of finances and general operations?
- ➢ Does the denomination contribute to the support of the institution?

Assignment by a church to another organization

Services performed by a minister for an organization which is neither a religious organization nor operated as an integral agency of a religious organization must be based upon a *substantive* assignment by a church or denomination. Assignments must be made prospectively to be effective. Even though the minister's service may not involve the conduct of religious worship or the ministration of sacerdotal functions, all of the services performed by the minister are considered to be in the exercise of ministry.

The following characteristics must be present for an effective assignment:

- ➢ A sufficient relationship must exist between the minister and the assigning church or denomination to justify the assignment of the minister.
- ➢ Sufficient relationship must exist between the assigning church or denomination and the organization to which the minister is assigned to justify the assignment.
- ➢ The assignment must be initiated solely by the church or denominational agency.
- ➢ The duties performed by the minister must further the progress of the assigning church or denominational agency.
- ➢ The services performed by the minister must be subject to the control of the assigning church or denominational agency.
- ➢ The assigning church or denominational agency must have a history of assigning ministers.

In addressing the relationship between the church or denomination and the organization, the question to ask is why the church or denomination should assign a minister to this particular organization. Essentially, the assignment must accomplish the ministry purposes of the church or denomination.

Caution

Too often, a denomination or church lists a minister as being assigned to a parachurch ministry, and the minister believes he or she meets assignment for tax purposes. But effective assignments are generally based on the substantive relationship and ongoing documentation of the assignment.

When a church or denomination considers the assignment of a minister, it is important to distinguish between the process of assigning and the documentation of the assignment. The process of assigning expresses the church's or denomination's theology, philosophy, and policy of operation—its way of doing ministry. The documentation of the assignment provides evidence that the church or denomination is providing ministry through the particular individual assigned.

The following are keys to a proper assignment:

Key Issue

An assigned minister is not required to conduct religious worship or sacerdotal functions to receive ministerial tax treatment.

- ➢ A written policy describing the specific requirements for the relationship of the church or denomination both to the minister being assigned and to the organization to which the minister is assigned. This would include the church's or denomination's theological and policy goals for the assignment.
- ➢ A formal review to confirm the qualifications of the minister and the proposed service with the organization.
- ➢ A written assignment coupled with guidelines explaining how the church or denomination should supervise the minister and how the organization should report to the church or denomination.
- ➢ A periodic (at least annual) formal review of the minister's activities to the church or denomination confirming that the assignment continues to comply with the policy.

If a housing allowance is designated for an assigned minister, it should be designated by the employing organization, not the assigning church or denomination.

Other service

If a minister is not engaged in service performed in the exercise of the ministry of a local church or an integral agency of a church, or if a minister is not serving under a substantive assignment from a church or denomination, then the definition of a qualifying minister becomes much narrower. Tax law and regulations provide limited guidance for ministers in this category.

Tax Court cases and IRS rulings suggest that an individual in the "other services" category will qualify for the special tax treatment of a minister only if the individual's services for the employer *substantially involve conducting religious worship or performing sacerdotal functions.* This definition might include preaching, conducting Bible studies, spiritual and pastoral counseling, conducting crusades, producing religious television and radio broadcasts, and publishing religious literature.

Caution

A minister employed by a parachurch ministry does not automatically qualify for ministerial tax treatment simply by virtue of being ordained, licensed, or commissioned.

How much time constitutes substantial involvement in conducting worship or administering the sacraments? This is difficult to say. However, in two IRS letter rulings, the IRS determined that 5% of the minister's working hours were not sufficient to qualify for tax treatment as a minister.

Based on IRS rulings, it is clear that ministers serving as chaplains in government-owned-and-operated hospitals or in state prisons fall in a special category. They are employees for Social Security (FICA) purposes and qualify for the housing allowance exclusion. If they have opted out of Social Security by filing Form 4361, the exemption does not apply to this employment.

Individuals Not Qualifying for Ministerial Tax Treatment

An individual does not qualify as a "minister" if he or she is:

- a theological student but does not otherwise qualify as a minister
- an unordained, uncommissioned, or unlicensed individual
- an ordained, commissioned, or licensed minister working as an administrator or on the faculty of a nonchurch-related college
- an ordained, commissioned, or licensed minister working as an executive of a nonreligious, nonchurch-related organization
- a civilian chaplain at a Veteran's Administration hospital (the tax treatment of ministers who are chaplains in the armed forces is the same as for other members of the armed forces)
- an ordained, licensed, or commissioned minister employed by a parachurch organization but does not perform sacerdotal functions or conduct religious worship

Income Tax Status of Ministers

Are ministers employees or self-employed (independent contractors) for income tax purposes? The IRS considers virtually all ministers to be employees for *income tax purposes*. The income tax filing status has many ramifications for what and how a church and the minister report to the IRS.

Employees report compensation on Form 1040, Line 1, not on Schedule C (used by self-employed individuals). Employees receive a Form W-2 each year from their employer, while Form 1099-NEC is used to report compensation received by a self-employed individual.

Employees may no longer deduct unreimbursed business expenses whether or not they are eligible to itemize deductions on Schedule A. Self-employed individuals deduct expenses on Schedule C whether or not they are eligible to itemize deductions. Only 50% of business meals and entertainment expenses are deductible on Schedule C. If expenses are deducted on Schedule C, they are still subject to the allocation rules. See pages 115, 172, 176, 184, and 186.

The IRS often applies a common-law test to individuals, including ministers, to determine whether they are employees or self-employed for income tax purposes. (While the IRS and the courts have applied other tests to determine the status of workers, the other tests generally reach the same conclusion as when the common law test is applied.) Ministers are generally considered employees for income tax purposes if they meet the criteria reflected under these three categories as outlined in IRS Publication 15-A:

1. **Behavioral control**

   The person:

   - follows the church's work instructions
   - receives on-the-job training
   - provides services that are integral to the church
   - hires, supervises, and pays assistants for the church
   - follows set hours of work
   - works full-time for the church
   - does their work in a church-determined sequence
   - submits regular or written reports to the church

Key Issue

The defining court case on the topic of income tax status for ministers was a 1994 case in which a Methodist minister claimed he was self-employed for income tax purposes. The Tax Court held that he was an employee for income tax purposes. A federal appeals court upheld the decision.

2. **Financial control**

   The person:

   - receives business expense reimbursements
   - receives routine payments of regular amounts

- needs the church to furnish tools and materials
- does not have a major investment in job facilities
- cannot suffer a loss from the services
- works for one church at a time
- does not offer services to the general public

3. **Relationship of the parties**

   He or she:

   - has an ongoing work relationship with the church
   - provides services that must be rendered personally
   - works on the church's premises
   - can be fired by the church
   - may quit work at any time without penalty

Caution

With rare exceptions, ministers should receive Form W-2 from the church or other employer. Few ministers qualify as independent contractors for income tax purposes (even though considered self-employed for Social Security tax purposes). A church generally has sufficient control that qualifies the minister for W-2 treatment.

Some of the factors above are often given greater weight than others. *Generally a minister is an employee if the church has the legal right to control both what and how work is done, even if the minister has considerable discretion and freedom of action.* The threshold level of control necessary for employee status is generally lower when applied to professional services than when applied to nonprofessional services.

Nearly every local church minister qualifies as an employee for income tax purposes and should receive Form W-2. Few ministers can adequately substantiate filing as self-employed for income tax purposes.

Even though the minister might take exception to this reporting by the church, the church still has a responsibility under the law to determine the proper filing method (Form W-2 vs. Form 1099-NEC) and proceed accordingly.

Importance of the Employee vs. Self-Employed Decision on Income Taxes

Documenting a minister's employee status for income tax purposes is important both for the church and the minister. This issue has a direct impact on several tax-related issues:

- ➢ Ministers must be given Form W-2 and report their compensation on page 1 of Form 1040.

➢ Expenses reimbursed under a nonaccountable plan must be included in compensation on Form W-2.

➢ Accident, long-term care insurance, and qualified group health insurance premiums paid directly by an employer are not reportable as income to the employed minister but must be reported as taxable income to the self-employed minister.

Ministers may deduct accident and long-term care insurance and qualified group health insurance premiums that they paid personally and were not reimbursed by the church, on Schedule A as a medical and dental expense, generally subject to a 7.5% limitation of adjusted gross income.

Key Issue

It is vital for churches and other employers to treat ministers as employees (Form W-2) for income tax purposes in nearly every instance. If the minister is not considered an employee for income tax purposes, it jeopardizes the tax-free treatment of many fringe benefits.

The impact of a minister being considered self-employed for income tax purposes is generally very significant even if only health insurance is considered. With health insurance premiums running thousands of dollars per year, reporting these premiums as taxable (self-employed minister for income purposes) versus tax-free (minister treated as employee) can significantly impact the minister's tax bill. If health insurance premiums are included in taxable income, a low-income minister might also have his or her earned income tax credit reduced or eliminated.

Example: The church has a qualified group health insurance plan and pays health insurance premiums of $12,000 for the minister (and his or her dependents). Since the church considers the minister an employee for income tax purposes, the payment of the group health insurance premiums are tax-free for income and Social Security tax purposes and are not reported on Form W-2. The minister's marginal federal and state income tax rates are 24% and 6%, respectively. For Social Security tax purposes, the minister's rate is 15.3% (all ministers are self-employed for Social Security tax purposes).

Therefore, the tax-free payment of the health insurance premiums saves the minister over 45%, or almost $5,500 (45.3% x $12,000). Conversely, if a

Warning

Employers should consult professional tax advisors before reimbursing medical expenses for employees. Under changes brought by the Affordable Care Act, non-compliant reimbursements may result in penalties of $100 per employee per day.

church pays health insurance premiums for a minister who is self-employed for income tax purposes, the total amount is taxable for income and Social Security tax purposes.

- Health savings accounts, health reimbursement arrangements, or flexible spending arrangements are only available to employees or ministers who are treated as employees. See Chapter 3 for a more detailed discussion.
- Group-term life insurance of $50,000 or less, provided by an employer, is tax-free to employees but represents taxable income for the self-employed.
- A voluntary arrangement to withhold income tax may be used by a minister treated as an employee but may not be used by the self-employed. The amount withheld as federal income tax, however, could be set high enough to cover a minister's self-employment Social Security tax (SECA).

Social Security Tax Status of Ministers

Ministers engaged in the exercise of ministry are *always* treated as self-employed for Social Security tax purposes. Self-employed individuals pay Social Security tax under the Self-Employment Contributions Act (SECA) instead of under the Federal Insurance Contributions Act (FICA).

Applying the correct method of contributing Social Security tax for ministers is often confusing. A church should *never* deduct FICA-type Social Security tax from the pay of a qualified minister. If the individual is a qualifying minister, SECA coverage is applicable. The type of Social Security coverage is not based on the desire of a minister. It is the responsibility of the church to determine the appropriate type of Social Security based on whether the individual qualifies as a minister in the eyes of the IRS.

If a church withholds and matches FICA-type Social Security tax for a qualified minister, the minister is incorrectly being treated as a lay employee for Social Security tax purposes. The FICA matched by the church is improperly treated as *tax-free* when it is *taxable* for both income and Social Security purposes. This results in the underreporting of compensation and the *evasion* of both income and Social Security taxes.

It is possible for a minister to be exempt from SECA in only a few situations. To claim a SECA exemption, a minister must be conscientiously opposed to receiving public insurance (including an opposition to receiving Social Security benefits) because of the minister's religious beliefs or because of the position of the minister's religious denomination regarding Social Security (see pages 117-22).

A minister's earnings from a church that are not from the exercise of ministry are generally subject to Social Security tax under FICA for nonministerial employment or SECA for nonministerial independent contractor earnings. And even if a minister has been approved for an exemption from self-employment Social Security taxes, this Social Security exemption does not apply to Social Security taxes on earnings as an employee or independent contractor resulting from work that is *not* in the exercise of ministry.

Caution

Social Security tax is a confusing issue for many ministers. FICA-type Social Security never applies to an individual who qualifies as a minister for tax purposes. Stated another way, if a housing allowance has been designated for a qualified minister, FICA tax should not be deducted from pay—the minister is responsible to determine Social Security tax by completing Schedule SE each year.

Example 1: Michael Leonard is an ordained minister. He serves as a maintenance employee at the church that he attends. He also does some itinerant preaching at other churches. The maintenance work that Michael does at the church is not in the exercise of ministry. Therefore, it is subject to FICA. On the other hand, any income received from itinerant preaching activities is generally subject to SECA-type Social Security.

Example 2: Maria Sanchez serves on the youth staff of a church. She is commonly referred to as Pastor Sanchez by the church staff and attendees, however, she has never been ordained, licensed or commissioned. She is subject to FICA-type Social Security tax and is ineligible for the special ministerial tax treatments such as the housing allowance.

Example 3: Carla Wright is an ordained minister that just transitioned as senior pastor from Church A to Church B. Church A considered her as an employee for Social Security tax purposes and she now requests Church B to do the same. Church A should have considered Carla self-employed for Social Security tax purposes. Church A's mistake has no bearing on Church B, which should consider her subject to SECA, not FICA.

- **Ministers who do not qualify for ministerial tax treatment as a minister in a local church.** While most ordained ministers employed by a local congregation qualify for special ministerial tax treatment, some do not. While a congregation may designate a housing allowance for an individual who does not qualify for ministerial tax treatment, the law and integrity require more.

- **Assignment of ministers to a parachurch organization.** Many ministers request an assignment from a local congregation in relation to their employment to a parachurch organization. Why are these requests made by ministers? It's very simple! If a minister has an effective assignment, he or she has a much lower threshold to meet to qualify as a minister for tax purposes with the parachurch organization.

  What should a congregation do when a minister requests an assignment to another organization? It should determine if an assignment of the minister can be done with integrity. An effective assignment is more than the congregation simply sending a letter of assignment to an organization. For example, does the church have a written policy which outlines the criteria for assignment of ministers? Does the assignment accomplish the ministry purposes of the church?

- **Ministers employed by a parachurch organization.** Unless a minister has a valid assignment from a church to a parachurch organization, qualifying for ministerial tax status with the parachurch organization is much more difficult than with a local church.

  In the non-assignment, non-church setting, a minister must perform substantial sacerdotal functions or conduct religious worship with respect to his or her employment with the parachurch organization to qualify for special ministerial tax treatment.

- **Proper Social Security treatment of ministers.** When an individual qualifies as a minister in the eyes of the IRS, he or she automatically becomes subject to Social Security under the self-employment (SECA) rules and is ineligible for FICA-type Social Security treatment. In other words, a church or other employer of a qualified minister should *never* deduct FICA Social Security tax from a minister's pay.

Compensation Planning

In This Chapter

- What is a minister's true salary?
- Plan the compensation package
- Use fringe benefits wisely
- Use accountable expense reimbursements
- Routinely evaluate compensation
- Checklist for churches demonstrating integrity in compensation-setting

"If you fail to plan, you are planning to fail." This familiar quote attributed to Benjamin Franklin is so applicable to the topic of compensation planning for ministers. Without a clear roadmap, it is very easy for churches to get lost and overwhelmed. A simple lack of planning can easily result in hundreds (or more!) of dollars in tax burdens on a minister every year.

The good news is that a little planning can go a long way, and it starts with determining the current compensation package. One of ECFA's excellent compensation planning resources is an eBook, *8 Essentials of Compensating Ministers.*

Key Issue

If a church does not increase the pastor's pay each year, it has, in effect, reduced the pay. Inflation is low today, but it still exists, even at a few percentage points. It does cost more each year to live. Just as laypersons expect their employers to provide them with a cost-of-living pay increase each year, a pastor should expect the same.

Even church board members often do not know their minister's true compensation. When a church financial report is prepared, the data may be presented in such a way that there is not a clear reflection of salary as contrasted with fringe benefits and expense reimbursements. Too often, all of these expense elements are added together, leaving the appearance that the pastor is making much more than he or she really is.

When evaluating the appropriate amount of compensation for a minister, it is often helpful to review compensation data for other ministers who serve churches of similar size in the same geographic area. While precise data based on all of these factors is difficult to determine, there are several annual surveys available of church staff compensation.

What Is a Minister's True Salary?

There is often confusion about how much a pastor is really paid. The tendency for churches is to consider everything that is paid to or for a pastor as salary. This often results in the perception that the minister's salary is much higher than it really is, which is detrimental to both the minister and the church.

In a general sense, a pastor's salary is everything except fringe benefits and expense reimbursements. An amount designated for housing allowance is a component of the salary, which receives favorable tax treatment.

The common miscommunication often begins with church financial reports that include pastoral salary, fringe benefits, and expense reimbursements in one category. Here's why that is a problem:

- The cost of church-provided group health, dental, vision, and disability insurance are not salary—they are fringe benefits.
- An amount paid to reimburse or provide an allowance for a minister's self-employment Social Security tax is not salary—it is a fringe benefit.
- Professional expense reimbursements paid to a minister under an accountable expense reimbursement plan are not salary or fringe benefits—they are simply a church ministry expense.

Using the worksheet found on page 23 will allow the minister and the church board to identify the amount that is truly salary and the amount of fringe benefits. You will note that reimbursements made under an accountable expense reimbursement plan are not reflected on the worksheet because they are neither salary nor fringe benefits—they are church ministry expenses.

Plan the Compensation Package

The entire congregation may ultimately approve the annual budget that includes pastoral pay and benefits. But the pay package needs to be carefully developed before it reaches the congregational approval stage. Even the entire church board or compensation committee is usually too large a forum for the initial compensation discussions. A representative or a small committee from the church board should meet with the pastor, talk about pay

Minister's Compensation Worksheet

	This Year	Next Year
Salary and Equivalent Compensation:		
A. Cash salary, less designated housing/furnishings allowance	$______	$______
B. If parsonage owned by church, fair rental value including utilities and any housing/furnishings allowance	______	______
C. If parsonage not owned by church, cash housing allowance provided (plus utilities, maintenance, or any other housing expenses paid directly by church)	______	______
D. Cash bonus	______	______
E. Other	______	______
Total Salary	$______	$______
Fringe Benefits:		
A. Tax-deferred employer payments (TSA/403[b], 401[k], IRA, 457)	$______	$______
B. Health reimbursement arrangement	______	______
C. Insurance premiums paid by church		
1. Group health	______	______
2. Disability	______	______
3. Long-term care	______	______
4. Group-term life	______	______
5. Dental/vision	______	______
6. Professional liability	______	______
7. Malpractice	______	______
D. Social Security (SECA) reimbursement or allowance	______	______
E. Other	______	______
Total Fringe Benefits	$______	$______

expectations, review past pay patterns, discuss the tax consequences of compensation components, then make recommendations to the appropriate body.

An annual review of a minister's pay is vital. The minister should know exactly what to expect from the church during the coming year. It is inexcusable to wait until after the new church year begins to decide the new pay plan for the minister.

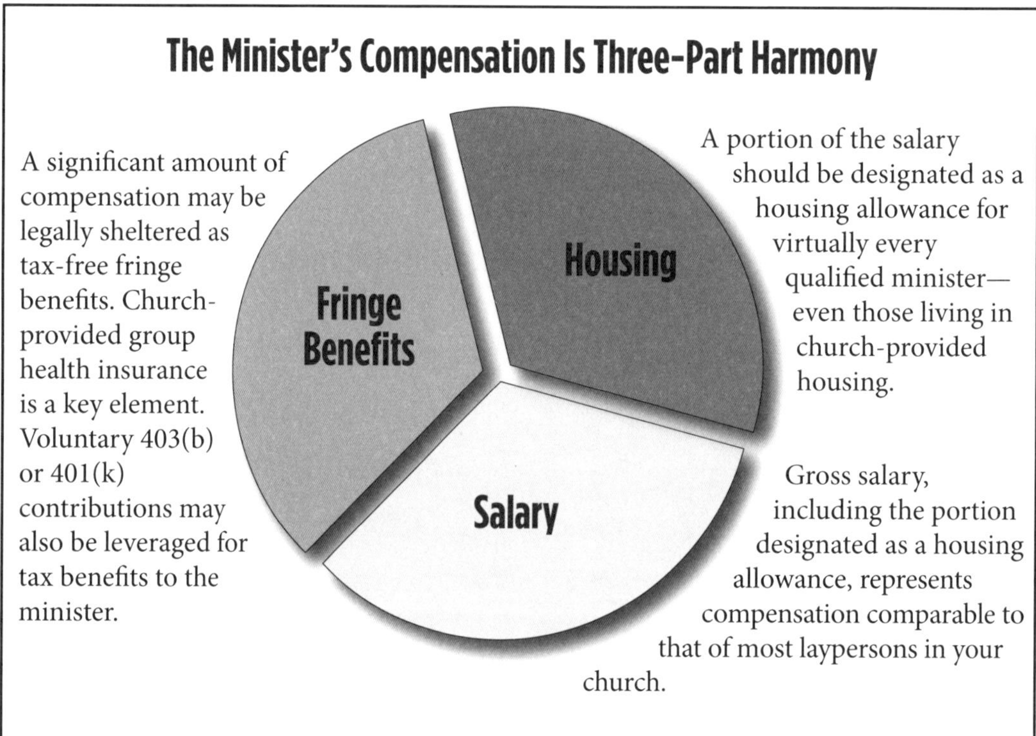

Note: Expense reimbursements are excluded from this graphic because they are not part of compensation when they are processed with an accountable reimbursement plan.

It is wise for the committee responsible for recommending compensation matters to build a plan for the upcoming church year well in advance of the start of the new church year. This allows the church board to act on the recommendations in enough time for the compensation package to be included in the church budget for the upcoming year. For example, if the church budget year starts on January 1, the committee might build a plan in August or September of the previous year, sending it to the board for action in September or October, to be included in the full church budget that is approved prior to the start of the new church year. The detailed elements of the pay plan, while fully disclosed to the church board or compensation committee, are often summarized for presentation to the congregation—perhaps summarized with the compensation data of the other church staff.

Some congregations may choose to boost the minister's salary 3% this year, leaving other elements of the pay package as they are. This practice presumes that the base salary for the previous year was adequate and that certain categories of compensation do not need any adjustment (*e.g.*, housing allowance designation). This may or may not have been true.

Remember

All of the elements of a minister's compensation plan should be annually evaluated. A thorough evaluation is much more than just adding an inflationary increase to gross pay. If the gross pay was inadequate before the increase, it is still too low after the inflationary increase.

For compensation planning, churches should consider salary ranges rather than fixed amounts. This will show the minister that, based on experience, longevity, and education, he or she could start at a higher rate and receive better periodic increases.

Consider goals and objectives

Does your church have goals and objectives? It is important to set goals. Perhaps goals include a percentage increase of worship attendance, growth in giving to missions, paying down or paying off the mortgage, or raising money for a building expansion.

Remember

Ministers who live in church-provided housing are penalized when residential real estate values are increasing. Even if real estate is modestly increasing, it is important for a church to provide an equity allowance. This annual payment in lieu of home ownership permits the pastor to invest the amount that might have been received through growth in the real estate market.

In a similar manner, have you stated the specific objectives of your minister's compensation policy? Here are a few examples:

- ➢ **Attraction.** Our goal is to attract a minister who has a record of leading churches that are growing spiritually and numerically.
- ➢ **Retention.** Our goal is to increase the average time a minister remains at our church to more than ten years.
- ➢ **Motivation and reward.** Our goal is to motivate our minister to do what is necessary to cause our church to meet its objectives as a congregation.

Taking your overall church goals and objectives and minister's compensation objectives into account, it may be helpful to establish a written compensation policy for the minister and ministerial staff.

Example: Based on our goals to develop three multi-site campuses in the next five years and to expand our international missions outreach, our compensation policy will attract, retain, reward, and motivate a pastor in a fair and equitable manner. This compensation policy will take into consideration reliable comparability data for similar positions.

Compare the job description to benchmarks of other jobs

The minister's job description should be compared to other jobs based on the following requirements: knowledge base, problem-solving ability, and personal accountability for results. How much are other well-educated professionals paid in the community or the area? A possible comparison may be to pay the minister similar to an elementary school principal, middle school principal, or high school principal in your area. This data is public information and can be readily obtained.

Recognize the motivational factors and job description

It is important to recognize factors that commonly motivate ministers. These include extrinsic factors (God's call to preach the Word), intrinsic factors (the pastoral role and relationships with church attendees and those in the community), and external factors (salary and benefits).

But the job description for most ministers is astounding! Typically, the job includes preaching the Word; equipping the saints for the work of ministry; administering the sacraments; visiting the sick and the needy; comforting those who mourn; correcting, rebuking, and encouraging; caring for the departments of the church; giving leadership to evangelism and education programs of the church; supervising the preparation of statistical reports; and so much more.

Key Issue

Few churches in America compensate ministers adequately. First, consider the minister's job description. Then, compare the job description to benchmarks of other jobs in the community based on the knowledge base, problem-solving ability, and personal accountability required for the minister.

Leverage the unique aspects of ministerial compensation

In too many congregations, the church leadership may say, "We can pay you $80,000. How do you want the money divided among salary, housing allowance, fringe benefits, and expense reimbursements?" The salary may be considered as $80,000 when it is really considerably less in "take-home" pay for the minister. Salary is just one component of compensation. And this approach lacks good stewardship as it almost always results in the minister paying more taxes than necessary—simply due to poor planning.

In another church, the church leadership may set the salary at $70,000, professional reimbursements at $4,000, and pension contributions at $2,000. Thus, the salary may be viewed as $76,000, rather than what it really is: $70,000.

Key Issue

Compensation paid to the minister should be fair and reasonable, including the congregation's evaluation of the minister's worth. Above all, compensation should reflect the congregation's assessment of how well the minister handles a multitude of challenges and effectively serves a diverse congregation. Pay should relate to the responsibilities, the size of the congregation, the economic level of the locale, and the experience of the pastor.

The various forms of compensation that a minister might receive can and should be leveraged to ensure the best financial outcome, both for ministers and in terms of responsible stewardship for the church.

As illustrated in this example, stewardship isn't only about *how much* a minister is compensated but also *how*, or the form in which a minister is compensated.

Example: Is it better stewardship for a church to pay its minister a cash salary of $70,000 and provide a professional expense allowance (nonaccountable plan) of $8,000 or pay its minister a cash salary of $70,000 and reimburse up to $8,000 of professional expenses under an accountable plan?

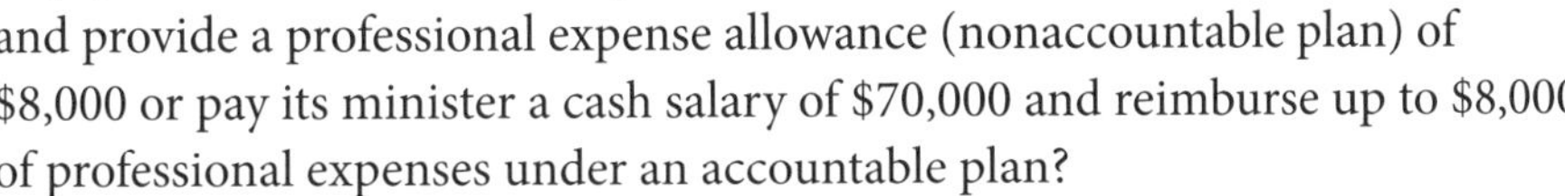

The church is going to spend the same amount of money either way ($78,000). However, the minister will almost always have less money in his or her pocket at the end of the year with the nonaccountable plan. This is because the $8,000 of professional expense allowance under a nonaccountable plan must be added to the minister's Form W-2 as taxable compensation, and it is not deductible for federal income tax purposes.

Use Fringe Benefits Wisely

Fringe benefit plans should be established by the church separately from housing allowance resolutions, accountable expense reimbursement arrangements, and compensation resolutions. There are different tax rules that apply to gross pay, the housing allowance, and the various fringe benefits. Too often, churches try to wrap too many plans into one resolution. This can result in improperly establishing important elements in the compensation plan.

There are several key fringe benefits that most churches should consider for ministers:

- **Tax-deferred accounts.** The minister should contribute as much as he or she can (see Chapter 3 for limitations) to tax-deferred accounts such as 403(b) tax-sheltered annuities (TSAs) or 401(k) plans. ***Caution:*** Do not exceed retirement plan limits! These change yearly based on inflation.

- **Life insurance.** Church-provided group life insurance coverage for a minister is an excellent fringe benefit. The first $50,000 of coverage under a nondiscriminatory plan is tax-free for the minister. Premiums for coverage over $50,000 are taxable to the minister.

- **Disability insurance.** The church can provide disability insurance coverage as part of the minister's taxable compensation, and disability insurance benefits are tax-free. Or, the church could pay the premiums as a tax-free fringe benefit. If the premiums are tax-free to the minister, disability insurance benefits are taxable.

Idea

A sound fringe benefit package almost always starts with the church or other employer paying for the minister's health insurance. This is vital because payments for coverage under the church's qualified group plan are tax-free. If the minister has to pay the health insurance premiums, they can be claimed on Schedule A but rarely produce a tax benefit.

- **Social Security (SECA) reimbursement.** All ministers pay self-employment Social Security tax of 15.3% on the first $137,700 of income in 2020. The Medicare tax of 2.9% is still due for all income above this limit, as well as an additional tax of 0.9% on wages above $200,000 for ministers filing as single and $250,000 for ministers married filing jointly. The only exception from paying self-employment Social Security tax is for the few ministers who qualify, file, and are approved for Social Security exemption.

Caution

An allowance to cover the minister's self-employment Social Security tax provides no tax benefit since the amount itself is fully taxable. However, paying at least one-half of the minister's Social Security tax, like lay employees, is important, so this amount can be properly shown as a fringe benefit for compensation analysis purposes.

Churches often provide a reimbursement or allowance to assist the pastor in paying a portion or all of the Social Security tax. The payments are taxable for income and Social Security tax purposes, whether paid directly to the minister or the IRS, and the payments should be included on the minister's Form W-2 in Box 1 as compensation. An even more generous approach is when the church chooses to "gross up" this Social Security reimbursement to also cover any taxes the minister incurs on the benefit so the minister is not left with any tax burden.

- ➢ **Sabbaticals.** Some churches choose to provide their ministers a sabbatical every few years either to focus on a project such as writing a book or as a respite for a certain number of years of service. This usually takes the form of an extended paid leave, and expenses are treated as additional compensation. A housing allowance is still appropriate if the minister otherwise qualifies. No other benefits would be impacted.

Use Accountable Expense Reimbursements

Since all ministers incur travel and other ministry-related expenses while conducting the ministry of the local church, an adequate accountable reimbursement plan is vital. Auto expenses of a minister's personally-owned vehicle are generally a minister's most significant ministry-related expense. If payments to the minister for these and other ministry expenses are not made subject to the accountable plan rules, the payments simply represent additional taxable compensation. The difference between treating several thousands of dollars of ministry-related expenses as tax-free under an accountable expense reimbursement plan or as fully taxable under a nonaccountable plan can be very significant in terms of dollars saved by the minister.

Remember

"Expense allowances" have no tax value to a minister—they simply represent fully taxable compensation. It is only through an accountable expense reimbursement plan that the reimbursement of expenses can be tax-free.

Ministers also incur other business expenses such as entertainment, professional books, magazines, online subscriptions, membership dues, and supplies. Some churches reimburse their ministers in full for these expenses. Other churches reimburse the minister for these expenses up to certain limits.

All churches should establish a fair and equitable reimbursement plan, comparable to most business situations. The reimbursement plan should meet the rules for accountable plans explained in Chapter 5. Full reimbursement of reasonable professional expenses should be the goal. If the church does not reimburse for 100% of professional expenses, the unreimbursed expenses are not deductible by the minister and therefore have no federal income tax value. Anything less than 100% reimbursement of church-related expenses is poor stewardship of the money entrusted to a church.

Some churches choose to provide for expense reimbursements up to a specified annual limit. If an expense limit is set, use one limit for all business and professional expenses (see Chapter 5). It is generally counterproductive to set expense plan limits by segments of expense like automobile, meals and entertainment, dues, and so on.

In addition to the adoption of an accountable reimbursement plan by the church, the minister must keep proper records and provide substantiation to the church for the expenditure of funds. The failure to adequately account for the expenses may be very expensive in terms of income taxes.

Avoid recharacterization of income

Some churches pay their employees' business (ministry) expenses through a salary reduction arrangement. These approaches generally violate the tax code and should be avoided.

Accountable expense reimbursement arrangements must meet the business connection, substantiation, and return of excess reimbursement requirements of the income tax regulations. But there is an additional requirement. If a church agrees to pay a minister (or other staff member) a specified annual income, and also agrees to reimburse the employee's business expenses out of salary reductions, the IRS takes the position that the church has arranged to pay an amount to an employee regardless of whether the employee incurs business expenses.

The following example illustrates the key principle:

Example: A church pays its minister an annual salary of $72,000 ($6,000 each month). Additionally, the church agrees to reimburse the minister's substantiated business expenses through salary reductions. The minister's business expenses for January were $1,000. She substantiates these expenses to the church treasurer during the first week of February. While the minister receives her monthly check of $6,000, only $5,000 of the check issued to the minister for February is treated as taxable salary and accumulated for purposes of reporting on the minister's Form W-2 at year-end. This is improper.

Based on the tax regulations, the entire $72,000 is reportable on the minister's Form W-2 because the minister would receive the entire $72,000 salary whether or not she incurred any business expenses.

Caution

Avoid paying for a minister's business expenses through a salary reduction arrangement that has no tax benefit.

While churches can pay for a minister's business expenses through salary reductions, such an arrangement is nonaccountable and, therefore, there are no tax advantages associated with such an arrangement.

Can a church prospectively reduce a minister's salary and increase the amount available for accountable business expense reimbursement? Can a church prospectively hold a minister's salary level and increase the amount available for accountable business expense reimbursement, when the minister otherwise would have received a salary increase? The answer to these questions may depend on whether the church has authorized the minister's salary and established the business expense reimbursement arrangement as two separate actions of the governing board or appropriate committee, without any indication that the reimbursements are being funded out of what otherwise would be the minister's salary.

Routinely Evaluate Compensation

Few people would deny that most ministers work very hard at their jobs, yet many churches prefer to avoid conversations about compensation and hope that it will somehow all work itself out. On the other hand, if a church has a broken window or faulty equipment that distracts during the service, immediate action is taken to keep the church performing at its best.

In the same way, employees of the church must be properly compensated to free them up for ministry unhindered by the trouble of paying rent or obtaining health care due to inadequate or poorly planned compensation. And, of course, it is our biblical mandate to provide for workers, including ministers.

Caution

Discomfort around discussing pay can lead to what is sometimes called a "conspiracy of silence" where no one wants to talk about compensation for church leaders.

All of this starts with open and productive discussion to help your church find and implement a sound compensation policy. To do this, it is vital to routinely evaluate and discuss the minister's compensation package. To ensure that total compensation is fair and reasonable, church leaders must be willing to engage in regular discussion. More than that, a church's compensation policy goes hand-in-hand with its culture, goals, and philosophy of ministry.

It is understandable that churches and ministers alike find it difficult to speak openly about their finances. Discomfort around discussing pay can lead to what is sometimes called a "conspiracy of silence" where no one wants to talk about compensation for church leaders, and therefore no one discusses it until there's a serious problem. With the principles outlined in this guide, it is our hope that your church and its leaders will be empowered to engage in the conversation and properly steward resources to bless your leaders and your ministry.

Income Tax Reporting and Expense Reimbursements

22222	VOID ☐	a Employee's social security number	For Official Use Only ▶ OMB No. 1545-0008	
b Employer identification number (EIN)			1 Wages, tips, other compensation	2 Federal income tax withheld
c Employer's name, address, and ZIP code			3 Social security wages	4 Social security tax withheld
			5 Medicare wages and tips	6 Medicare tax withheld
			7 Social security tips	8 Allocated tips
d Control number			9	10 Dependent care benefits
e Employee's first name and initial	Last name	Suff.	11 Nonqualified plans	12a See instructions for box 12 Code
			13 Statutory employee ☐ Retirement plan ☐ Third-party sick pay ☐	12b Code
			14 Other	12c Code
				12d Code
f Employee's address and ZIP code				

15 State	Employer's state ID number	16 State wages, tips, etc.	17 State income tax	18 Local wages, tips, etc.	19 Local income tax	20 Locality name

Form **W-2** Wage and Tax Statement **2020**

Department of the Treasury—Internal Revenue Service

For Privacy Act and Paperwork Reduction Act Notice, see the separate instructions.

Cat. No. 10134D

Copy A—For Social Security Administration. Send this entire page with Form W-3 to the Social Security Administration; photocopies are **not** acceptable.

Do Not Cut, Fold, or Staple Forms on This Page

The IRS treats most ministers as employees for income tax purposes. Churches must issue Form W-2 to ministers.

Box 1 will be completed for all ministers. Box 2 will reflect any voluntary withholding the minister chose for the ministry to withhold from their pay. Boxes 3 through 11 should be blank. Per IRS Publication 517, the housing allowance amount may be reflected in Box 14.

Every church should adopt an accountable expense reimbursement plan. Expenses paid under an accountable plan are not includible on the minister's Form W-2. The expenses are not reported in any manner on the minister's Form 1040.

Ministers without accountable reimbursement plans will generally pay unnecessary income taxes.

Checklist for Churches Demonstrating Integrity in Compensation-Setting

Follow steps 1-3 for *all* churches:

1. **Approval of compensation for the lead pastor** – The full church board *(i.e.,* entire corporate governing body) or a an independent committee authorized by the board annually approves total compensation of the lead pastor or comparable position.

2. **Notification of family members' compensation** – The full church board or an independent committee authorized by the board is notified annually of the total compensation of any of the lead pastor's family members who themselves are employed by the church.

3. **Documentation** – Approval (Step 1) and Notification (Step 2, if applicable) are documented in the board minutes.

Follow Step 4 for churches where the lead pastor's total compensation is $150,000 or more, and *recommended* for all churches regardless of the lead pastor's compensation amount:

4. **Additional due diligence** – In setting the lead pastor's compensation, the board or a committee authorized by the board should

   - *Exclude* anyone with a conflict of interest from the decision-making process.
   - *Obtain* reliable comparability data for similar churches (at least within the past five years or when considering a significant increase).
   - *Determine* appropriate compensation considering the comparability data and factors unique to the lead pastor (skills, talents, education, experience, performance, knowledge, etc.).
   - *Document* these additional due-diligence steps, the board's decision regarding total compensation, and, if applicable, its rationale for establishing compensation at a level exceeding that which is supported by the comparability data.

All of the above steps are required to meet the "ECFA Policy for Excellence in Compensation-Setting and Related-Party Transactions" (ECFA Standard 6).

- **Compensation approval basics.** Churches can demonstrate integrity in the compensation approval process by following three basic steps:
  - **Independent compensation approval.** While the governing body or congregation may consult with a minister concerning financial needs, the formal approval of a minister's compensation should be done independently of the minister. In other words, a minister should be recused from the meeting in which his or her compensation is approved.
  - **Documenting the compensation package.** A minister's compensation package should be formally documented in the minutes of the approving body. The details of the package may be recorded in a document separate from the meeting minutes (see the 2021 edition of the *Church and Nonprofit Tax & Financial Guide* for a sample form to record compensation).
  - **Obtaining competitive compensation data.** It is appropriate to periodically obtain comparability data before approving a minister's compensation package. Rarely is the data necessary to avoid paying excessive compensation to a minister, but more often it will reveal that a minister's pay is below that of a similar position in a similar church in the same geographic region.
- **Working with the congregation to optimize the stewardship opportunities.** Stewardship is generally maximized for the congregation and minister by initially focusing on tax-favored or tax-free fringe benefits and accountable expense reimbursements, then the housing allowance, and finally cash compensation.
- **Accountability over expenses authorized by the lead pastor.** The church board should give careful attention to exercising appropriate oversight regarding the lead pastor's ministry budget and discretionary expense account, if one has been provided by the church. This oversight responsibility should be assumed by the board chair or an independent member of the governing body, so expenses are objectively reviewed by someone who is not related to the pastor or in a staff reporting relationship to the pastor. One of the key objectives of this periodic review (*e.g.*, monthly or quarterly) is to ensure that all expenses serve a legitimate ministry purpose. Any expenses that are of a personal nature for the pastor should be reported as taxable income.

The Pay Package

In This Chapter

- Avoiding the nondiscrimination rules
- Tax treatment of compensation elements
- Reporting compensation, fringe benefits, and reimbursements

Ask many ministers about their compensation and they will tell you the amount of their weekly check, perhaps including a cash housing allowance, but there is more to it than that. Care should be given in identifying what portion of the compensation package is subject to tax. Not only is the salary subject to tax, but so are many "fringe benefits" that may be received.

What are fringe benefits? A fringe benefit is any cash, property, or service that an employee receives from a church in addition to salary. The term "fringe benefits" is really a misnomer because employees have come to depend on them as a part of their total compensation package. All fringe benefits are taxable income to employees unless specifically exempted by the Internal Revenue Code.

Many fringe benefits can be provided by a church to a minister without any dollar limitation (group health insurance is an example), while other fringe benefits are subject to annual limits (dependent care is an example). The annual limits by fringe benefit type are reflected in this chapter.

And then, certain fringe benefits are tax-deferred. The most common tax-deferred benefit is the retirement plan. Tax-deferral of a fringe benefit is less valuable to an employee than a benefit that is tax-free. However, paying tax on a benefit at a later date instead of the current date is advantageous because of the present value of the dollar.[1]

For a summary of taxable, non-taxable, and tax-deferred elements of compensation, see the table located at the end of this chapter.

---

[1] The present value of a dollar is the current worth of a future sum of money given a specified rate of return. This is also sometimes called the time value of money principle.

Avoiding the Nondiscrimination Rules

To qualify for exclusion from income, many fringe benefits must be provided in a nondiscriminatory manner. In other words, the benefits must be offered to all employees or all employees in the same class. A fringe benefit that is offered only to the senior pastor or other highly compensated employee when other individuals are employed by the church could trigger the nondiscrimination rules.

Failure to comply with the nondiscrimination rules does not disqualify a fringe benefit plan entirely. Only the tax-free nature of the benefit is lost to the highly compensated employee. Still that outcome would not be welcomed.

The nondiscrimination rules apply to several types of fringe benefit plans, including:

- qualified tuition and fee discounts (see page 57-58)
- educational assistance benefits (see page 42)
- dependent care assistance plans (see page 40)
- tax-sheltered annuities (TSAs), 401(k) plans, and other deferred compensation plans (see pages 53-55)
- group-term life insurance benefits (see pages 49-50)
- certain group medical insurance plans (see page 46-47)
- health reimbursement arrangements (see pages 47-48)
- health savings accounts (see pages 48-49)
- qualified small employer health reimbursement arrangement (see pages 47-48)
- cafeteria plans (see pages 43-44), including a flexible spending account dependent care plan (see page 40), and a health care flexible spending account (see pages 43-44)

For purposes of the nondiscrimination rules, a "highly compensated employee" for 2020 is someone paid more than $130,000 in the previous year and is in the top 20% of employees when ranked by pay for the preceding year.

On these and other fringe benefits questions, you may find IRS Publication 15-B helpful, the "Employee Tax Guide to Fringe Benefits." Another resource is ECFA's *9 Essentials of Church Fringe Benefits*.

Tax Treatment of Compensation Elements

For the fringe benefits discussed below that are considered taxable income to the minister, we assume that the minister is classified as an employee for income tax purposes and that any taxable income will be reported for the minister on Form W-2 for employees.

➢ **Adoption assistance programs.** A church can provide adoption assistance on a tax-favored basis, with the church financially assisting or reimbursing employees for expenses related to the adoption of a child. An "eligible child" is a person who has not reached age 18 as of the time of the adoption or who is physically or mentally incapable of caring for himself or herself.

A church can determine whether an adoption assistance policy will apply only to employees who finalize the adoption or also to those with unsuccessful adoption efforts. The church also has discretion over the amount of financial assistance and/or paid leave provided, and employee eligibility requirements.

Adoption expenses paid or reimbursed must be included in the employee's taxable income if it exceeds the tax exclusion limit. For 2020, the excludable dollar limit is $14,300 and the excludable amount begins to phase out for high-bracket taxpayers.

To compute the dollar limitation, qualified adoption expenses claimed and paid for an unsuccessful domestic adoption effort must be combined with qualified adoption expenses paid in connection with a subsequent domestic adoption attempt, whether or not the subsequent attempt is successful. It should be noted that the tax credit cannot be claimed for an unsuccessful foreign adoption.

Most churches use the IRS definition of "reasonable and necessary expenses directly related to the adoption of a child," and includes adoption fees, court costs, attorney's fees, traveling expenses (include meals and lodging) while away from home, and other expenses that are directly related to, and have as their principal purpose, the legal adoption of an eligible child.

If the church pays or reimburses some of the adoption expenses, the employee can use any excess adoption expenses to claim the adoption tax credit. The employee simply cannot "double-dip" by obtaining a church reimbursement and an adoption tax credit for the same expense.

➢ **Awards.** If ministers receive cash or cash equivalent awards based on performance, such awards are generally taxable income unless the value is insignificant. If an award is made to the minister in goods or services, such as a vacation trip, the fair market value of the goods or services is taxable income.

➢ **Bonuses.** A bonus paid by a church to an employee for outstanding work or other achievements is taxable income and reportable on Form W-2.

➢ **Books.** A church may reimburse a minister for ministry-related books. To avoid confusion, it is wise for churches to have a policy covering who owns those books (and other property with a useful life longer than one year) paid for by the church.

➢ **Business and professional expenses reimbursed *with* adequate accounting.** If the church reimburses the minister under an accountable reimbursement plan for employment-related professional or business expenses (for example, auto, other travel, subscriptions, entertainment, and so on), the reimbursement is not taxable compensation and is not reported to the IRS by the church or the minister (see pages 82-84). Per diem allowances up to IRS-approved limits also qualify as excludable reimbursements (see page 89). A minister's tithes and charitable contributions to the church are not reimbursable as business expenses.

Idea

The goal of every minister should generally be to have all or most employment-related expenses reimbursed by the employer under an accountable plan. Covering all of these accountable expenses may be more advantageous to a minister than a pay raise, which is taxable.

Reimbursing employees' business expenses through a salary reduction arrangement is prohibited by IRS Regulations (see pages 30, 32).

➢ **Business and professional expense payments *without* adequate accounting.** Many churches pay periodic allowances or reimbursements to ministers for business expenses with no requirement to account adequately for the expenses. These payments do *not* meet the requirements of an *accountable* expense reimbursement plan.

Allowances or reimbursements under a *nonaccountable* plan must be included in a minister's taxable income on Form W-2, and there is no income tax deduction for unreimbursed business expenses related to W-2 income.

➢ **Cell phones.** Cell phones and similar devices provided to employees are excludable from an employee's income as a fringe benefit and are not subject to stringent recordkeeping requirements in certain situations. The cell phones must be provided for "substantial reasons relating to the employer's business, other than providing compensation to the employee." Cell phones provided for employee morale or goodwill, or to recruit prospective employees, are not provided for "noncompensatory business purposes."

If the church does not have a substantial noncompensatory business reason for providing a cell phone to an employee, or reimbursing the employee for business use of his or her personal cell phone, the value of the use of the phone or the amount of the reimbursement is taxable income, reportable on Form W-2, and is subject to employment tax withholding for lay employees.

- **Clothing.** Ordinary clothing worn in the exercise of a minister's duties for the church is a personal expense and is not reimbursable by the church under an accountable plan.

  If a minister wears clothing that is of a type specifically required as a condition of employment and is not adaptable to general use or continued usage to the extent that it could take the place of ordinary clothing, such as vestments, the cost is reimbursable as a business expense.

- **Club dues and memberships.** Dues for professional organizations (such as ministerial associations) or public service organizations (such as Kiwanis, Rotary, and Lions clubs) are generally reimbursable.

  Other club dues are generally not reimbursable (including any club organized for business, pleasure, recreation, or other social purposes). If the church pays the health, fitness, or athletic facility dues for a minister, the amounts paid are generally fully includible in the minister's income as additional compensation.

- **Computers and laptops.** The treatment of church-provided computers, laptops, and other peripheral equipment follows the same rules as cell phones discussed on page 38. As long as the church has provided the computer equipment primarily for non-compensatory business reasons, it is treated as a tax-free fringe benefit.

- **Conventions.** Expenses incurred by a minister to attend a church-related convention or seminar are generally reimbursable. (See pages 88-89 for rules for the travel expenses of spouses and children.) Social or sightseeing expenses are personal and not reimbursable.

  If the convention is held outside North America, expenses are reimbursable only if attendance is ministry-related and is considered reasonable (see IRS Publication 463 for factors considered as part of the reasonableness test).

  When a minister travels away from home to attend a convention and combines personal activities with ministry activities, only the ministry-related expenses are eligible to be reimbursed by the church.

- **Deferred compensation.** A church may maintain a retirement or other deferred compensation plan for employees that is not qualified under the Internal Revenue Code and is not a 403(b) tax-sheltered annuity (see pages 53-55) or a "Rabbi Trust" (see page 54-55). If the plan is unfunded (the church makes a promise, not represented by a note, to pay at some time in the future), contributions to the plan are generally not taxable currently.

  Funds placed in an investment account under the church's control (other than in a tax-sheltered annuity or "Rabbi Trust") to provide retirement funds for the minister have no tax consequence to the minister until the funds are available to the minister.

- **Dependent care.** If a church pays or reimburses child or dependent care services, the minister can exclude the amount of this benefit from income within certain limits (see also page 44 for a flexible spending account dependent care plan). The dependent must be your child under 13 years old, or your spouse who is physically or mentally incapable of self-care. In certain circumstances, sometimes other dependents may qualify. The amount excludable is generally limited to the smallest of these three:

  - ☐ the minister's earned income
  - ☐ the spouse's earned income
  - ☐ $5,000 ($2,500 if married filing separately)

  The dependent care assistance must be provided under a separate written plan of the church that does not favor highly compensated employees and that meets other qualifications.

  Dependent care assistance payments are excluded from income if the payments cover expenses that would be deductible if the expenses were not reimbursed. If the minister is married, both spouses must be employed. There are special rules if one spouse is a student or incapable of self-care.

Tip

Under the current 403(b) plan contribution limits, relatively few ministers will need to look for other retirement plan options. However, if the church funds an unqualified plan (such as purchasing an annuity contract) that is not a tax-sheltered annuity or a Rabbi Trust, the contributions are generally taxable when made.

- **Dependent educational benefits.** If a church provides educational benefits for the minister's children when they attend college or a pre-college private school, the funds are taxable income to the minister. If the church withholds money from pay and forwards the funds to a college for the education of the minister's child, the amount withheld does not reduce taxable compensation. See the 2021 edition of the *Church and Nonprofit Tax & Financial Guide* for more information on scholarship funds established by churches.

- **Disability insurance.** If a church pays the disability insurance premiums (and the minister is the beneficiary) as a part of the compensation package, the premiums are excluded from income. However, any disability policy proceeds must be included in taxable income. The amount included in income depends upon who paid the premiums for the policy covering the year when the disability started. If the premiums are shared between the church and the minister, then the benefits are taxable in the same proportion as the payment of the premiums.

Idea

Statistics suggest that a minister is seven times more likely to need disability insurance than life insurance before age 65. When a church provides the maximum disability insurance as a tax-free benefit, it could reduce the awkwardness of a pastoral transition should the minister become disabled while serving the congregation.

Conversely, if a minister pays the disability insurance premiums or has the church withhold the premiums from salary, then the minister receives no current deduction, and any disability benefits paid under the policy are not taxable.

A third option is for the church to pay the disability premiums. But instead of treating the premiums as tax-free, the church treats the premiums as additional employee compensation. Benefits received under this option are tax-free.

How do you determine whether disability benefits are taxable if the disability insurance premiums are paid by the church for some years and by the minister for other years? Taxability of the benefits generally depends on who paid the premiums for the policy year in which the disability benefit payments begin.

➢ **Discretionary fund.** Churches sometimes establish a fund to be disbursed upon the discretion of a minister. If the funds are used for church-related purposes or the needs of individuals associated with the church in a benevolent manner, and if a proper accounting is made, there is no tax impact on the minister. If it is permissible to distribute some of the funds to the minister, even if the minister does not benefit from the fund, *all* money placed in the fund becomes additional taxable income to the minister in the year the money is transferred by the church to the discretionary fund. To avoid this unfortunate result, a church should expressly prohibit the use of the discretionary fund for the minister's personal use.

Caution

Discretionary funds often serve a useful purpose for the pastoral staff—giving them the flexibility to provide immediate financial assistance, generally in small amounts, to those in need (larger amounts should be handled through a formal benevolence fund). An adequate accounting (dates, names, amounts, and need) must be maintained by the church in every instance.

➢ **Dues, ministerial.** Ministers often pay an annual renewal fee to maintain their credentials. These and other similar professional expenses may be reimbursed tax-free by the church.

- **Educational assistance benefit plans.** An educational assistance program is a separate written plan of a church to provide educational assistance to employees, generally including books, equipment, fees, supplies, and tuition. Excludible expenses are meals, lodging, transportation, and supplies that could be retained for use after the course of instruction is completed.

  A program may include courses whether or not they are job-related. Graduate-level courses are covered under the program.

  The program must be nondiscriminatory. Other requirements include giving reasonable notice of the availability and terms of the program to eligible employees and not allowing employees to choose to receive cash or other benefits that must be included in gross income instead of educational assistance.

  No benefits may be provided to the employee's spouse or dependents. The church should exclude from income the first $5,250 of any qualified educational assistance paid for a minister during the year.

- **Educational reimbursement plans.** If a church requires the minister to take educational courses or job-related courses, and the church either pays the expenses directly to the educational organization or reimburses the minister for the expenses after a full accounting, the minister may not have to include in income the amount paid by the church. (See page 153-54 for three types of education credits.)

  While there are no specific dollar limits on educational expenses paid under a non-qualified reimbursement plan, the general ordinary and necessary business expense rules do apply. These types of payments may be discriminatory (see page 36).

  Though the education may lead to a degree, expenses may be deductible or reimbursable if the education:

  - ☐ is required by the church to keep the minister's salary, status, or job (and serves a business purpose of the church)
  - ☐ maintains or improves skills required in the minister's present employment

  Even when the requirements above are met, expenses do not qualify if the education is:

  - ☐ required to meet the minimum educational requirements of the minister's present work
  - ☐ part of a program of study that will qualify the minister for a new occupation

- **Embezzled funds.** If a minister (or staff member) embezzles funds from a church, the amount embezzled is reportable as taxable income on the minister's tax return.

If the embezzlement occurred during prior years, amended tax returns should be filed by the minister for each year when the embezzlement occurred. Even if embezzled funds are refunded to the church, the act of embezzlement is complete and the full amount embezzled is taxable income.

The precise amount embezzled usually cannot be determined. However, if the church knows the exact amount misappropriated, the amount should be reported as compensation on Form W-2. When the exact amount embezzled is indeterminable, the church should consider filing Form 3949-A, "Information Referral." The form may be used to report suspected illegal activity, including embezzlement.

- **Entertainment expenses.** Entertainment expenses that represent an ordinary and necessary business expense generally qualify for reimbursement under an accountable expense reimbursement plan. For information on business meals, see pages 101-2.

- **Equity allowance.** If a minister lives in a church-owned parsonage, the minister is not building up equity. If the church provides a cash allowance for the minister to purchase a home, the minister may establish some equity.

  An equity allowance is an amount paid to a minister living in a church-owned parsonage. This allowance may partially or fully offset the equity that the minister would have accumulated in a personally owned home.

  An equity allowance is fully taxable when it is paid to the minister and not excludable as a housing allowance. However, the church could make the equity payments to a tax-sheltered annuity (TSA) or 401(k) plan. This would be consistent with the desire of a congregation to provide funds for housing at retirement. The funds received at retirement from church-sponsored TSA or 401(k) plans may be eligible for tax-free treatment as a housing allowance (see pages 75-76).

- **Flexible spending account (FSA).** "Cafeteria" or FSAs are plans used to reimburse employees for certain personal expenses. They are provided by employers in conjunction with group health plans to pre-fund dependent care, medical, or dental expenses (often called a health care flexible spending account) in pre-tax dollars (see the 2021 edition of the *Church and Nonprofit Tax & Financial Guide* for more information on FSAs).

  The only taxable benefit that a cafeteria or FSA can offer is cash. A nontaxable benefit to the participant includes any benefit that is not currently taxable upon receipt. Examples of these benefits are group-term life insurance up to $50,000, coverage under an accident or health plan, and coverage under a dependent care assistance program.

A cafeteria or flexible spending plan cannot discriminate in favor of highly compensated participants for contributions, benefits, or eligibility to participate in the plan. While only larger churches generally offer cafeteria plans because of the complexity and cost, many churches could feasibly offer an FSA.

The FSA contribution limit for 2020 is $2,750 per person per year. During the plan year, the money is available for use by the account holder. Ultimately, the employer owns the account and any unused balance at the end of either the plan year or any administrative grace period is forfeited to the employer.

An administrative grace period may be adopted before the beginning of an FSA plan year as a way to provide relief without running afoul of the prohibition on deferred compensation. Under this provision, employees are permitted a grace period of 2½ months immediately following the end of the plan year to use the funds. Expenses for qualified benefits incurred during the grace period may be paid or reimbursed from benefits or contributions remaining unused at the end of the plan year.

Example: A minister's plan year ends on December 31, 2020, and at that point, the minister still has $150 left in unused funds in an FSA. On February 5, 2021 (during the grace period), the minister incurs $400 in eligible medical expenses. After the claim is submitted, the remaining $150 from the 2020 plan is used first for reimbursement, and the other $250 is taken out of the funds from the 2021 plan.

There is also the option of rolling over any unused FSA dollars into the next plan year, but this option is subject to a $500 limit. *Note:* If an administrative grace period is offered, the $500 rollover may not be used, and vice versa.

➢ **Flexible spending account dependent care plan.** Generally, a dependent care flexible spending account (FSA) is designed to pay for the care of dependent children under age 13 by a babysitter, in a day care center, or in a before-school or after-school program. The maximum amount that may be funded through a dependent care FSA is $5,000 (married, filing jointly), earned income, or spouse's earned income, whichever is lowest.

➢ **Frequent flyer awards.** Free travel awards used personally that were received as frequent flyer miles on business travel paid by the church are not taxable when the awards are used for travel. However, if these awards are converted to cash, they are taxable.

Churches should obtain professional guidance before allowing a minister to use a personal credit card to purchase church assets (like a car or computers) for the purpose of diverting frequent flyer miles to his or her personal account.

➢ **Gifts/personal.** Money that a minister receives directly from an individual is usually considered a personal gift and may be excluded from income if the payments are intended for the personal benefit of the minister and not in consideration of any services rendered. If the gift is a check, it should be made payable directly to the minister (not the church) to qualify for tax exclusion for the minister. A personal gift of this nature will not qualify as a charitable contribution by the giver.

Idea

The IRS formerly took the position that an individual had tax liability because he or she had received or used frequent flyer miles or other promotional benefits related to the individual's business travel. However, the IRS has reversed, saying these benefits are generally tax-free.

➢ **Gifts/special occasion.** Christmas, anniversary, birthday, retirement, and similar gifts are often paid by a church to a minister or lay employee. To qualify as a nontaxable gift, the payment must be based on detached and disinterested generosity, out of affection, respect, admiration, charity, or like impulses. The giver's intention is the most critical factor. Also, the gift must be made without consideration of services rendered.

Some examples may be helpful to distinguish some of the facts and circumstances related to gifts.

Example 1: A church attender slips two $100 bills into the minister's hand on the way out the door after the close of the Sunday morning service. This gratuitous and occasional gift generally qualifies as a tax-free gift. However, if the gift is provided by a family member after a wedding or funeral, the money may be taxable to the minister as consideration for services rendered.

Filing Tip

An occasional check payable to the church designated for the benefit of a minister typically represents taxable income when paid to the minister. Such payments may not qualify as charitable contributions because of the conduit/pass-through potential of the payments. It is highly preferable for payments of this nature to be made directly to the minister instead of "running them through the church" to try to get a tax deduction.

Example 2: The church announces that it will receive funds as a special gift for the benefit of the senior pastor. The funds are not given directly to the church but rather given directly to the pastor. While these may be tax-free gifts to the minister, the more regularly (more than two or three times a year) such special offerings are received and the more significant the amounts the offerings are in relation to the pastor's annual salary, the more likely the amounts will be taxable income to the pastor. Either way the gifts generally do not qualify for a charitable gifts acknowledgment.

Example 3: A church receives an annual offering for the pastoral staff on Pastor Appreciation Day. Checks are made payable to the church. The church issues gift acknowledgments and the board determines how much to distribute to each pastor. The amounts paid to the pastor are taxable compensation and should be added to Form W-2. Gifts to the church qualify for a charitable contribution acknowledgment.

If the church gives a minister a turkey, ham, or other item of nominal value at Christmas or other holidays, the value of the gift is not income. If an individual gives a minister cash or gift cards, these represent tax-free gifts to the minister and they are not deductible by the donor.

If the church gives the minister cash or an item that can easily be exchanged for cash, such as a gift card, the gift is taxable compensation regardless of the amount involved.

- **Gym membership.** See "Club dues and memberships" above.

- **Health care sharing arrangements.** Certain non-insurance arrangements (for example, health care sharing ministry plans) are used by some ministers. Since such plans are typically described as non-insurance, the payments by a church to these plans (or to reimburse a minister's payments to these plans) are generally fully taxable. *Note:* The IRS has proposed expanding the definition of medical expenses to include payments to health care sharing arrangements. If this proposal passes, payment by churches to or on behalf of an employee as part of an HRA could qualify for tax-free treatment.

Caution

Certain non-insurance arrangements (for example, health care sharing ministry plans) are used by some ministers. Since such plans are typically described as non-insurance, the payments by a church to these plans (or to reimburse a minister's payments to these plans) are generally fully taxable.

- **Health insurance.** If the church pays a minister's qualified group health insurance premiums directly to the insurance carrier, the premiums are tax-free to the minister. Insurance may be provided or made available for purchase by the employees for medical, dental, and vision coverage. Premiums paid by the employer for the employee, including dependents, are excluded from income for income tax purposes as well as Social Security and Medicare.

Ministries may reimburse employees tax-free for their medical expenses, including individual health insurance premiums under either a qualified small employer health reimbursement arrangement (QSEHRA) or a individual coverage health reimbursement arrangement (ICHRA).

The similarities of the two arrangements are as follows:

- **Employees purchase health care.** Employees buy health insurance, products and services they want. Any expense listed in IRS Publication 502 can be reimbursed.
- **Employees submit reimbursement requests.** Employees submit expense documentation to the church.
- **Churches review and reimburse.** Churches review the documentation submitted, and if approved, reimburses employees tax-free.

Now for the differences between the arrangements:

- **Number of employees.** To offer a QSEHRA, a ministry must have fewer than 50 full-time employees, and it cannot offer a group insurance policy. However, churches of all sizes can offer an ICHRA. Employers can offer a group health insurance policy to one class of employees and an ICHRA to another class of employees, provided they meet minimum class size standards.
- **Employee eligibility.** With a QSEHRA, all full-time employees and their families are eligible for the benefit and the church can choose to extend eligibility to part-time employees. With an ICHRA, the church can structure their eligibility requirements based on a given set of employee classes.
- **Allowance caps.** With a QSEHRA, churches cannot offer allowance amounts that exceed annual caps set by the IRS. For 2020, those caps are $5,250 for single employees and $10,600 for employees with a family. Balances in the QSEHRA can roll over month to month and year to year, though total reimbursements cannot exceed that year's IRS cap. With the ICHRA, there are no annual contribution caps and allowance amounts can roll over month-to-month and year-to-year without restriction.

➢ **Health reimbursement arrangement (HRA).** A properly designed, written HRA under which the church pays the medical expenses of the minister, spouse, and dependents may be nontaxable to the minister.

Funding by choosing a salary reduction is not permitted. Excess money in a church-funded HRA can be carried over to a future year without any tax implications to the minister. Because benefits can be carried over indefinitely, the only danger of losing the balance in an HRA account is at retirement or other separation of employment.

Typical expenses covered by such a plan are deductibles, coinsurance, and noncovered amounts paid by the individual.

HRAs may not discriminate in favor of highly compensated employees with regard to either benefits or eligibility. HRAs are only available to employees.

Caution

An HRA may reimburse health care expenses under a plan in which the employer decides how much will be available for each employee. This amount is generally the same for all eligible employees because the nondiscrimination rules apply. Account balances may be carried forward to increase the maximum reimbursement amount in subsequent coverage periods.

- **Health savings account (HSA).** HSAs are individual, portable, tax-free, interest-bearing accounts (typically held by a bank or insurance company) through which individuals with a high-deductible health plan (HDHP) save for medical expenses. The purpose of an HSA is to pay what basic coverage would ordinarily pay.

Within limits, HSA contributions made by employers are excludable from income tax and Social Security wages and do not affect the computation of the earned income credit. Earnings on amounts in an HSA are not currently taxable, and HSA distributions used to pay for medical expenses are not taxable.

Tip

HSAs are confidential. Employees are not required to provide medical bills to their employer or to the trustee or custodian of the plan. The employee is responsible to reconcile withdrawals from the HSA with unreimbursed medical expenses.

HSAs can be funded up to $3,550 for individuals and $7,100 for families to cover health care costs (2020 limits). In addition to the maximum contribution amount, catch-up contributions may be made by or on behalf of individuals between age 55 and 65. Individuals who have reached age 55 by the end of the tax year are allowed to increase their annual contribution limit by $1,000.

The HSA is often compared with an FSA (see pages 43-44). While both accounts can be used for medical expenses, some key differences exist between them. For example, unused funds in the FSA during a given tax year are forfeited once the year ends and any applicable grace period or rollover. Also, while the elected contribution amount for the year can be changed by an employee with an HSA any time during the year, the elected contribution for an FSA is fixed and can only be changed at the beginning of the following tax year.

Only employees who are enrolled in qualifying HDHPs may participate in an HSA. A HDHP has at least $1,400 annual deductible for self-only coverage and $2,800 deductible for family coverage (2020 limits). Additionally, annual out-of-pocket expenses for HSAs must be limited to $6,900 for individuals and $13,800 (2020 limits) for families. A state high-risk health insurance plan (high-risk pool) qualifies as an HDHP if it does not pay benefits below the minimum annual deductible under the HSA rules.

HSA withdrawals do not qualify to cover over-the-counter medications (other than insulin and over-the-counter medication purchased with a prescription). Additionally, there is an excise tax for nonqualified HSA withdrawals (withdrawals not used for qualified medical expenses) of 20%.

➢ **Housing allowance.** A properly designated housing allowance may be excluded from income subject to certain limitations (see Chapter 4). The fair rental value of a parsonage provided to a minister is not taxable for income tax purposes but is includible for Social Security tax purposes.

Any housing allowance paid to a minister that is more than the excludable amount is taxable compensation. The excess must be determined by the minister and reported on Form 1040, page 1. The church does not have a reporting requirement to the minister or the IRS regarding any portion of the designated housing allowance that exceeds the amount actually excluded.

➢ **Life insurance/group-term.** If the group life coverage provided under a non-discriminatory plan does not exceed $50,000 for the minister, the life insurance premiums are generally tax-free to the minister. Premiums for group-term life insurance coverage of more than $50,000 provided to the minister by the church are taxable under somewhat favorable IRS tables. Group-term life insurance is term life insurance protection that:

- ☐ provides a general death benefit that can be excluded from income
- ☐ covers a group of employees (a "group" may consist of only one employee)
- ☐ is provided under a policy carried by the employer
- ☐ provides an amount of insurance for each employee based on a formula that prevents individual selection

Caution

If the church pays the premium on a whole life or universal life policy (in contrast to a term policy) on the life of the minister and the minister names personal beneficiaries, all the premiums paid are taxable income to the minister.

If a minister pays any part of the cost of life insurance, the entire payment reduces, dollar for dollar, the amount the church would otherwise include in income.

If the minister's group-term life insurance policy includes permanent benefits such as a paid-up or cash surrender value, the minister must include in income the cost of the permanent benefits, reduced by the amount the minister paid for them.

Retired ministers should include in income any payments for group-term life insurance coverage over $50,000 that were made by a former employing church, unless the minister otherwise qualifies to exclude the payments.

➢ **Loan-grants.** Churches may provide a loan-grant to a minister relating to moving expenses, the purchase of a car, or the purchase of other property. In these instances, compensation is reported on Form W-2 for the minister based on the amount of the loan forgiven in a calendar year. The rules on compensation-related loans (see below) apply to loan-grants over $10,000.

➢ **Loans.** Some churches make loans or transfer property to ministers. The loans are often restricted to the purchase of land or a residence, or the construction of a residence. Before a loan is made, the church should consult with legal counsel to determine if the transaction is legal under state law. Such loans are prohibited in many states.

If a church makes a compensation-related loan to a minister at below-market rates, the minister may have additional taxable income. A "compensation-related" loan is any direct or indirect loan of over $10,000 made at below-market interest rates that relates to the performance of services between a church and a minister. There is an exception for certain employee-relocation loans.

For term loans, additional compensation equal to the foregone interest over the entire term of the loan is considered as compensation received on the date the loan was made. For demand loans, the foregone interest is added to compensation each year that the loan is outstanding. The additional compensation is reportable on Form W-2, Box 1.

If the loan proceeds are used for housing, and the loan is secured and properly recorded, and the minister itemizes deductions, then the minister may be able to deduct the imputed interest as mortgage interest. However, term loan interest must be prorated over the term of the loan. The interest is also eligible for inclusion in housing expenses for housing allowance purposes.

➢ **Long-term care insurance.** Long-term care or nursing home insurance premiums paid or reimbursed by the church are tax-free. If the premiums are paid by the minister and not reimbursed by the church, they are deductible as medical expenses subject to annual limits based on age.

➢ **Meals.** If meals are furnished to the minister by the church on the church premises for the church's convenience (*e.g.*, having a minister on call or if there are few or no restaurants nearby) and as a condition of employment, a church does not include their value in income, if the benefits are nondiscriminatory. The "convenience" test is met if the meals furnished on church premises are provided to at least half of the employees. *Note*: the benefits are taxable to a minister in computing self-employment for Social Security tax.

If meals provided by the church are simply a means of giving the minister additional pay and there is no other business reason for providing them, their value is considered taxable income. The value of church-provided snacks for staff is excluded from employee compensation as a *de minimus* fringe benefit.

➢ **Minimal fringe benefits.** If fringe benefits are so small (*de minimis*) in value that it would be unreasonable or impractical to account for them, the church does not have to include their value in income. If the value of the benefit is not small, its entire value must be included in income.

De minimis fringe benefits for ministers might include traditional holiday gifts with a low fair market value, occasional typing of personal letters by the church secretary, or occasional personal use of the church copy machine.

Example: A minister uses the church copy machine for personal items. The machine is used at least 85% of the time for business purposes since the church restricts personal use of the copy machine. Though the minister uses the machine for personal purposes more than other employees, the use is *de minimis* and not taxable.

Caution

Churches may still pay or reimburse moving expenses for employees, but these amounts are now considered taxable income. Churches may wish to "gross up" the moving expense payments so that employees are not left with the related tax burden.

➢ **Moving expenses.** If employee moving expenses are paid by the church (regardless of whether they are paid to the employee or to the moving company), they are includible in the employee's taxable income. Moving expenses paid by the minister are not tax-deductible.

➢ **Parking.** Ministers do not have to include in income the value of free parking facilities provided on or near the church premises if it is $270 or less per month for 2020. This also applies for reimbursements from the church for renting a parking space on or near the church premises. A church can also sell transit passes or tokens to ministers at discounts of up to $270 (2020 limit) per month tax-free to the minister or give cash up to $270 for passes and tokens tax-free.

➢ **Pre-employment expense reimbursements.** Prospective ministers may be reimbursed for expenses related to seeking a position with a particular church. Substantiated expenses related to interviews (meals, lodging, and travel) are not includible in the prospective employee's gross income whether or not the minister is subsequently employed.

➢ **Property transfers/restricted.** To reward good work, a church may transfer property to a minister subject to certain restrictions. The ultimate transfer of the property will occur only if the restrictions are met at a later date.

Property that is subject to substantial risk of forfeiture and is nontransferable is not substantially vested. No tax liability will occur until title to the property is vested with the minister. This simply represents a deferral of the tax consequences.

For tax planning purposes, the "vesting" of a restricted property transfer to a minister may be staggered over several years. The reporting of a sizable restricted gift in one year may have significant tax consequences.

When restricted property becomes substantially vested, the minister must include in income, for both income and Social Security tax purposes, an amount equal to the excess of the fair market value of the property at the time it becomes substantially vested, over any amount the minister pays for the property. The church should report the additional income on the minister's Form W-2.

Example: A church transfers a house to a minister subject to the completion of 20 years of pastoral service to the church. The minister does not report any taxable income from the gift until the year that includes the twentieth anniversary of the agreement.

➢ **Property transfers/unrestricted.** Some transfers of property by a church to a minister may trigger tax reporting:

- **Unrestricted transfers.** If a church transfers property (a car, a residence, a computer, furniture, music equipment, etc.) to a minister at no charge, this constitutes taxable income to the minister. The amount of income is typically the fair market value of the property transferred.

- **Property purchased from the church.** If the church allows a minister to buy property at below fair market value, the

Caution

Don't forget to evaluate intellectual property transfers. These may also result in taxable income to the minister. See eBook *6 Essentials of Copyright Law for Churches* at *www.ECFA.church/eBooks*.

minister is subject to taxable income for the difference between the property's fair market value over the amount paid and liabilities assumed by the minister.

➢ **Recreational expenses.** A minister may incur expenses that are primarily recreational, *e.g.*, softball or basketball league fees, greens fees, and so on. Even if there is an element of ministry purpose, the reimbursement of such fees as business expenses is generally not justified.

➢ **Retirement gifts.** Gifts made to a minister at retirement by the employing church are usually taxable compensation. Personal retirement gifts made by an individual directly to a minister may be tax-free to the minister, but they will not qualify as charitable contributions by the donor.

➢ **Retirement plans**

☐ **401(k) plans.** A church may offer a 401(k) plan to its employees. Under a 401(k) plan, an employee can elect to have the church make tax-deferred contributions, up to $19,500 for 2020 (in addition to catch-up contributions).

☐ **403(b) plans.** Ministers, who are employees for income tax purposes, may have a Section 403(b) salary reduction arrangement based on a written plan.

A minister's housing allowance or the fair rental value of church-provided housing is not included in gross income for income tax reporting purposes. Thus, the definition of computing the limit on 403(b) contributions is generally considered to exclude the portion of a minister's compensation designated as housing allowance *or* the fair rental value of church-provided housing.

Compliance with special nondiscrimination rules may be a condition to a minister benefiting from the Section 403(b) exclusion allowance. Churches and elementary or secondary schools controlled, operated, or principally supported by a church or convention or association of churches are not subject to the nondiscrimination rules.

Both nonelective (for example, payments by a church into a denominational 403[b] other than funded through a salary reduction agreement) and elective (funded through a salary reduction agreement) contributions for a minister to a 403(b) are excludable for income and Social Security tax (SECA) purposes. While permissible, after-tax employee contributions are the exception.

There are two separate yet interrelated limitations on the amount of contributions to a 403(b) plan that are excludable from gross income:

- **Salary reduction limitation.** This limitation is $19,500 for 2020. Employees over age 50 can make a "catch-up" contribution of $6,500 in 2020.

- **Maximum exclusion allowance.** For 2020, the maximum exclusion allowance is $57,000 or 100% of compensation, whichever is less.

Caution

A designated housing allowance generally must be excluded from compensation when calculating tax sheltered annuity contribution limits.

A minister can roll funds tax-free from one 403(b) to another 403(b) and from a 403(b) to an IRA. Rollovers are not subject to annual limits.

Withdrawals from a denominationally sponsored 403(b) plan may qualify for designation as a housing allowance and are not subject to Social Security (SECA) tax (see pages 75-76).

For a comparison between 403(b) and 401(k) plans, see the 2021 edition of the *Church and Nonprofit Tax & Financial Guide.*

☐ **457 deferred compensation plans (also known as Rabbi Trusts or Top Hat plans).** Churches may make cash contributions to 457 deferred compensation plans to fund their future obligation to pay deferred compensation benefits. The funds contributed are tax-deferred in a similar manner to other tax-deferred vehicles such as a 403(b) plan.

In some instances, depending on a participant's includible income (generally, includible income is a participant's salary without including parsonage), churches can make contributions that exceed the IRS maximum annual contribution limits for a 403(b) plan.

These plans are intended to provide a degree of certainty that accumulated deferred compensation benefits will actually be paid. Amounts contributed to an irrevocable plan should not revert to the church until all nonqualified deferred compensation benefits have been paid to eligible participants.

Because trust assets are subject to the claims of the church's creditors in the case of insolvency or bankruptcy, the creation of a 457 plan does not cause the arrangement to be treated as "funded" for income tax purposes.

Distribution rules for 457 plans are not as flexible as for 403(b) accounts. For example, money in a 457 plan is not eligible to be rolled over into qualified retirement plans such as 403(b) plans or IRAs.

☐ **Individual retirement accounts.** Amounts contributed by a church for a minister's Individual Retirement Account (IRA) are includible in the employee's compensation on the Form W-2 and are subject to self-employment tax. IRA contributions may fall into one of the following categories:

- **Contributions to a regular IRA.** Each spouse may, in the great majority of cases, make deductible contributions to his or her IRA up to the dollar limitation (*e.g.*, $6,000 reduced by adjusted gross income limits for 2020). The adjusted gross income phaseout ranges for 2020 are $104,000 to $124,000 for married taxpayers and $65,000 to $75,000 for singles. (The phaseout amounts are different if the minister is not an active participant but his or her spouse is.) Catch-up contributions of $1,000 may be made by taxpayers age 50 and over.

- **Contributions to a Roth IRA.** Nondeductible contributions may be made to a Roth IRA. The buildup of interest and dividends within the account may be tax-free depending on how and when you withdraw the money from the account.

☐ **Keogh plans.** If a minister has self-employment income for income tax purposes, a Keogh plan (also called "qualified retirement plans") may be used. Amounts contributed to a Keogh plan are not taxed until distribution if the contribution limits are observed. If a minister withdraws money from a Keogh plan before reaching the age of 59½, the minister will be subject to a 10% early withdrawal penalty.

➢ **Sabbatical pay.** Churches often provide a sabbatical, a period of time away from the church every few years for rest, writing, and study. A pastor typically receives full or part pay during the sabbatical. If sabbatical payments qualify as a nonqualified deferred compensation plan, plan requirements—such as documentation, elections, funding, distributions, withholding, and reporting—must be considered. Otherwise, sabbatical pay generally represents taxable pay reportable on Form W-2. A housing allowance is still appropriate for the sabbatical period.

A church sometimes reimburses travel expenses (for example, transportation, meals, and lodging) for the pastor during the sabbatical. The portion of the travel expenses that is for a bona fide business purpose and are ordinary, necessary, and reasonable generally do qualify for reimbursement under an accountable reimbursement plan and would not be added to compensation on Form W-2 (subject to IRS limitations on certain types of expenses, such as meals), while personal travel expenses do not qualify for reimbursement under an accountable expense reimbursement plan and should not be reimbursed.

➢ **Salary.** The cash salary (less the properly designated and excludable housing allowance amount) is taxable income to the minister.

➢ **Severance pay.** A lump-sum payment for cancellation of a minister's employment contract is income in the tax year received and must be reported with other compensation. An exception applies for damages received for personal physical injuries or physical sickness.

Severance paid to lay employees are subject to federal income tax and FICA withholding.

Key Issue

The U. S. Supreme Court has confirmed that severance payments constitute taxable wages and are subject to FICA.

- **Sick or disability pay.** Amounts ministers receive from their employer while sick or disabled are part of their compensation (sick or disability pay is distinguished from payments for injury provided under Workers' Compensation insurance, which are normally not taxable). Also see Disability Insurance on pages 40-41.

- **Simplified employee pension plan (SEP).** Through a SEP, an employer may contribute amounts to a minister's IRA. But there are many nondiscriminatory limitations on SEP contributions that most churches will find insurmountable.

- **Social Security tax reimbursement or allowance.** Churches and other employers commonly reimburse ministers or provide an allowance for a portion or all of their self-employment Social Security (SECA) tax liability. Any Social Security reimbursement must be reported as taxable income for income tax purposes, and it is includible in the Social Security tax (SECA) computation.

  Ministers who have opted out of SECA do not pay any Social Security tax. Therefore, in these situations, there is not a logical basis for a Social Security reimbursement or allowance.

  Because of the deductibility of the self-employment tax in both the income tax and self-employment tax computations, a full reimbursement is effectively less than the gross 15.3% rate:

Minister's Marginal Tax Rate	Effective SECA Rate
0%	14.13%
12	13.28
22	12.58
24	12.43

  It is usually best to reimburse the minister for self-employment tax on a monthly or quarterly basis. An annual reimbursement may leave room for misunderstanding between the church and the minister if the minister moves to another church before the reimbursement is made.

Caution

An allowance to cover the minister's self-employment Social Security tax provides no tax benefit since the allowance itself is fully taxable. However, the SECA is deductible in computing income tax. Paying at least one-half of the minister's SECA tax is important so this amount can be properly shown as a fringe benefit.

For missionaries who, due to the foreign earned income exclusion, are not eligible for the income tax deduction of one-half of the self-employment tax, the full reimbursement rate is effectively 14.13%.

Example: A church provides a cash salary of $80,000 and provides a parsonage that has an annual fair rental value of $15,000. Even though a full reimbursement of the minister's SECA is slightly less than 15.3%, the church decides to reimburse at the 15.3% rate for simplicity.

The church grosses up the monthly pay by $1,211.25 (15.3% times $95,000, or $14,535 divided by 12).

➢ **Subscriptions.** A church may reimburse a minister for ministry-related print or online subscriptions as a tax-free benefit.

➢ **Travel expenses.** Travel expenses are reimbursable as business expenses if they are ordinary and necessary and are incurred while traveling away from the minister's tax home for business-related reasons. Expenses that are for personal or vacation purposes, or that are lavish or extravagant, are not reimbursable as business expenses.

Travel expenses incurred outside the United States may be subject to a special business vs. personal travel-expense allocation of the transportation costs to and from the business destination. This allocation can apply even when foreign travel expenses are incurred primarily for business purposes. Expenses incurred for travel as a form of education, such as a tour of the Holy Land, are generally not reimbursable (see pages 87-88).

If a minister incurs travel expenses for a spouse or child, the minister may receive a tax-free reimbursement for the spouse's and children's expenses only if they qualify for employee treatment and

☐ the travel of the spouse and/or children is for a bona fide business purpose, and

☐ the minister substantiates the time, place, amount, and business purpose of the travel under an accountable business expense reimbursement plan.

Caution

The travel expenses of an employee's spouse and children often do not qualify for tax-free reimbursement. To be tax-free, there must be a bona fide business purpose for the spouse and children to travel, in addition to substantiation of expenses.

➢ **Tuition reduction programs.** Some churches operate schools. The school may provide for either a full or a partial tuition reduction for the employees of the church.

The amount received under a nondiscriminatory qualified tuition reduction program is not includible in the gross income of an employee or a dependent who is receiving the education *if* the school is a program of the church. If a school is separately incorporated from a church, tax-free tuition reductions are only available to school employees and are not available to church employees. If the school is unincorporated and operated by a church, tuition reductions may apply to employees of the church and the school. It is possible that individuals may qualify for a tax-free tuition program if they are employed by both a church and a separately incorporated school.

A tuition reduction program is a very attractive benefit for a school, but it is particularly beneficial for a school that cannot afford to pay its employees competitive salaries. The cost to the school for providing tuition reductions is generally far less than the amount of the tuition reduction itself.

A tax-free qualified tuition reduction may be provided for any of the following people:

- an employee;
- a retired employee;
- an employee who separated from service due to disability;
- the surviving spouse of a deceased employee;
- the spouse of an employee;
- the dependent children of an employee; and
- the children (who have not attained age 25) of a deceased employee, if both parents are dead.

Filing Tip

Tax-free tuition and fee discounts are only available to the dependents of an employee of a school. Discounts provided to church employees are taxable. This is true if the school is operated as part of the church, is a subsidiary corporation under the church, or is separately incorporated.

The portion of tuition that an employee pays to a school cannot be treated as tax-free under a pre-tax salary reduction arrangement.

➢ **Vacation pay.** Payments made by the church to a minister for vacations are taxable income.

➢ **Vehicles/personal use of employer-owned vehicle.** One of the most attractive fringe benefits for a minister is for the church or other employer to own or lease a vehicle for the minister to use. The church generally makes the lease payments or car loan payments, if any, plus paying for all gas, oil, insurance, repairs, and other related expenses. Unless the vehicle is always parked on the church premises (*e.g.*, where business trips start) and is never used for personal purposes, the minister must maintain a log to document any personal use of the vehicle. The church must report the value of the personal use of the vehicle as taxable income on Form W-2. See pages 94-96 for the rules a ministry can use to determine the personal use value of a vehicle for inclusion in income as a noncash fringe benefit.

➢ **Vehicle use/nonpersonal.** The total value of a qualified nonpersonal-use vehicle is excluded from income as a working condition fringe benefit. The term "qualified nonpersonal-use vehicle" means any vehicle that is not likely to be used more than a small amount for personal purposes because of its nature or design.

Example: A church provides the minister with a vehicle to use for church business. The minister does not qualify for a home office and leaves the car parked at the church when it is not being driven for business purposes. There is a written agreement with the church that prohibits personal use of the vehicle. Only in an emergency is the car driven for personal benefit. This vehicle should qualify under the nonpersonal-use provision, and the entire value of the nonpersonal use of the vehicle would be excluded from income.

➢ **Withholding.** Amounts withheld from pay or put into a minister's bank account under a voluntary withholding agreement for income tax are compensation as though paid directly to the minister. These amounts must be included on Form W-2 in the year they were withheld. The same is generally true of amounts withheld for taxable fringe benefits.

If the church uses wages to pay a minister's debts, or if wages are garnished, the full amount is compensation to the minister.

➢ **Workers' compensation.** A minister who receives workers' compensation benefits due to his or her job-related injuries or sickness may generally exclude the benefits from gross income. In addition, the minister is not taxed on the value of the insurance premiums paid by the church.

Ministers are subject to workers' compensation laws in many states. It is often important to cover ministers under workers' compensation insurance even if it is not a state requirement. For work-related injuries of ministers, many health benefit plans will not pay medical expenses unless the minister is covered by workers' compensation insurance.

Reporting Compensation, Fringe Benefits, and Reimbursements for Income Tax Purposes*

Compensation, fringe benefit, or reimbursement	Minister
Bonus or gift from church	Taxable income/Form W-2
Business and professional expenses reimbursed *with* adequate accounting	Tax-free
Business and professional expense reimbursed *without* adequate accounting	Taxable income/Form W-2
Club dues paid by the church	Taxable income/Form W-2 (except for dues for professional organizations and civic and public service groups)
Compensation reported to minister by church	Taxable income/Form W-2
Dependent care assistance payments	Tax-free, subject to limitations
Educational assistance programs	May be eligible to exclude qualified assistance
401(k) plan	Eligible for 401(k) (either tax-deferred or taxable with tax-free growth)
403(b) plan	Eligible for 403(b) (either tax-deferred or taxable with tax-free growth)
Gifts/personal (not handled through church)	Tax-free
Housing allowance	Tax-free
Health reimbursement arrangement	Tax-free
Health savings account	Tax-free
Health care flexible spending account	Tax-free
IRA payments by church	Taxable income/Form W-2, may be deducted
Insurance, disability. Paid by church, minister is beneficiary	Premiums are tax-free, but proceeds are taxable
Insurance, disability. Paid by minister, minister is beneficiary	Premiums paid after-tax, proceeds are tax-free
Insurance, group-term life. Paid by church	Premiums on first $50,000 of coverage is tax-free

** Many of these compensation elements are conditioned on plans having been properly established and/or subject to annual limits.*

Compensation, fringe benefit, or reimbursement	Minister
Insurance, health	Tax-free if directly paid by church as part of a qualifying group plan. If paid by minister and not reimbursed by church, deduct on Schedule A subject to limitations
Insurance, life, whole or universal. Church is beneficiary	Tax-free
Insurance, life, whole or universal. Minister designates beneficiary	Taxable income/Form W-2
Insurance, long-term care	Tax-free if directly paid by church or reimbursed to minister on substantiation. If paid by minister and not reimbursed by church, deduct on Schedule A subject to limitations
Loans, certain low-interest or interest-free to minister over $10,000	Imputed interest (the difference between the IRS-established interest rate and the rate charged) is taxable income/Form W-2
Moving expenses paid by the church	Taxable (not deductible by the minister)/Form W-2
Pension payments to a denominational plan for the minister by the church	Tax-deferred. No reporting required until the funds are withdrawn or pension benefits are paid
Per diem payments for meals, lodging, and incidental expenses	May be used for travel away from home under an accountable reimbursement plan
Professional income (weddings, funerals)	Taxable income/Schedule C
Property transferred to minister at no cost or less than fair market value	Taxable income/Form W-2
Retirement or farewell gift to minister from church	Generally taxable income/Form W-2
Salary from church	Taxable income/Form W-2
Social Security reimbursed by church to minister	Taxable income/Form W-2
Travel paid for minister's spouse by the church	May be tax-free if there is a business purpose
Tuition and fee discounts	May be tax-free in certain situations
Value of home provided to minister (parsonage)	Tax-free
Vehicles/personal use of church-owned auto	Taxable income/Form W-2
Voluntary withholding	Eligible for voluntary withholding agreement

- **Reimbursing out-of-pocket medical expenses.** Sadly, most ministers do not have one of the plans under which out-of-pocket medical expenses may be reimbursed on a tax-free basis.
  - **Cafeteria plan.** Generally only very large churches can justify establishing and maintaining a cafeteria plan. These plans can cover much more than medical expenses—for example, dependent care, life insurance, and disability insurance.
  - **Health Savings Account (HSA).** This concept is valid, but it has grown very slowly.
  - **Health reimbursement arrangement (HRA).** The same HRA benefit must be provided to all employees. This makes this concept very limiting since out-of-pocket costs significantly vary employee-to-employee.
  - **Flexible spending account (FSA).** The FSA should generally be the plan of choice for many ministers and churches. The FSA is simple to establish and easy to administer by the church.
  - **Other options.** Smaller churches may also be able to offer a qualified small employer health reimbursement arrangement (QSEHRA) or individual coverage health reimbursement arrangement (ICHRA) as possibilities for helping ministers with health insurance and other medical expenses.
- **The impact of the nondiscrimination rules on ministers.** While the nondiscrimination rules do not impact many fringe benefits, these rules do apply to most of the plans under which out-of-pocket medical expenses (see above) may be reimbursed.

  Often a church will want to reimburse out-of-pocket medical expenses for the staff at varying levels, *e.g.*, up to $1,000 for the senior pastor, up to $500 for the associate pastor, and up to $300 for a secretary under an HRA. This arrangement fails the nondiscrimination test.
- **Discretionary funds.** If a church provides a minister with discretionary funds (funds to provide benevolence assistance as needs are identified by the minister), the accounting to the church for these funds is vital. Unless a minister documents the date the funds were spent, the recipient of the funds, and the benevolent need, discretionary funds are generally taxable to the minister as compensation.

Housing Exclusion

In This Chapter

- Types of housing arrangements
- Establishing and modifying the housing designation
- Reporting the housing allowance to the minister
- Accounting for the housing exclusion
- Other housing exclusion issues
- Housing exclusion worksheets

The housing exclusion was originally enacted in 1921, allowing ministers to exclude from income the annual rental value of a church-owned parsonage provided to them as part of their compensation for serving the church. This provision only applied to in-kind housing and typically applied to ministers who lived on-site.

In 1954, Congress overhauled the Tax Code and allowed ministers to continue receiving tax-free housing even if they lived off-site or if the housing were explicitly intended as compensation.

In 1984, in preparation for what ultimately became the Tax Reform Act of 1986, the Treasury Department proposed eliminating the housing exclusion. However, Congress chose to retain the exclusion.

In 2002, litigation arose as to whether ministers could exclude unlimited amounts of cash compensation allocated to and actually spent on housing, or whether the amount excludible should be limited to the rental value of the housing. The Tax Court sided with the minister, and the IRS appealed the decision to the Ninth Circuit, which began questions on the provision's constitutionality. In response to an outcry from religious organizations, the government quickly moved to protect the exemption. Congress amended the statute explicitly to limit the allowance to the fair rental value of the home and other associated expenses.

In recent years, the Freedom From Religion Foundation (FFRF) has fought to have the ministerial housing exclusion deemed unconstitutional. FFRF was successful in seeing the

Employer-Provided Housing

The fair rental value of the housing plus utilities (if the utilities are paid by the church) is

- Excludable for federal income tax purposes, and
- Includible for Social Security (SECA) purposes.

A housing allowance may also be provided to a minister living in church-provided housing as a designation of the cash salary. A minister may utilize the housing exclusion to exclude certain housing expenses paid by the minister (see the worksheet on page 77).

Minister-Provided Housing

The housing allowance is excluded for federal income tax purposes. The entire housing allowance is taxable for Social Security tax (SECA) purposes. See the worksheets on pages 78 and 79 for excludable expenses. In this case, the housing exclusion (which doesn't exceed reasonable compensation) is the *lowest* of these three factors:

1. Amount used from current ministerial income to provide the home
2. Amount prospectively and officially designated by the church
3. Fair rental value of the home including utilities and furnishings

Any excess over the lowest of these factors is reportable as additional income for income tax purposes on Form 1040, page 1, Line 1.

exclusion struck down in 2013 in a District Court for the Western District of Wisconsin, only to see it reversed by an appeals court in 2014. FFRF filed another lawsuit in 2015, and in 2017, the same Wisconsin District Court determined the exclusion was an unconstitutional preference for religion. Then, an appeals court reversed the District Court's decision and affirmed the constitutionality of the housing exclusion.

Today, qualified ministers (see Chapter 1 for who is a qualified minister under tax law) continue to be eligible to receive lodging from a church or a cash housing allowance free of income tax liability by excluding dollars from gross income. Maximizing housing benefits requires careful planning, though. Used properly, the housing allowance can truly be the minister's best tax friend.

If the church properly designates a portion of the minister's cash salary for expenses of a *home he or she provides*, it is commonly referred to as a "housing allowance." If the church properly designates a portion of the minister's cash salary for expenses they incur in relation to *church-provided housing*, it is often called a "parsonage allowance." In either instance, it is an exclusion from federal income tax, but not from self-employment Social Security tax.

Nearly every qualified minister gets a tax advantage by having a portion of salary designated as a housing allowance. For church-owned housing, the housing exclusion covers expenses such as furnishings, personal property insurance on contents, as well as utilities, potentially saving hundreds of dollars of *income taxes*. For ministers living in their own homes or rental housing, a properly designated housing allowance may be worth thousands of dollars of *income tax* saved.

The designated housing allowance should be subtracted from compensation before the church completes Form W-2, Box 1. The housing allowance is often shown in Box 14 of Form W-2. The housing allowance is not entered on Form 1040 or related schedules, except Schedule SE, since it is not a deduction for income tax purposes. However, any unused portion of the housing allowance must be reported as income on Form 1040, page 1, Line 1.

Key Issue

Understanding the distinction between a housing allowance designation and the housing exclusion is fundamental. The *designation* is officially made by the church or other employer. The *exclusion* is the amount the minister actually excludes for income tax purposes after applying the limitations outlined in this chapter.

Ministers are eligible to exclude the fair rental value of church-provided housing for income tax purposes without any official action by the church. However, a cash housing allowance related to housing, either church-provided or minister-provided, is only excludable under the following guidelines:

- ➢ The allowance must be officially designated by the church. The designation should be stated in writing, preferably by resolution of the top governing body, in an employment contract, or by a committee of the board. If the only reference to the housing allowance is in the church budget, the budget should be formally approved by the top governing body of the church. See the 2021 edition of the *Church and Nonprofit Tax & Financial Guide* for examples of housing allowance resolutions.

Tax law does not specifically say that an oral designation of the housing allowance is unacceptable. In certain instances, the IRS has accepted an oral housing designation. Still, the lack of a written designation significantly weakens the defense for the housing exclusion upon audit.

➢ The housing allowance must be designated prospectively by the church. This means that any cash housing allowance payments made prior to a designation are fully taxable. Also, carefully word the resolution so that it will remain in effect until a subsequent resolution is adopted, *i.e.*, "This resolution shall remain in effect until subsequently changed."

➢ All actual housing expenses paid during the calendar year can be excluded from income. Any amounts received in a housing allowance that exceeded amounts actually used as proper housing expenses must be declared as income. Moreover, the source of the funds used to pay for a minister's housing expenses must be compensation received by the minister in the exercise of ministry in the current year.

➢ Only an annual comparison by a minister of housing expenses to housing allowance is required. For example, if the housing allowance designation is stated in terms of a weekly or monthly amount, only a comparison of actual housing expenses to the annualized housing allowance is required. However, if there is an adjustment during the year in the housing allowance amount that was designated by the church, the minister must determine if the actual expenses were incurred before or after the housing allowance amount was changed when determining the amount for exclusion.

Key Issue

A minister with a designated housing allowance must compare it to his/her actual expenses annually and exclude from declared income only the amount actually used for housing, the rest is declared as income.

➢ The housing allowance exclusion cannot exceed the fair rental value of the housing, including furnishings plus utilities.

Another useful resource is the ECFA eBook *10 Essentials of the Minister's Housing Exclusion.*

Types of Housing Arrangements

Minister living in church-provided housing

If a minister lives in a church-owned parsonage or housing rented by the church, the fair rental value of the housing is not reported for income tax purposes. The fair rental value is subject only to self-employment tax.

However, the minister may also request a housing allowance to cover expenses incurred in maintaining church-owned or church-rented housing. A cash housing allowance that is not more than reasonable pay for services is excludable for income tax purposes, subject to the lowest of (1) actual housing expenses paid from current ministerial income, or (2) the amount prospectively and officially designated. If the actual expenses exceed the housing allowance designated by the church, the excess amount does not qualify as an exclusion from income. The types of expenses shown on the worksheet on page 77 qualify as part of the housing exclusion for a minister living in housing owned or rented by the church.

Tip

The designation of a housing allowance for a minister living in church-provided housing is often overlooked. While the largest housing allowance benefits go to ministers with mortgage payments on their own homes, a housing allowance of a few thousand dollars is often beneficial to a minister in a church-provided home.

It is appropriate for the minister's out-of-pocket expenses for the maintenance of a church-owned parsonage to be reimbursed by the church. These reimbursements are not excludable as part of a housing allowance. If such expenses are not reimbursed, they may be excluded from income under a housing allowance.

If the church owns the parsonage, the church may wish to provide an equity allowance to help compensate the minister for equity not accumulated through home ownership. An equity allowance is taxable for both income and Social Security tax purposes *unless* directed to a 403(b) tax-sheltered annuity, 401(k) plan, or certain other retirement programs.

Minister owning or renting their own home

If ministers own or rent their own home, they may exclude, for income tax purposes, a cash housing allowance that is not more than reasonable pay for services and that is the lowest of (1) the amount used to provide a home from current ministerial income, (2) the amount prospectively and officially designated, or (3) the fair rental value of the furnished home, plus utilities.

The types of expenses shown on the worksheet on page 78 qualify as part of the housing allowance for a minister owning or buying a home. Page 79 shows a similar worksheet for a minister renting a home.

Many ministers make the mistake of automatically excluding from income (for income tax purposes) the total designated housing allowance, even though the fair rental value of the furnished home or actual housing expenses are less than the designation. This practice may cause a significant underpayment of income taxes.

The housing expenses related to a minister-owned house should not *be reimbursed* by the church. These are personal expenses that should be covered by the minister under a cash housing allowance paid by the church.

Example: A minister lives in a personally owned home. The church prospectively designates $28,000 of the minister's salary as housing allowance. The minister spends $27,000 for housing-related items. The fair rental value of the home is $29,000.

Since the amount spent for housing expenses is lower than the designated housing allowance or the fair rental value, the excludable portion of the housing allowance is $27,000. Therefore, $1,000 ($28,000 less $27,000) must be added to taxable income on the minister's Form 1040, page 1, Line 1. Unless the minister has opted out of Social Security, the entire $28,000 is reportable for Social Security purposes on Schedule SE ($1,000 which was added to income, and $27,000 which ws excludable as income).

Establishing and Modifying the Housing Designation

Before paying compensation

The church should take the following steps to specify a housing designation before paying compensation:

- Verify the qualified tax status of the minister. Does the minister meet the tests found on pages 14-19?
- Verify the qualified nature of the minister's services, *e.g.*, administering sacraments; conducting religious worship; performing management responsibilities for a church, a denomination, or an integral agency of a

Warning

It is the responsibility of the church—not the minister—to determine if an individual qualifies as a minister in the eyes of the IRS and, therefore, qualifies for a housing designation. Simply being ordained, licensed, or commissioned is not enough to qualify for this status.

church or denomination; or the services performed for a parachurch or other organization (see pages 14-19).

- Determine the extent to which the payment of housing expenses will be the responsibility of the minister. For example, will the utilities for a church-owned parsonage be paid by the church or the minister?
- Request that the minister estimate the housing-related expenses expected in the coming year which are the minister's responsibility.
- Adopt a written designation based on the minister's estimate. This designation may be included in minutes or resolutions of the top governing body, an employment contract, the church's annual budget, or another appropriate document if official action on the document is recorded.

During the calendar year

The following actions should be taken during the year (after the housing designation is made):

- The minister should keep records of allowable housing expenses incurred.
- The minister should make regular payments to the IRS to cover the self-employment tax (SECA) on the entire housing allowance (and other income subject to SECA) plus federal income tax on any anticipated unexpended portion of the allowance and other taxable income. This may be accomplished by submitting quarterly tax installments with Form 1040-ES, voluntary income tax withholding by the church, or spousal income tax withholding.
- The minister should identify any significant change in housing expenses and estimate the amount by which the total actual expenses may exceed the amount designated as the housing allowance.
- When housing expenses are running higher than anticipated—or are expected to do so—and the fair rental value will exceed actual housing expenses, the minister should ask the church to prospectively increase the housing allowance designation. A retroactive housing allowance increase is ineffective.
- The church should prospectively amend the minister's housing allowance as appropriate to reflect the anticipated change in housing expenses (see page 71).

After each calendar year

The following actions should be taken after the close of each calendar year with respect to the housing allowance:

- The church should provide the minister with copies of Form W-2. An approved housing allowance paid to the minister may be included on Form W-2 in Box 14 with the explanation: "Housing Allowance." As an option, the church may provide the minister with a separate statement showing the amount of any housing allowance paid to or for the minister and omit the data from Form W-2, Box 14.

  The minister who provides his or her own housing should compare reasonable compensation, the amount designated for housing, actual housing expenses, and the fair rental value. The lowest of these amounts is excluded for income tax purposes.

  Ministers living in church-provided housing must compare reasonable compensation, the amount designated, and actual housing expenses, and exclude the lowest of these amounts.

Designation limits

Caution

How high is too high? Can even 100% of a minister's cash salary be designated as a housing allowance? Yes, but only in limited situations. The fair rental value and actual housing expense limitations usually make the 100% designation inappropriate.

The IRS does not place a limit on how much of a minister's compensation may be designated as a housing allowance by a church. In a few instances, as much as 100% of the cash compensation may be designated. *But practical and reasonable limits apply.*

A housing allowance must not represent "unreasonable compensation" to the minister. Unfortunately, neither the IRS nor the courts have provided a clear definition of unreasonable compensation. When determining reasonable compensation, the IRS generally considers the total compensation package, including the housing allowance and taxable and nontaxable fringe benefits.

It is generally unwise for the employing church to exclude 100% of compensation, unless the amount to be designated as a housing allowance is justified based on anticipated housing expenses within the exclusion limitations.

Example 1: A minister provides her own housing. The fair rental value, furnished plus utilities, is $25,000. She anticipates spending $28,000 on housing. Should the church designate a housing allowance of $25,000 or at least $28,000? Based on these facts, the church does not have a sound basis to designate more than $25,000, since the minister cannot exclude more than this amount.

Example 2: A bi-vocational minister receives a salary of $20,000 per year from the church and provides his home. Actual housing costs are $30,000. If the church sets the housing allowance at 100% of compensation, or $20,000, the minister may exclude $20,000 for federal income tax purposes. If the church had set the housing allowance at 50% of compensation, or $10,000, only $10,000 could be excluded.

Example 3: A minister has a voluntary withholding arrangement with the church, and the church sets the housing allowance at 100% of compensation. Form W-2 should show no salary (ignoring other compensation factors) but would reflect any federal income tax and possibly state income tax withheld. While the Form W-2 would be correctly stated, its appearance would be most unusual.

It is often best to over-designate your housing allowance by a reasonable amount, subject to the fair rental value limitation, to allow for unexpected housing expenses and increases in utility costs. Any excess housing allowance designated should be shown as income on Form 1040, page 1, Line 1, with the notation "Excess housing allowance."

More than one housing allowance?

Based on a Tax Court ruling, a minister may only exclude housing expenses of one home, the principal residence. This ruling is important to many ministers because it is not unusual for a minister to own two homes at the same time. Multiple ownership most often occurs when a minister buys a new home and has not yet sold a former home. *Based on the Tax Court ruling, there is no basis to exclude housing expenses of two homes owned concurrently.*

Amending the housing designation

If a minister's actual housing expenses are or will be higher than initially estimated and designated, the church may prospectively amend the designation during the year, subject to the fair rental value limitation.

Example: The church sets the housing allowance at $2,000 per month on January 1. On July 1, the church approves an increase in the housing allowance to $2,400 per month. Therefore, the housing allowance for the year totals $26,400 ($12,000 for the first six months and $14,400 for the last six months). Actual housing costs are $2,100 per month for the first six months and $2,300 per month for the last six

Remember

The housing allowance designation may be prospectively amended at any time during the year, regardless of whether a calendar or fiscal year is used. Changing the designation to cover expenses that have *already* been paid (almost all ministers use the cash basis for tax purposes) is not acceptable.

months. The fair rental value of the home is $2,500 per month. The minister excludes $25,800 for federal income tax purposes: $12,000 for the first six months (limited by the designation) and $13,800 for the last six months (limited by the actual housing costs).

Housing allowance adopted by denomination

If the local congregation employs and pays a minister, a resolution by a national or area office of that denomination does not constitute a housing allowance designation. The local congregation must officially designate a part of the minister's salary as a housing allowance. A resolution of a denomination can designate a minister's housing allowance if the minister is employed and paid by a national or area office or if a retired minister receives a retirement distribution from a denominational retirement plan.

Reporting the Housing Allowance to the Minister

The designated housing allowance may be reflected on Form W-2 in Box 14 with the notation, "Housing Allowance." Though not required, this reporting method is suggested by IRS Publication 517.

Alternatively, a church can report the designated housing allowance to a minister by providing a written statement separate from Form W-2. The statement should not be attached to your income tax returns when they are sent.

A church might erroneously include the housing allowance on the minister's Form W-2, Box 1. If this happens, the church should correct this using Form W-2c.

There is no requirement for the minister to account to the church for the actual housing expenses, with the housing allowance designation limited to documented actual expenses. Additionally, many ministers consider this as an intrusion into their personal finances.

Accounting for the Housing Exclusion

Determining fair rental value

The determination of the fair rental value of church-provided housing for self-employment Social Security tax purposes is solely the responsibility of the minister. The church is not responsible to set the value. The fair rental value should be based on comparable rental values of other similar residences in the immediate community, comparably furnished, plus utilities.

One of the best methods to establish the fair rental value of the minister's housing is to request a local realtor to estimate the value in writing (this is not a formal appraisal). A minister can place the estimate in a personal tax file and annually adjust the value for inflation and other local real estate valuation factors.

There is no definitive guidance regarding whether the fair rental value limitation refers to a furnished home or the fair rental value of an unfurnished home *plus* the fair rental value of furniture used in the home.

Housing allowance in excess of actual expenses or fair rental value

Some ministers erroneously believe that they may exclude every dollar of the housing *designation* adopted by the church without limitation. The housing designation is merely the starting point in calculating the housing exclusion. If reasonable compensation, actual expenses, or the fair rental value is lower, the *lowest* amount is eligible for exclusion from income.

> ***Example:*** A minister living in a personally owned home receives cash compensation from the church of $80,000. The church prospectively designates $25,000 as a housing allowance. The fair rental value is $26,000. Actual housing expenses for the year are $24,000. The amount excludable from income is limited to the actual housing expenses of $24,000 (the lowest of these amounts).

Determining actual expenses

The actual amount expended for housing and furnishings is limited to amounts expended in the current calendar year. Amounts expended in a prior year cannot be carried forward to a following year by depreciating the cost of the home or by carrying forward actual current-year expenses that exceeded amounts designated in a prior year. Unused housing expenses from prior years simply have no value in future years.

Home equity loans and second mortgages

Without a home mortgage, a minister has no mortgage principal and interest amounts to exclude under a housing allowance. Also, there would be no "double benefit" of the mortgage interest as an itemized deduction and as a housing expense for purposes of the housing allowance exclusion.

What is the treatment of principal and interest payments on a second mortgage or a mortgage that has been refinanced and increased the

Warning

Loan payments on home equity loans and second mortgages qualify as housing expenses only in certain instances. The use of the loan proceeds as housing expenses vs. non-housing expenses determines whether the loan payments may be excluded for income tax purposes.

indebtedness? This issue has not been addressed by the IRS or courts. However, it appears that an allocation of the loan payments between excludable housing expenses and nonexcludable personal expenses would be required based on the use of the additional loan proceeds.

Do principal and interest payments on a home equity loan qualify as excludable housing expenses? The Tax Court has ruled that the loan or mortgage payments are excludable as housing expenses only if the loan proceeds are used for housing expenses. The exclusion is not available if the loan proceeds are used for personal expenses such as the purchase of an auto or for a child's college education. The interest is deductible on Schedule A if the loan proceeds are used to buy, build, or substantially improve the minister's home that secures the loan.

Example: A home equity loan of $20,000 was obtained by a minister, secured by the residence. The money was used as follows: $10,000 for a new car and $10,000 to add a deck and screened-in porch to the minister's home. The home equity loan payments relating to funds used to purchase the new car are not excludable as housing expenses. Since the other $10,000 was used for housing, the payments relating to this portion of the loan qualify as housing expenses.

Other Housing Exclusion Issues

Payment of the housing allowance to the minister

It is immaterial whether the payment of a properly designated cash housing allowance is a separate payment or is part of a payment that also includes other compensation. A cash housing allowance is usually included with the minister's salary check.

Cost of the housing allowance to the church

Some churches mistakenly believe that providing a housing allowance to their minister will increase the church budget. This is not true. If a portion of the compensation already being paid to the minister is designated as a housing allowance, it costs the church nothing and simply increases the "take home pay" of the minister.

Example: A church pays a minister $75,000 per year but does not presently designate a housing allowance. The minister provides the home. The minister requests that the church designate a housing allowance of $30,000 per year. The church adopts a resolution reflecting compensation of $75,000 per year, of which $30,000 is a designated housing allowance. Before the designation, Form W-2 for the minister would have shown compensation of $75,000. After the designation, Form W-2 would reflect compensation of $45,000. The money spent by the church is the same before and after the designation, and the minister saves a significant amount of income taxes.

"Double benefit" of interest and taxes

Ministers who own their homes and itemize their deductions are eligible to claim mortgage interest and property taxes on Schedule A even though these items are also excluded from taxable income as part of the housing allowance. This is also referred to as a "double benefit" or "double deduction."

Housing allowances for retired ministers

Pension payments, retirement allowances, or disability payments paid to a retired minister from an established plan are generally taxable as pension income. However, most denominations designate a housing allowance for retired ministers to compensate them for past services to local churches of the denomination, to the denomination itself, or in denominational administrative positions. The housing allowance designated relates only to payments from the denominationally-sponsored retirement program.

Withdrawals from a denominationally sponsored 403(b) plan, also called a tax-sheltered annuity (TSA), or from a 401(k) plan qualify for designation as a housing allowance. Withdrawals from a 403(b) or 401(k) plan not sponsored by a denomination or a church are not eligible for designation as a housing allowance.

Retired ministers may also exclude the rental value of a home furnished by a church or a rental allowance paid by a church as compensation for past services.

Can a local church (as contrasted with a denomination) or a nondenominational local church designate a housing allowance for a *retired* minister for the church's contributions to a minister's 403(b) plan? While IRS rulings in this area are not specific, a church has a reasonable position to make the designation.

Remember

Payments to ministers from denominational retirement plans are generally designated as housing allowance. While a local church may designate a housing allowance for a retired minister, it is unclear if the IRS will honor the designation on the minister's tax return.

If a denomination reports the gross amount of pension or TSA payments on Form 1099-R and designates the housing allowance, the minister may offset the housing expenses and include the net amount on Line 5c of Form 1040, page 1. A supplementary schedule such as the following example should be attached to the tax return:

Pensions and annuity income (Form 1040, Line 5a)	$10,000
Less housing exclusion	8,000
Form 1040, Line 5b	$ 2,000

For a retired minister, the amount excluded for income tax purposes is limited to the lowest of (1) the amount used to provide a home, (2) the properly designated housing allowance, or (3) the fair rental value of the furnished home, plus utilities.

A surviving spouse of a retired minister cannot exclude a housing allowance from income. If a minister's surviving spouse receives a rental allowance from a church, it is includible in gross income.

Housing allowances for honoraria

Ministers may treat a portion of speaking fee honoraria received as an excludable housing allowance to the extent that the paying church designates all or a portion of the honorarium as a housing allowance in advance of payment. Honoraria payments of $600 or more in a calendar year to a minister require the church to issue Form 1099-NEC. The $600 reporting threshold is after excluding any properly designated housing allowances and the net of expense reimbursements based on adequate substantiation.

Example: William Dalton preaches at Westside Church for a weekend conference. Westside Church paid Dalton $3,000 consisting of $500 documented travel expenses and a properly designated housing allowance of $1,000. Since the non-excludable portion of the honorarium exceeded $600, the church issued Dalton a Form 1099-NEC for $1,500.

Housing allowances for teachers or administrators

Ministers employed as teachers or administrators by a church-sponsored school, college, or university perform ministerial services for purposes of the housing exclusion. However, if the minister performs services as a teacher or administrator on the faculty of a non-church college, he or she cannot exclude from income a housing allowance.

Housing Exclusion Worksheet

Minister Living in Housing Owned by or Rented by the Church

Minister's name: ______________________________________

For the period ____________________, 20___ to ____________________, 20_____

Date designation approved ________________________, 20___

Allowable Housing Expenses *(expenses paid by minister from current income)*

	Estimated Expenses	Actual
Utilities *(gas, electricity, water)* and trash collection	$ ________	$ ________
Decoration and redecoration	________	________
Structural maintenance and repair	________	________
Landscaping, gardening, and pest control	________	________
Furnishings *(purchase, repair, replacement)*	________	________
Personal property insurance on minister-owned contents	________	________
Personal property taxes on contents	________	________
Umbrella liability insurance	________	________
Subtotal	________	
10% allowance for unexpected expenses	________	
TOTAL	$ ________	$________(A)
Properly designated housing allowance		$________(B)

The amount excludable from income for federal income tax purposes is the lower of A or B (or reasonable compensation).

Housing Exclusion Worksheet

Minister Living in Home
Minister Owns or Is Buying

Minister's name: ______________________________

For the period __________________, 20___ to __________________, 20_____

Date designation approved ______________________, 20___

Allowable Housing Expenses *(expenses paid by minister from current income)*

	Estimated Expenses	Actual
Down payment on purchase of housing	$ ________	$ ________
Housing loan principal and interest payments	________	________
Real estate commission, escrow fees	________	________
Real property taxes	________	________
Personal property taxes on contents	________	________
Homeowner's insurance	________	________
Personal property insurance on contents	________	________
Umbrella liability insurance	________	________
Structural maintenance and repair	________	________
Landscaping, gardening, and pest control	________	________
Furnishings *(purchase, repair, replacement)*	________	________
Decoration and redecoration	________	________
Utilities *(gas, electricity, water)* and trash collection	________	________
Homeowner's association dues/condominium fees	________	________
Subtotal	________	
10% allowance for unexpected expenses	________	
TOTAL	$ ________	$ ________ (A)
Properly designated housing allowance		$ ________ (B)
Fair rental value of home, including furnishings, plus utilities		$ ________ (C)

The amount excludable from income for federal income tax purposes is the lowest of A, B, or C (or reasonable compensation).

Housing Exclusion Worksheet
Minister Living in Home
Minister Is Renting

Minister's name: ____________________

For the period ______________, 20___ to ______________, 20_____

Date designation approved ______________, 20___

Allowable Housing Expenses *(expenses paid by minister from current income)*

	Estimated Expenses	Actual
Housing rental payments	$ ______	$ ______
Personal property insurance on minister-owned contents	______	______
Personal property taxes on contents	______	______
Umbrella liability insurance	______	______
Structural maintenance and repair	______	______
Landscaping, gardening, and pest control	______	______
Furnishings *(purchase, repair, replacement)*	______	______
Decoration and redecoration	______	______
Utilities *(gas, electricity, water)* and trash collection	______	______
Other rental expenses	______	______
Subtotal	______	
10% allowance for unexpected expenses	______	
TOTAL	$ ______	$ ______(A)
Properly designated housing allowance	______	$ ______(B)

The amount excludable from income for federal income tax purposes is the lower of A or B (or reasonable compensation).

- **Determining housing allowance eligibility.** The designation of a portion of cash compensation as a housing allowance is the responsibility of the church or other nonprofit ministry, and it is only available to certain ministers. Ordination, licensure, or commissioning of a minister alone is not enough. Improperly claiming an exclusion for housing expenses could result in the minister paying significant back taxes, interest, and penalties.

  The various rules for ministers serving a local church, serving as missionaries, assigned by a church, or functioning in other service positions are discussed in Chapter 1.

- **Confirm that a housing allowance has been officially designated.** The wise minister will receive a copy of the annual housing allowance formally designated by the board or an authorized committee. The housing allowance resolution should be placed in the minister's tax file for future reference, if audited by the IRS.

- **Applying the limits on the exclusion.** The designation of a housing allowance for a qualified minister is an action required by a church, formally and prospectively. However, it is the *minister's* responsibility to determine how much of the housing allowance designation qualifies for exclusion from federal, and perhaps state, income taxes. Remarkably, the IRS does not require the reporting of the application of the housing exclusion limits. But the law and integrity require the limits be applied.

  For the vast majority of ministers, the most overlooked test is the fair rental value, including furnishings, plus utilities. The fair rental value, including furnishings, plus utilities is admittedly a "soft" number because the guidance provided by the IRS is vague on this topic. But an honest effort to reasonably determine this number is essential.

  The excess housing allowance, which is the designated housing allowance minus the lowest of the housing exclusion limitations (see pages 70-71), must be reported on Form 1040, page 1, Line 1. This results in the excess housing allowance being subjected to federal, and perhaps state, income taxes.

Business Expenses

In This Chapter

- Accountable and nonaccountable expense reimbursement plans
- Substantiating and reporting business expenses
- Travel and transportation expenses
- Auto expense reimbursements
- Other business expenses
- Allocation of business expenses

Most ministers spend several thousand dollars each year on church-related business expenses. For example, the ministry-related portion of auto expenses is often a major cost. Business and professional expenses fall into three basic categories: (1) expenses reimbursed under an accountable plan, (2) expenses reimbursed under a nonaccountable plan, and (3) unreimbursed expenses. Neither of the last two categories provide any income tax benefit to a minister.

The reimbursement of an expense by the church to the minister *never* changes the character of the item from personal to business. Business expenses are business expenses whether or not they are reimbursed. Personal expenses are always nondeductible and nonreimbursable. If a personal expense is inadvertently reimbursed by the church, the minister should immediately refund the money to the church.

Key Issue

Combining an accountable expense reimbursement plan with a housing allowance or any other fringe benefit plan is not permissible. These concepts are each covered under separate sections of the tax law and cannot be commingled.

To be reimbursable, a business expense must be both ordinary and necessary. An ordinary expense is one that is common and accepted in your field. A necessary expense is one that is helpful and essential for your field. An expense does not have to be indispensable to be considered necessary.

You may find this additional ECFA resource helpful: *5 Essentials of Reimbursing Ministerial Expenses.*

Accountable and Nonaccountable Expense Reimbursement Plans

An accountable plan is a reimbursement or expense allowance arrangement established by the church that requires (1) a business purpose for the expenses, (2) substantiation of expenses to the employer, and (3) the return of any excess reimbursements. A sample plan is included in the 2021 edition of the *Church and Nonprofit Tax & Financial Guide.*

The substantiation of expenses and the return of excess reimbursements must be handled within a reasonable time. The following methods meet the "reasonable time" definition:

Caution

Documentation for business expenses must be submitted to the church on a timely basis—within 60 days after the expense was paid or incurred. While the 60 days is a timeliness "safe harbor" versus a fixed time limit, it is clear that documentation submitted semiannually or annually should not be reimbursed under an accountable plan.

- The *fixed date method* applies if:
  - ☐ an advance is given no more than 30 days before an expense is paid or incurred
  - ☐ an expense is substantiated to the church within 60 days after the expense is paid or incurred
  - ☐ any excess amount is returned to the church within 120 days after the expense is paid or incurred
- The *periodic statement method* applies if:
  - ☐ the church provides employees with a periodic statement that sets forth that the advance or reimbursement was more than substantiated expenses under the arrangement
  - ☐ the statements are provided at least quarterly
  - ☐ the church requests that the employee provide substantiation for any additional expenses that have not yet been substantiated and/or return any amounts remaining unsubstantiated within 120 days of the statement

Business expenses that are substantiated and reimbursed are not included on Form W-2. Business expenses that are reimbursed *but not* substantiated are included on Form W-2 in Box 1.

Example 1: The church adopts an accountable reimbursement plan using the "fixed date method." The church authorizes salary of $76,000 and in a separate action, without an indication that the reimbursements are being funded out of what otherwise would be the minister's salary, agrees to pay business expenses up to $10,000.

During the year, the minister substantiates $9,000 of expenses under the accountable guidelines. The church provides a Form W-2 reflecting compensation of $76,000. The substantiated expenses of $9,000 are not reported to the IRS by the church or on the minister's tax return.

The church retains the $1,000 difference between the amount budgeted by the church and the amount reimbursed to the minister. (See pages 84-85 for an example where the church pays the balance to the minister in the expense reimbursement plan.)

Example 2: The church authorizes a salary of $63,000 and additionally authorizes allowances of $5,000 for auto expenses and $3,000 for other business expenses. The church does not require or receive any substantiation for the auto or other business expenses. This is a nonaccountable reimbursement plan.

The church should provide a Form W-2 reflecting compensation of $71,000. The minister is ineligible to claim the auto and other business expenses as a deduction for income tax purposes.

The IRS disallows deductions for any portion of unreimbursed business expenses on Schedule C on the premise that the expenses should be allocated to the minister's excludable housing allowance (see allocation of business expenses on pages 102-3). This is another reason that every minister should comply with the accountable expense reimbursement rules. The goal should be to eliminate all unreimbursed business expenses.

Accountable expense reimbursement plans should not be combined with other fringe benefit plans or a housing allowance. Ministers are sometimes advised that the church can establish an overall reimbursement account to cover business expenses, housing expenses, dependent care expenses, and educational expenses. While all of these items can be handled in a tax beneficial manner for a minister, they are subject to separate rules in the tax law. Some of the items are subject to the nondiscrimination rules, while others are not. Dollar limits must be separately established in some instances, but not in others. Housing expenses for a minister-owned home are not reimbursable at all.

Warning

Many ministers are paid expense "allowances." These payments accomplish nothing in terms of good stewardship. "Allowances" are fully taxable for income and Social Security tax purposes.

The timing of documenting expenses for reimbursement is of utmost importance. Under the fixed date method (see page 82), the IRS provides a safe harbor of 60 days after the expense is paid or incurred. Does this mean that the IRS will disallow expenses reimbursed on the 61st day? Not necessarily. It simply means 60 days is a safe harbor as a "reasonable time."

> ***Example:*** A church approves $75,000 of compensation for the pastor and says to let the church know at the end of the year how much has been spent on business expenses, and they will show the net amount on Form W-2. Is this valid? No. The salary *must* be established separately from expense reimbursements and should be one before the year begins. Further, even if an accountable expense reimbursement plan is used, the annual submission of expense documentation would fail the timeliness test for expenses incurred in all but the last portion of the year.

Nonaccountable expense reimbursement or allowance

If a minister does not substantiate expenses to the church, or if the amount of the reimbursement exceeds the actual expenses and the excess is not returned to the church within a reasonable period, the minister's tax life becomes more complicated.

Nonaccountable reimbursements and excess reimbursements above IRS mileage or per diem limits must be included in the minister's gross income and reported as wages on Form W-2.

If the church pays an "allowance" in lieu of reimbursing substantiated business expenses, it represents taxable compensation. The term "allowance" implies that the payment is not based upon substantiated expenses, does not meet the adequate accounting requirements for an accountable plan, and must be included in the minister's income.

The unused "balance" in an accountable expense reimbursement plan

If the church pays the unused balance in an accountable expense reimbursement plan (perhaps calling the payment a "bonus"), the expense reimbursement plan becomes nonaccountable for the entire year. (This is also referred to as a "recharacterization of income.") All payments under a nonaccountable plan are reportable as compensation on Form W-2.

> ***Example:*** A church sets the minister's salary at $80,000 and agrees to reimburse

Caution

The best expense reimbursement plan for a minister is one that pays 100% of church-related expenses. Too often, churches place dollar limits on these plans. With a dollar limit, any money left in the plan at the end of the year must stay with the church for reimbursements to be tax-free. If the balance is paid to the minister, all payments for the year become taxable.

business expenses under an accountable plan for up to $10,000. The reimbursed expenses are $9,000, and the church gave a bonus for the $1,000 difference. Because of the "bonus" arrangement, all reimbursements made under the plan are generally considered to be nonaccountable. The entire $90,000 is reported by the church as compensation on Form W-2.

Substantiating and Reporting Business Expenses

Substantiating business expenses

For expenses to be treated as reimbursable, a minister must show that money was spent and that it was spent for a legitimate business reason. To prove that the money was spent, generally documentary evidence must be provided that can be confirmed by a third party. Canceled checks, credit card, or other receipts are an excellent starting point. To the IRS, third-party verification is important. If business expenses are paid in cash, be sure to get a receipt.

Documenting a business expense can be time-consuming. The IRS is satisfied if the five Ws are noted:

- ➢ Why (business purpose)
- ➢ What (description, including itemized accounting of cost)
- ➢ When (date)
- ➢ Where (location)
- ➢ Who (names of those for whom the expense was incurred, e.g., Pastor Mark Smith)

Remember

When a minister provides a listing of business expenses to the church or other employer—this is only a report, not documentation. Documentary evidence is much more than a report. It involves detailed support of the five Ws (why, what, when, where, and who).

The only exception to the documentation rules is if the individual's outlays for business expenses, other than for lodging, come to less than $75. The IRS does not require receipts for such expenses, although the five Ws are still required for adequate substantiation. A receipt for lodging expenses will always be needed, regardless of the amount. An employer may apply a documentation threshold lower than $75.

Use of a church credit card can be helpful to charge church-related business expenses. However, the use of a credit card does not automatically provide substantiation without additional documentation of the expense; *e.g.*, business purpose and business relationship.

CASH EXPENSE REPORT

Name: Pastor Frank Morris

Address: 3801 North Florida Avenue

Miami, FL 33168

Period Covered: From: 7/1/20 To: 7/14/20

DATE	TRAVEL								OTHER *		ACCOUNT to be Charged
	City	Purpose of Travel	Brkfast	Lunch	Dinner	Snack	Lodging	Trans.	Description	Amount	
7/2/20									Lunch w/Bob Cox	18.21	544-20
7/6/20	Atlanta, GA	Continuing Ed. Sem.		10.80	13.40	2.10	90.50	265.08	Tips	8.00	549 20
7/6/20	" "	" " "	6.40								544-20
7/6/20									Lunch w/Al Lane	12.80	544-80
7/14/20									Lunch w/Sam Lee	11.12	544 40
		TOTAL CASH EXPENSES	6.40	10.80	13.40	2.10	90.50	265.08		50.13	

*If this is entertainment, please use the entertainment worksheet on the back of this form.

Frank Morris 7/16/20
Signature (person requesting reimbursement) Date

Bob Davis 7/16/20
Approved by Date

Total cash expenses	438.41
Personal auto business mileage (Complete worksheet on the back of this form.) 188.6 miles X 57.5¢ per mile	108.45
Less travel advance	(300.00)
Balance due	246.86
Refund due organization	

When a minister is traveling out of town as an employee, the church may use a per diem for reimbursements instead of actual costs of meals (see page 89).

Only the portion of business and professional expenses directly attributable to Schedule C income (self-employment activities) should be deducted on Schedule C.

For more detailed information, refer to IRS Publication 535, *Business Expenses*, and Publication 463, *Travel, Entertainment, Gift, and Car Expenses.*

Travel and Transportation Expenses

The terms "travel" and "transportation" are often used interchangeably, but each has a distinct meaning for tax purposes. Travel is the broader category, including not only transportation expenses, but the cost of meals, lodging, and incidental expenses as well. To qualify for a travel business expense reimbursement or deduction on Schedule C—including expenses incurred for meals, phone calls, cab fares, and so forth—the business purpose must take the minister away from home overnight or require a rest stop. If the minister does not spend the night, only transportation costs qualify.

Travel expenses

Many different expenses can add up on a business trip: air and taxi fares, costs of lodging, baggage charges, rental cars, tips, laundry and cleaning, and telephone expenses. The minister can be reimbursed for these expenses incurred while he or she was away, provided certain guidelines are met:

- the trip must have a business purpose,
- the expenses cannot be "lavish and extravagant," and
- the time away from home is long enough to require sleep or rest.

Deriving some personal pleasure from a trip doesn't disqualify it from being deductible. The IRS does, however, apply some important limitations to the tax treatment of foreign travel expenses.

If the travel is within the United States, all transportation costs can be reimbursed, plus the costs of business-related meals and lodging, as long as business was the primary reason for the trip. If a Saturday night stay is needed to get a lower airfare, the hotel and meal expenses for Saturday will generally be deductible. If the trip is primarily personal, none of the transportation costs can be deducted, but other business-related travel expenses can be deducted.

International travel

Costs are reimbursable if a minister takes an international trip for business reasons. If the trip is seven days or less, he or she can deduct the entire airfare even if most of the time is spent on personal activities. If some days are spent for personal reasons, the hotel, car rental, and meal costs are not reimbursable for those days. If the trip is more than seven days and more than 25% of the time is spent on personal activities, all expenses must be allocated between business and personal time.

Trips to the Holy Land

Ministers often travel to the Holy Land to more closely identify with the area where Christ taught, preached, and ministered. In spite of all the obvious ministerial advantages of visiting the Holy Land, the applicability of tax-free reimbursements for such trips is not as clear.

Generally, no reimbursement is allowed for travel as a form of education. However, travel expense may be reimbursable if the travel is necessary to engage in the education activity.

A number of factors must be considered before the tax status of a Holy Land trip may be determined. To qualify as a reimbursable ministry-related expense, the trip must meet the general educational expense rules outlined on page 42. Holy Land trips are also subject to the international travel rules as described above.

If the answer to the following questions is "Yes," the expenses more likely qualify for reimbursement:

- Did the employing church require or strongly suggest that the minister make the trip to the Holy Land?
- Is this the minister's first trip to the Holy Land? If he or she has a pattern of making the pilgrimage every few years, the trip is less likely to qualify as an educational expense.
- Will the minister be receiving college credit for the trip from a recognized educational institution? Is there a course syllabus?
- Is the trip organized for the purpose of study in the Holy Land and led by a Bible scholar?
- Did the minister take notes and pictures of places visited? If most of the photos include family members and friends, the trip is less likely to qualify as an education expense.

Reimbursement by a church for a minister's trip to the Holy Land should be made only after careful consideration of the facts and circumstances and the applicable tax rules.

Furlough travel

A missionary on furlough may qualify for travel status. The purpose of the travel must be primarily business, such as deputation (resource raising), reporting to constituents, or education, and the missionary's primary residence must remain in another country. Incidental costs for personal travel such as vacation, nonbusiness spousal and children costs are non-reimbursable. If personal expenses are paid by a church, the amounts represent taxable income.

Travel expenses of the minister's spouse or children

If the minister's spouse or children accompany him or her on the business trip, their expenses are nonreimbursable unless they qualify for employee treatment and

- the travel of the spouse or dependent is for a bona fide business purpose; and

- ➢ the employee substantiates the time, place, amount, and business purpose of the travel under an accountable business expense reimbursement plan.

If there is not a bona fide purpose or the payments are not made under an accountable plan, the expenses are includible as income on Form W-2.

The IRS and the courts evaluate the following criteria to determine whether a bona fide business purpose exists:

- ➢ The spouse's and children's function must be necessary; *i.e.*, results in desired business (ministry) benefits to the church.
- ➢ The spouse's and children's contributions to the church must be those which cannot be efficiently performed (or performed at all) by the minister alone.
- ➢ The spouse's and children's services must augment the minister's purpose for the trip.
- ➢ The benefit to the church must be substantial.

Remember

Spouses and children often accompany ministers to conferences and other work-related meetings. Their expenses are reimbursable under an accountable plan or deductible *only if* the minister can document a business (ministry) purpose (for example, a minister's spouse attends certain meetings at a conference and reports to the church on those meetings).

Per diem allowance

The IRS has provided per diem allowances under which the amount of away-from-home meals and lodging expenses may be substantiated. These rates may not be used to claim a reimbursement for unreimbursed expenses. Higher per diem rates apply to certain locations annually identified by the IRS. For more information on these rates, see IRS Publication 1542.

Travel expenses for ministers with interim appointments

Many ministers accept or are appointed to temporary ministerial positions with churches. For example, a semiretired minister may own his or her own home and decide not to relocate for a temporary assignment. So the minister commutes each week to serve a church that does not have a resident minister. Or, a minister may have secular employment in a city where he or she lives and is invited to preach each Sunday on an interim basis for a church. The minister is able to maintain the secular job and fill the ministerial assignment with periodic trips to the church.

If a minister temporarily changes his or her job location, the minister's tax home does not change to the new location. This means that the minister can be reimbursed for his or her travel expenses (auto or public transportation expense and meals) to and from the temporary location. If the minister stays overnight at the temporary location, food and lodging expenses at the temporary location become reimbursable.

When is a job location temporary? A minister will be treated as being temporarily away from home during any period of employment that is realistically expected to last and actually does last a year or less. Daily transportation expenses are reimbursable by the church if the minister qualifies for temporary work status. These rules may also apply to a minister serving more than one church (a circuit arrangement).

Caution

If a minister temporarily changes his or her job location, the minister's tax home does not change to the new location. This means that the minister can be reimbursed for his or her travel expenses (auto or public transportation expense and meals) to and from the temporary location. If the minister stays overnight at the temporary location, food and lodging expenses at the temporary location become reimbursable.

However, if employment away from home is realistically expected to last for more than one year, the employment will be treated as indefinite, regardless of whether it actually exceeds one year. In this case, daily transportation expenses are not reimbursable by the church.

Example 1: A minister lives in Town A and accepts an interim pulpit assignment in Town B, which is 60 miles away from Town A. The assignment in Town B is realistically expected to be completed in 18 months, but in fact it was completed in 10 months. The employment in Town B is indefinite because it was realistically expected that the work in Town B would last longer than one year, even though it actually lasted less than a year. Accordingly, travel expenses paid or incurred in Town B are not reimbursable.

If, initially, employment away from home in a single location is realistically expected to last for one year or less, but at some later date the employment is realistically expected to exceed one year, that employment will be treated as temporary (in the absence of facts and circumstances indicating otherwise) until the date that the minister's realistic expectation changes.

Example 2: An interim assignment began as a temporary assignment (a six-month assignment that was extended for a second six-month period), but at the 365th day of employment it was apparent that the contract would be extended for an additional period. At that time, the minister no longer has a realistic expectation that his or her employment would last for one year or less. Thus, the expenses the minister incurred *after* that 365th day are not reimbursable.

When a minister's realistic expectation changes—*i.e.*, when the minister realistically expects the initially temporary employment to exceed one year—the employment becomes indefinite for the *remaining* term of employment. In other words, the employment can become indefinite before the end of the one-year period if, before the end of that period, the minister realistically expects that his or her employment will exceed one year.

Example 3: A minister accepted a temporary ministerial assignment, which the minister realistically expected would be completed in nine months. After eight months, the minister was asked to remain for seven more months (for a total stay of 15 months). Although the minister's employment is temporary for the first eight months and travel expenses during that period are reimbursable, the minister's employment for the remaining seven months is indefinite, and the minister's travel expenses for that seven-month period are not reimbursable.

If, after working on the assignment only three months, the minister was asked to extend his or her employment for 10 months, only the travel expenses incurred during the first three months would be reimbursable.

In effect, the IRS takes the position that part of a period of employment that is more than a year will still be treated as temporary if the taxpayer reasonably expected that the employment would last for a year or less when the employment started. The employment won't be treated as indefinite until the taxpayer's expectation changes.

If a minister is not told how long an assignment is expected to last, other factors will have to be taken into account to determine whether it can reasonably be expected to last more than one year. Merely being classified as an interim minister by a church does not justify indefinite status. Also, the fewer connections that a minister keeps with his or her former work location, the less likely it is that the new assignment will be treated as merely temporary.

Auto Expense Reimbursements

A minister's car expenses are reimbursable to the extent that they are for business rather than personal use. Generally, only those expenses that are necessary to drive and maintain a car that is used to go from one workplace to another are deductible. However, in some limited situations, the expense of driving between home and a workplace is reimbursable (see pages 96-98).

Business-related auto expenses incurred by an employee and reimbursed under an accountable plan are excludable from the employee's gross income. Unreimbursed employee business-related auto expenses are only deductible on Schedule C (related to *self-employment* income from speaking, funerals, weddings, etc.) for income tax purposes.

Mileage and actual expense methods

In determining the amount eligible for reimbursement for the business use of a personal car, a minister may use one of two methods to figure the amount: (1) the standard mileage rate, or (2) the actual expense method. Generally, the minister can choose the method that gives the greater deduction. If he or she uses the actual expense method and accelerated depreciation for the first year his or her car was placed in service, the minister may not use the standard mileage method in a subsequent year. However, if the standard mileage method is used for the first year the car was placed in service, either method may be used in subsequent years.

Standard mileage rate method

If the minister is reimbursed the maximum mileage rate of 57.5 cents per mile (2020 rate), and he or she provides the time, place, and business purpose of the driving for each instance, the minister has made an adequate accounting of the automobile expenses, qualifying for a tax-free reimbursement.

If the church does not reimburse the minister for auto expenses or reimburses under a nonaccountable plan, the minister may not deduct the expenses for income tax purposes except on Schedule C (related to self-employment income).

The standard mileage rate, which includes depreciation and maintenance costs, is based on the government's estimate of the average cost of operating an automobile. Depending upon the make, age, and cost of the car, the mileage rate may be more or less than your actual auto expense. If you use the mileage rate, you may also be reimbursed for parking fees and tolls and the business portion of personal property tax.

Remember

The standard mileage rate may generate a lower deduction than using actual expenses in some instances. But the simplicity of the standard mileage method is very compelling.

The standard mileage rate may also be used for leased autos (see page 96 for additional information, "Leasing your car").

- **Conditions on use of mileage rate.** The mileage rate may not be used if:
  - ☐ the minister has claimed depreciation under Modified Accelerated Cost Recovery (MACRS), Accelerated Cost Recovery (ACRS), or another accelerated method
  - ☐ the minister has claimed first-year expenses under Section 179 of the tax code

- **Use of mileage rate in first year.** If the minister chooses the standard mileage rate for the first year the car is in service, he or she may use the standard mileage rate or actual expense method in later years. If the minister does not choose the standard mileage rate in the first year, he or she may not use it for that car in any following year.

  By choosing to use the mileage rate in the first year the car is in service, the minister may not use the MACRS method of depreciation for the car in a later year. Also, he or she may not claim a deduction under Section 179. If the minister switches to the actual expense method in a later year before the automobile is fully depreciated, he or she must use the straight-line method of depreciation.

Warning

You have an important decision to make the first year you put a car into service. You will generally want to use the standard mileage rate in that first year. If you do not use the standard mileage rate in the first year, you may not use it for that car in any following year.

Actual expense method

The actual expense method is an alternative method permitted for ministers. This method may be preferential when operating costs exceed the amount allowed under the standard mileage rate method. However, even when the actual expense method exceeds the mileage method, the simplicity of the mileage method may outweigh the tax savings.

Allowable expenses under the actual expense method include gas and oil, interest on an auto loan, repairs, lease payments, tires, automobile club membership, batteries, car washes and waxes, insurance, license plates, parking fees and tolls, and supplies, such as antifreeze.

Filing Tip

While the actual expense method is one option for obtaining a reimbursement, it requires significantly more recordkeeping than the standard mileage method. And the minister still needs to maintain a mileage log to prorate costs between business and personal miles.

If accurate records have been kept, determining the amount eligible for reimbursement for most expenses should be straightforward. Generally, the amount of depreciation the minister may be reimbursed and the method used to calculate it depend on when the auto was purchased and was first used for ministerial purposes.

Under the actual expense method, the minister can use either accelerated or straight-line depreciation. As the names imply, the accelerated method front-loads the depreciation, giving larger reimbursements sooner. The straight-line method gives the same depreciation deduction every year.

Driving an employer-provided vehicle

When a church provides a car to a minister, the church must report the personal use of the car as income on Form W-2. However, when a minister pays the church the fair market value for the personal use of the car, there is no income tax impact to the minister. Partial payment to the church reduces the minister's taxable income by the amount of the payment.

When a car is used for both business and personal purposes, an allocation between the two types of use must be made based on the number of miles driven. The amount included in the minister's compensation is generally based on one of the following three valuation rules (for more information, see the 2021 edition of the *Church and Nonprofit Tax & Financial Guide)*:

➢ **Cents-per-mile valuation rule.** Generally, this rule may be used if the employer reasonably expects that the vehicle will be regularly used for church business and if the vehicle is driven at least 10,000 miles a year and is primarily used by employees. This valuation rule is available only if the fair market value of the vehicle, as of the date the vehicle was first made available for personal use by employees, does not exceed a specified value set by the IRS. For 2020, this value is $50,400 (including cars, vans, and trucks).

Personal use value of the vehicle is computed by multiplying the number of miles driven for personal purposes by the current IRS standard mileage rate (57.5 cents per mile for 2020). For this valuation rule, personal use is "any use of the vehicle other than use in the employer's trade or business of being an employee of the employer."

Caution

One of the best fringe benefits for a minister is when the church or other employer provides a vehicle. However, unless the car is parked at the church when not in use, it still requires maintaining a mileage log. Personal (including commuting) miles driven must either be reimbursed to the employer or the tax value must be placed on Form W-2.

This amount is then considered as income and reflected on Form W-2

➢ **Commuting valuation rule.** This rule may be used to determine the value of personal use only where the following conditions are met:

- ☐ The vehicle is owned or leased by the church and is provided to one or more employees for use in connection with church business and is used as such.

- ☐ The church requires the employee to commute to and/or from work in the vehicle for bona fide noncompensatory business reasons. One example of a such a reason is the availability of the vehicle to an employee who is on-call and must have access to the vehicle when at home.

- ☐ The church has a written policy that prohibits employees from using the vehicle for personal purposes other than for commuting or *de minimis* personal use such as a stop for a personal errand on the way home from work.

- ☐ The employee required to use the vehicle for commuting is not a "control" employee of the church. A control employee is generally defined as any director or employee who is an officer of the employer whose compensation equals or exceeds a level annually set by the IRS.

The personal use of a church-provided vehicle that meets the above conditions is valued at $1.50 per one-way commute, or $3.00 per day.

➢ **Annual lease valuation rule.** Under this rule, the fair market value of a vehicle is determined, and that value is used to determine the annual lease value amount by referring to an annual lease value table published by the IRS. The annual lease value corresponding to this fair market value, multiplied by the personal use percentage, is the amount to be added to the employee's gross income. If the church provides the fuel, 5.5 cents per mile must be added to the annual lease value. Amounts reimbursed by the employee are offset against the annual lease value.

Business Miles Do Not Start at Home If—

- ❑ You have a personal computer in your home office and you or another member of your family occasionally uses the personal computer for personal use.

- ❑ Your home office is in your bedroom, your living room, or any other room where the space is shared for both church work and family living.

- ❑ The church has an adequate office. You do most of your work there but work at home once in a while.

- ❑ The church expects you to use the church office for your work, but you prefer to work at home because it is convenient to you.

The fair market value of a vehicle owned by a church is generally the church's cost of purchasing the vehicle (including taxes and fees). The fair market value of a vehicle leased by an employer is generally either the manufacturer's suggested retail price less 8%, the dealer's invoice plus 4%, or the retail value as reported in a nationally recognized publication that regularly reports automobile retail values.

Leasing a car

A minister who leases a car and uses it in connection with the work of the church is generally eligible to have part or all of lease payments reimbursed as a rental expense. However, business use is typically less than 100%. Therefore, the rental amount is scaled down in proportion to the personal use. For example, a minister who uses a leased car 80% for business may be reimbursed for only 80% of the lease payments.

Additionally, the tax law is designed to bring lease payments in line with the "luxury auto" limits (annually determined by the IRS) placed on depreciation deductions for purchased cars (most cars meet the "luxury" definition). So, leasing a "luxury" car may not give you a tax break over buying one. However, nontax considerations may be important in the lease versus buy decision.

The mileage method may also be used for the reimbursement of expenses for a leased car.

Commuting

Personal mileage is never reimbursable. Commuting mileage is personal mileage.

Travel to and from home and church (a regular work location) for church services and other work at the church is commuting and is not reimbursable. The same rule applies to multiple trips made in the same day.

On the other hand, the cost of traveling between home and a temporary work location is generally reimbursable. Once the minister arrives at the first work location, temporary or regular, he or she may be reimbursed for trips between work locations.

A regular place of business is any location at which the minister works or performs services on a regular basis. These services may be performed every week, for example, or merely on a set schedule. A temporary place of business is any location at which services are performed on an irregular or short-term basis.

If a minister makes calls in a certain hospital or nursing home nearly every day, it qualifies as a regular work location. However, if he or she only visits the hospital or nursing home a few days each month, it generally qualifies as a temporary work location.

Commuting vs. Business Miles

When are transportation expenses deductible?

Most employees and self-employed persons can use this chart. (Do not use this chart if your home is your principal place of business.)

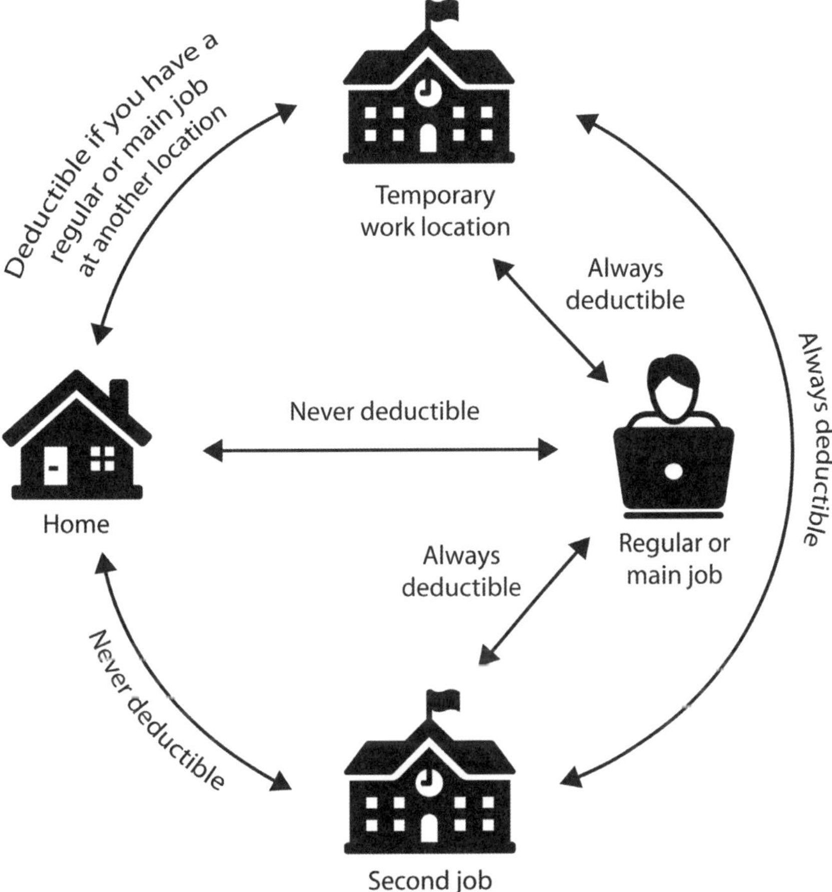

Home: The place where you reside. Transportation expenses between your home and your main or regular place of work are personal commuting expenses.

Regular or main job: Your principal place of business. If you have more than one job, you must determine which is your regular or main job. Consider the time you spend at each, the activity you have at each, and the income you earn at each.

Temporary work location: A place where your work assignment is realistically expected to last (and does in fact last) one year or less. Unless you have a regular place of business, you can only deduct your transportation expenses to a temporary work location outside your metropolitan area.

Example 1: A minister, not qualifying for an office at home, drives from home to the church. This trip is commuting and treated as personal mileage.

The minister leaves the church and drives to a hospital to call on a member. From the hospital, the minister drives to the home of a prospect to make a call. These trips qualify for business mileage regardless of whether the hospital qualifies as a regular or a temporary work location.

From the prospect's house, the minister drives home. This trip is also eligible for reimbursement since the minister is driving home from a temporary work location.

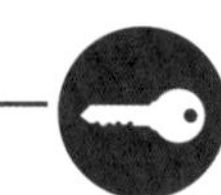

Key Issue

Churches and ministers often struggle to define commuting miles. It is a very important issue because commuting miles should not be reimbursed by an employer. The key to understanding commuting miles is defining regular and temporary work locations.

Example 2: A minister, not qualifying for an office at home, drives from home to a hospital to call on a member. The hospital is typically a temporary work location. This trip is eligible for reimbursement.

The minister then drives to a member's office to make a call and then returns to the minister's office at the church. The trips to this point are eligible as business expenses because they are all trips between work locations. The minister then drives to his home. This trip is commuting and is not reimbursable because the minister is driving from a regular work location to a nonwork location.

Documentation of auto expenses

To support the automobile expense reimbursement, automobile expenses must be substantiated by adequate records. A weekly or monthly mileage log that identifies dates, destinations, business purposes, and odometer readings in order to allocate total mileage between business and personal use is a basic necessity if the minister uses the mileage method. If he or she uses the actual expense method, a mileage log and supporting documentation of expenses are required. In either case, a mileage log is required.

Remember

For records to withstand an IRS audit, the minister should use a daily mileage log to document business vs. personal mileage. Whether a notepad is kept in the car or tracked on a smartphone, some type of log is the best approach to submitting data for reimbursement.

Reporting auto expenses

If the minister is reimbursed for automobile expenses under an accountable expense plan, it eliminates the need for income or Social Security tax reporting by the church or the minister.

Other Business Expenses

In addition to travel and transportation expenses, there are other business and professional expenses a minister may submit to the church for reimbursement under an accountable plan:

➢ **Business gifts.** Up to $25 per donee can be reimbursed as ministry gifts to any number of individuals every year. Incidental costs, such as for engraving, gift wrapping, insurance, and mailing, do not need to be included in determining whether the $25 limit has been exceeded.

The gifts must be related to the ministry. Gifts to church staff or board members would generally be reimbursable, subject to the $25 limit. Wedding and graduation gifts generally do not qualify as business expenses.

➢ **Cell phones**. The IRS treats the value of a church-provided cell phone and similar telecommunications equipment (including the value of any personal use by the employee) as excludible from the employee's income, as long as the cell phone is provided to the employee primarily for a noncompensatory business reason (such as the employer's need to contact the employee at all times for work-related emergencies). Providing a cell phone to promote morale or goodwill, to attract a prospective employee, or to furnish additional compensation to an employee is evidence that there is no noncompensatory business reason.

Remember

For a cell phone to be excludible from an employee's income, the phone must be provided primarily for noncompensatory business reasons.

Church staff may be reimbursed for the business use of a cell phone, but the church should generally require the employee to submit a copy of the monthly bill and evidence that the bill has been paid.

As a minister, the use of a cell phone must be for the "convenience of the church" and required as a "condition of employment." The "convenience of the church" test will generally be met if the cell phone is furnished for substantial "noncompensatory business reasons." Whether a minister (or other church employee) passes the "condition of employment" test is based on all the facts and circumstances and is not determined merely by an employer's statement that the use of the cell phone is a condition of employment.

If a church does not have a substantial noncompensatory business reason for providing a cell phone to an employee or reimbursing the employee for business use of his or her personal cell phone, then the value of the use of the phone or the amount of the reimbursement is includible in gross income and reportable on Form W-2. For lay employees, the amount of the reimbursement is subject to employment tax withholding.

- **Clothing.** Ordinary clothing worn in the exercise of a minister's duties for the church is a personal expense and is not reimbursable by the church under an accountable plan.

  If a minister wears clothing that is of a type specifically required as a condition of employment and is not adaptable to general use or continued usage to the extent that it could take the place of ordinary clothing, such as vestments, the cost is reimbursable as a business expense.

- **Computers.** If a computer is provided by the church in the church office but the minister prefers to work at home on a personal computer, the personal computer is not being used for the church's convenience. If the minister meets the "convenience of employer" and "condition of employment" tests but does not use the computer (and related equipment) more than 50% of the time for work, he or she must depreciate these items using the straight-line method to calculate the amount for reimbursement purposes.

  Adequate records of the business use of a personal computer should be maintained to substantiate deductions.

- **Education-related interest.** Up to $2,500 of interest paid during the tax year on any qualified education loan is deductible as an

Warning

If a minister purchases a computer *and* uses it primarily for church work *and* meets the "condition" and "convenience" tests, only the depreciation on the business portion of the computer can be reimbursed by the church, not the business portion of the cost, based on the Section 179 first-year write-off rules.

Caution

If the education is required to meet the minimum educational requirements of your work, educational expenses are not deductible.

adjustment to gross income on Form 1040. The taxpayer must have incurred the debt solely to pay qualified higher education expenses.

Warning

The one-time equipment write-off cannot be used as part of a minister's accountable expense reimbursement plan. If a minister personally owns a computer that is partially used for his or her employer, the business portion of the computer can be reimbursed under an accountable plan based on annual depreciation. The business portion of the cost of the computer cannot be reimbursed in one year under the one-time write-off rules.

- **Entertainment.** Entertainment expenses may qualify for reimbursement under an accountable expense reimbursement plan if they represent an ordinary and necessary business expense.

- **Interest expense.** For a minister, all auto-related interest expense is personal interest, which is not reimbursable. However, this interest expense may be claimed on Schedule A.

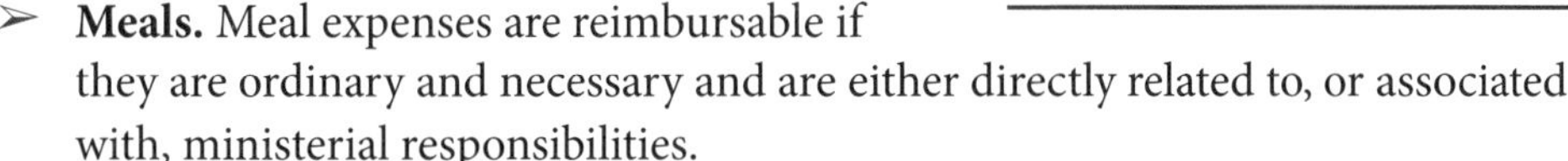

- **Meals.** Meal expenses are reimbursable if they are ordinary and necessary and are either directly related to, or associated with, ministerial responsibilities.

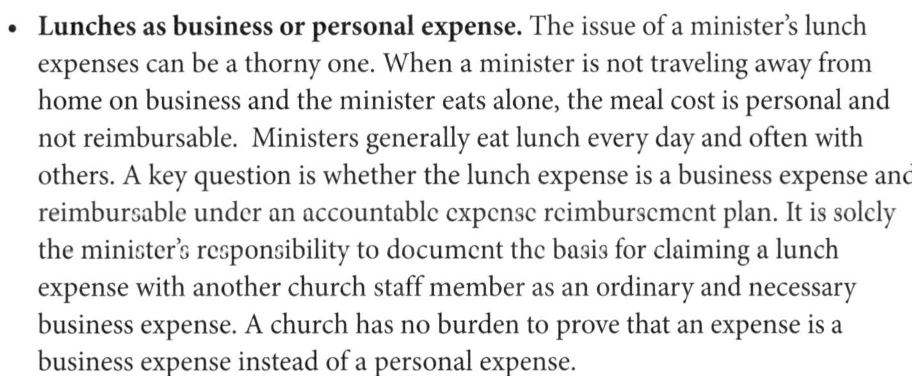

  - **Lunches as business or personal expense.** The issue of a minister's lunch expenses can be a thorny one. When a minister is not traveling away from home on business and the minister eats alone, the meal cost is personal and not reimbursable. Ministers generally eat lunch every day and often with others. A key question is whether the lunch expense is a business expense and reimbursable under an accountable expense reimbursement plan. It is solely the minister's responsibility to document the basis for claiming a lunch expense with another church staff member as an ordinary and necessary business expense. A church has no burden to prove that an expense is a business expense instead of a personal expense.

  - **Lunches with non-church staff members.** If these lunches are occasional and there is a church business connection, these lunches may qualify for reimbursement under an accountable expense reimbursement plan. For example, a pastor may have lunch once a month with the pastor of another church across town to discuss how each other handles certain issues in a church. A lunch of this type likely qualifies as a reimbursable business expense. Similar principles apply to the scenario of a minister having a meal with church volunteers.

  - **Lunches with other church staff.** Ministers often eat lunch with one or more other church staff members. If the minister picking up the tab turns the expense in for reimbursement under an accountable expense reimbursement plan, should the church treasurer consider the amount as an ordinary and necessary business expense and reimburse the expense and consider the amount tax-free? Or, should the church treasurer pay the expense and include it in compensation on Form W-2 as a personal expense? Or, should the church treasurer consider it a personal expense and refuse to pay the amount, since the church does not reimburse any personal expenses?

While an occasional meal with another church staff member may represent an ordinary and necessary business expense, frequent meals of this nature will rarely meet the business expense test. A monthly meeting with one or more staff members to discuss planning and church operational issues could meet the ordinary and necessary business expense test. However, a daily, every-few-days, weekly, or bi-weekly meeting with the same staff members is unlikely to meet the business expense test.

Certain meal expenses incurred in the minister's home may be reimbursable if they are ordinary and necessary business expenses. The minister should keep a log including date(s), names of guests, ministry purpose, and actual cost (not comparable value if purchased at a restaurant). Some ministers claim reimbursements for providing overnight lodging for church-related guests based on the value of motel lodging. There is no basis for such reimbursements since no out-of-pocket expense was incurred.

- ➢ **Moving expenses**. If employee moving expenses are paid by the church (regardless of whether they are paid to the minister or to the moving company), they are includible in the employee's taxable income (subject to income and self-employment Social Security taxes) and are not deductible by the minister on Form 1040. They are also subject to employment taxes for a lay employee.

- ➢ **Subscriptions and books.** Subscriptions to ministry-related resources are reimbursable. The cost of books related to the ministry may be reimbursed.

Allocation of Business Expenses

The IRS takes the position that the deduction of unreimbursed business expenses on Schedule C for self-employment income is limited to the extent that they are allocable to an excluded housing allowance or the fair rental value of church-provided housing (see pages 176 and 186). The IRS applies what is often referred to as the "Deason rule" (referring to a 1964 Tax Court Memorandum).

IRS Publication 517, *Social Security and Other Information for Members of the Clergy and Religious Workers,* explains this topic in detail and includes the concept in a completed tax return example. The most recent *Tax Guide for Churches and Other Religious Organizations* and *Minister Audit Technique Guide*, both issued by the IRS, clearly apply the expense allocation concept.

Since the housing allowance is not tax-exempt for self-employment purposes, the IRS takes the position in its *Minister Audit Technique Guide* that the Deason rule does not apply to the computation of a minister's self-employment taxes.

Under the IRS guidelines, if a minister excludes a housing allowance or is provided housing by the church, the minister cannot deduct expenses that are allocable to the minister's excluded rental or parsonage allowance. Home mortgage interest and real estate taxes are still deductible on Schedule A as itemized deductions even though the same amounts are excluded for income tax purposes under the housing allowance rules.

Caution

The allocation of unreimbursed expenses only applies to ministerial-related expenses reflected on Schedule C. This is because unreimbursed expenses related to Form W-2 income are no longer deductible on Schedule A.

- **Personal vs. business expenses.** Integrity in expense reimbursements or deductions starts by determining if the expenses are truly business expenses. A business expense must be ordinary (one that is common and accepted in a particular field) and necessary (one that is helpful and appropriate for a particular field). The law and integrity require the faithful application of the "ordinary" and "necessary" rule.

  The reimbursement of an expense never affects the character of the expense. Simply reimbursing an expense does not change its character from personal to business. Personal expenses are never eligible for reimbursement.

- **An accountable expense reimbursement plan.** The substantiated reimbursement of business expenses represents good stewardship for the minister and the employing church. A reimbursement is a tax-free payment.

  A formal reimbursement plan is the fundamental starting point. The plan provides the boundaries for compliance with the tax law for business expense reimbursements.

- **Substantiation vs. reporting of expenses.** Substantiating business expenses is much more rigorous than simply reporting expenses. Substantiation generally involves providing documentary evidence that can be confirmed by a third party. Canceled checks, credit card, or other receipts are an excellent starting point. But the substantiation is not complete without the "why" (business purpose), "what" (description, including itemized account of cost), "when" (date), "where" (location), and "who" (names of those for whom the expense was incurred, e.g., Pastor Mark Smith).

- **Reimbursing 100% of a minister's business expenses.** This is critical from the congregation's stewardship standpoint *and* from a minister's income tax viewpoint.

Retirement and Social Security

In This Chapter

- Preparing for retirement
- The fundamentals of Social Security
- Taking out retirement money
- The two Social Security tax systems
- Computing the self-employment tax
- Both spouses are ministers
- Self-employment tax deductions
- Use of income tax withholding to pay Social Security taxes
- Opting out of Social Security
- Working after retirement
- Canada Pension Plan

What does the Bible have to say about retirement for those who minister faithfully to God's people?

Consider this text from the Old Testament that relates to the Levites. They were the role models for God's people, whose service was attached to the House of the Lord.

"The Lord said to Moses, 'This applies to the Levites: Men twenty-five years old or more shall come to take part in the work at the tent of meeting, but at the age of fifty, they must retire from their regular service and work no longer. They may assist their brothers in performing their duties at the tent of meeting, but they themselves must not do the work. This, then, is how you are to assign the responsibilities of the Levites'" (Numbers 8:23–26).

The New Testament speaks to the role of the church in caring for ministers: "The elders who direct the affairs of the church well are worthy of double honor, especially those whose work is preaching and teaching" (1 Timothy 5:17). The idea "double honor" implies extending to them appropriate financial support and relationship support as they lead the church.

Taken together, at least three ideas come into view when considering the topic of retirement for ministers and churches: (1) longevity, (2) changing roles, and (3) planning.

Longevity is a reality. Life expectancy has been steadily increasing for many years. It is quite possible one can live to the age of 90 years old. This could mean that a minister who retires at age 65 could live 25 years or more *after* retirement. It is vital for a church to give consideration to how they prepare their minister for these retirement years.

With age, the role of a minister changes. In the Old Testament example of the Levites, they shifted from doing the heavy lifting to assisting the next generation. In the same way today, ministers must understand and prepare for the season when their role will change.

Planning for retirement is perplexing and complex. The goal is to provide a framework, a way of thinking about, and a way to successfully address retirement to show "double honor" to those who labor as ministers. In approaching the issue of retirement, there is an interdependence between the church and the minister. When they are both in tune, the resulting music will be beautiful. When they are not, the discord will be painfully evident.

For additional information for ministers' retirement, see ECFA's eBook, *8 Essentials of Retirement Planning for Ministers and Churches* at *www.ECFA.Church.*

Preparing for Retirement

How much income will be needed?

Being financially prepared for retirement is simply a function of time and money: the less we have of one, the more we need of the other.

What is the biggest excuse ministers use when they are not saving for retirement? They say they need every penny to pay their bills now—but they'll start saving once the bills are paid off. Paying off debts is a worthy goal, but most people never pay them all off.

Most ministers cannot save a fortune by the time they reach retirement. On a minister's pay, it is difficult to squirrel away as much as many experts insist is needed for a comfortable retirement. But there is one inescapable truth: The sooner we start saving, the better. Saving for retirement isn't like climbing one great peak. It's really like climbing several smaller ones.

Many financial planners suggest 70% to 80% pre-retirement income is needed. But ministers may be able to significantly reduce the income requirement just by moving from an area with a high cost of living to a lower-cost one.

How long is retirement going to be?

The major concern of retirees today is the fear of outliving their income. Today, a 66-year-old male is expected to live 18 more years, and a female is expected to live 24 more years. But life expectancies are averages, and planning on an "average" retirement can be dangerously shortsighted for anyone in good health. It makes sense for healthy people from long-lived families to plan for a retirement stretching at least to age 85, and women are likely to live longer than men.

Idea

While few ministers do, they should be contributing up to the limits allowed into a retirement plan. With the changes in retirement plan contribution limits, ministers can contribute more than ever before.

Investing for retirement

The best advice for ministers is the simplest: Put as much into a 403(b) tax-sheltered annuity plan as possible. Why? Consider these two special benefits for ministers:

- ➢ Prior to retirement, all nonelective and elective employer contributions to a 403(b) plan are excludable for income and Social Security tax (SECA) purposes. For ministers who have not opted out of Social Security (see pages 117-22), this means an immediate 15.3% tax savings on all monies contributed to a 403(b)(9) church plan. For those who have opted out, it is advisable to contribute 15.3% of salary to the retirement plan.
- ➢ The minister's housing exclusion is one of the great tax benefits available to ministers. It gets better because after retirement, a minister can take distributions from their denominationally-sponsored or church-sponsored 403(b)(9) retirement plan as part of an ongoing housing allowance, subject to the regular housing allowance limitations (see pages 75-76).

Example 1: After retirement, a minister receives a $20,000 distribution from a 403(b)(9) plan. The entire $20,000 was designated by the denominational pension plan as a housing allowance. The $20,000 distribution would be excluded for income tax purposes if the full $20,000 is spent on housing. Income and Social Security taxes were saved with the original contributions, and now there are no income or Social Security taxes when the funds are received as a distribution. This is a double benefit.

Example 2: After retirement, the approved housing allowance is $20,000. The distribution from the 403(b)(9) plan is $20,000. Actual housing expenses are $15,000, leaving $5,000 taxable for income tax purposes. The full $20,000 is not taxable for Social Security purposes.

What if the minister has already contributed the maximum to a tax-sheltered annuity plan? A $6,000 contribution to a nondeductible Roth IRA or a regular deductible IRA is a good option for the next retirement-savings dollars. How to decide? Young ministers will tend to benefit more from a Roth IRA because it thrives on long-term compounding. If the minister is nearing retirement and is in a 24% or higher income tax bracket but expects to drop to the 10% bracket at retirement, the minister should stay with a deductible IRA.

In addition to a tax sheltered annuity plan, there are other retirement vehicles for ministers. "Rabbi trusts" are non-qualified deferred compensation arrangements. The invested funds are held as an asset of the church with a corresponding liability reflected for the amount held. The church can't use these funds, but they are available to creditors if the church becomes insolvent.

When the tax-beneficial options have been exhausted, the minister may consider a taxable investment. The key to choosing taxable investments for retirement savings is to keep expenses down and get the most benefit from the capital gains rate (the rate is often zero for many ministers).

Asset allocation—the division of savings among different investment vehicles—is a key part of any retirement strategy. Not only is it necessary to decide what kind of investment account to use, the minister must also decide which specific investments should go into which account.

Proper diversification entails much more than simply spreading contributions evenly among the available choices. It is influenced strongly by how long the minister will continue to work and how much has already been invested elsewhere. In general, the more time the minister has, the more aggressive he or she can afford to be in asset allocation.

Insurance choices as retirement approaches

Approaching retirement, a minister's insurance needs are often different from when the minister was in his or her 30s and 40s. Here are some insurance policies that may be needed and policies that can probably be done without:

- **Life insurance.** The need for life insurance usually declines or disappears once the minister is in or near retirement. The minister's children are probably financially independent. And by then enough assets may have been accumulated to cover the spouse's future needs. This means the minister might want to drop some life

Countdown to Retirement

This table can help ministers make the timely decisions that ensure a comfortable retirement. Since only the minister knows when he or she plans to retire, it is organized according to the number of years until then. If plans change, this checklist can be compressed into the time available.

CATEGORY	FIVE YEARS BEFORE RETIREMENT	TWO YEARS BEFORE RETIREMENT	THREE MONTHS BEFORE RETIREMENT	IN RETIREMENT
BUDGET	Draw up two budgets, current expenses and expected expenses in retirement. Plan to pay off debts by retirement.	Update your current and future budgets.	Merge your two budgets, deleting career expenses and adding any new retiree expenses.	Fine-tune your budget every year so that your projected spending matches your actual spending.
PENSION Defined-benefit plan	Ask your pension office to project your pension monthly and in a lump sum.	Decide how to take your pension; if as a lump sum, decide how to invest it.	Set up the investments you have chosen for your lump sum.	Invest your lump sum immediately to avoid the tax consequences.
403(b), 401(k) plans	Put the maximum in your plan. Wait as long as possible to tap the money so earnings grow tax deferred.	Keep contributing the maximum. If you will take a lump sum, ask an accountant how to minimize taxes (e.g., housing allowance distribution).	Decide how to take your money. At 59½ you may start penalty-free lump-sum withdrawals.	At 72 you may have to start minimum withdrawals from tax-deferred retirement plans (unless working).
SOCIAL SECURITY	Set up a "my Social Security" account at *www.ssa.gov/myaccount/* to check your earnings and be sure your employers contributed the right amounts.	Double-check your "my Social Security" account.	Decide when after age 62 to start receiving Social Security.	At retirement age, there is no limit on the income you can earn without reducing your Social Security benefits.
INVESTMENTS	Meet with a financial planner to discuss your goals and adjust your investment selection to meet them.	Adjust the balance between aggressive and conservative investments to reduce your market risk and increase income.	Make further reductions in market risk—more conservative, less aggressive.	Generally, keep some of your money in stocks to offset inflation.
EMERGENCY FUND	Stash an amount equal to three months' expenses in a money market fund or fixed account.	Set up (or renew) a home-equity line of credit that you can tap in case of an emergency.	Your cash and home-equity line of credit should amount to one full year of expenses.	Keep one year's expenses in the fund; tap it only when you must.
HOUSE Sell vs. keep	Decide whether to keep your present house or sell it. If you sell, decide whether to buy another or rent.	If you plan to move after retiring, visit potential locations during vacations.	If you are selling, put your house on the market three to six months before retirement.	Your gain on the house is tax-free up to $500,000 (married), $250,000 (single).
Repairs and improvements	Renovate now; it's easier to borrow if you're employed.	Budget now for any big-ticket repairs you may need after you retire.		
MEDICAL INSURANCE	Ask your pension office what your medical benefits will be in retirement.	If you need individual coverage, start shopping for it now.	Apply for the coverage one month prior to retiring.	Medicare starts at 65. Six months before then, shop for Medigap insurance.

insurance coverage.

If life insurance is needed for estate planning or to protect dependents financially for at least 15 years, the minister should probably buy cash-value insurance so he or she can lock in the premium. If the minister owns a term life policy that is no longer needed, he or she can stop paying premiums and let the policy lapse.

➢ **Long-term care insurance.** Long-term care (LTC) insurance is a way to pay for nursing home costs while protecting your financial assets. LTC policies have improved significantly in recent years, but they are expensive.

Long-term care policies cover nursing home stays only, home care only, or both. A good LTC policy will cover skilled or intermediate care, or custodial help in any type of facility, with no prior hospitalization required.

Remember

Consider long-term care plans that provide the same coverage for home health care and nursing facilities. The employer can pay or reimburse LTC premiums tax-free. The premiums are generally the minister's responsibility from after-tax dollars after he or she retires.

➢ **Medical insurance.** The minister's medical insurance may stop when he or she becomes eligible for Medicare at full retirement age. A minister old enough for Medicare should call the Social Security Administration to enroll. The minister may be eligible to remain in a group policy for 18 months after leaving your current employment, if the plan is based on COBRA rules. A retiring minister will need to budget not only for Plan B but also for Medigap insurance.

The Fundamentals of Social Security

Ignore any scary stories about Social Security not being available at retirement. The truth is, the benefits for most ministers will remain largely intact for many years.

The age for collecting the full Social Security benefit used to be 65—but no longer. Full retirement is gradually being increased from age 65 to 67. Here, by year of birth, is the age at which ministers can expect to collect the full Social Security retirement benefit:

Age for Collecting

Year of Birth	Full Retirement Benefit
Before 1938	65
1938	65 and two months
1939	65 and four months
1940	65 and six months
1941	65 and eight months
1942	65 and ten months
1943–1954	66
1955	66 and two months
1956	66 and four months
1957	66 and six months
1958	66 and eight months
1959	66 and ten months
1960 and later	67

Filing Tip

If the minister works while receiving Social Security benefits, he or she must still pay Social Security and Medicare taxes regardless of age. Additional earnings can result in increasing the benefit if the earnings are higher than those of a previous year used in the earlier calculation.

Income taxes on benefits

Social Security benefits are income-tax-free for the majority of beneficiaries. However, those with high total incomes must include up to 85% of their benefits as income for federal income tax purposes. Special step-rate “thresholds” determine the amount that may be taxed:

- Single persons: $25,000 and $34,000
- Married couples filing a joint return: $32,000 and $44,000

Working after reaching retirement age

If the minister is under full retirement age (FRA), he or she loses $1 of Social Security benefits for every $2 earned over a certain limit, which increases annually ($18,240 in 2020). Once FRA is reached, one can earn as much as desired with no cut in benefits. The earnings test looks only at money you earn from a job or self-employment, not income from investments or other sources. However, amounts excluded as housing allowance are included in the earnings test.

Checking on benefits

Ministers should complete a request for an earnings and benefit estimate statement every year. This information can be accessed by setting up an account at *www.ssa.gov/myaccount*. The Social Security Agency should be notified of any discrepancies.

Taking Out Retirement Money

Ministers spend their entire lives putting money into retirement plans. When and how money is withdrawn from tax-deferred retirement plans are among the most important financial decisions.

Capital builds up in retirement plans, free of taxes. But the federal, state, and local governments are looking for their share whenever money is withdrawn. And Congress has devised a host of hurdles and penalties:

- Workers generally cannot start withdrawing until they reach 59½. If they do, they must pay a 10% tax penalty in addition to the standard income tax rates. The Roth IRA is an exception because money can be withdrawn, under certain conditions, without penalty if the funds have been left in the Roth IRA for at least five years.

- For church plans, the minister must start withdrawals at age 72 or the date of retirement, whichever is later. For other retirement plans, withdrawals must start when the minister reaches age 72. If not, the minister will have to pay a 50% penalty tax on the amount not withdrawn. There is no age requirement for starting to withdraw funds from a Roth IRA.

The Two Social Security Tax Systems

Social Security taxes are collected under two systems. Under the Federal Insurance Contributions Act (FICA), the employer pays one-half of the tax and the employee pays the other half. Under the Self-Employment Contributions Act (SECA), the self-employed person pays all the tax (self-employment tax) as calculated on the taxpayer's Schedule SE. IRS Publications 517 and 1828 provide information on Social Security taxes for ministers.

Warning

Churches commonly subject ministers to the wrong type of Social Security. If a minister qualifies for a housing allowance, he or she is not subject to FICA-type Social Security. The inappropriate use of FICA instead of SECA may result in the underpayment of a minister's income taxes.

You may also find ECFA's eBook helpful, *10 Essentials of Social Security for Ministers.*

Ministers are always self-employed for Social Security purposes, subject to SECA under the tax law with respect to services performed in the exercise of their ministry, whether employed by a church, integral agency of a church, or a parachurch organization. Ministers are self-employed for Social Security purposes regardless of how their church categorizes them for income tax purposes. Ministers are never subject to FICA-type Social Security taxes, even though they report their income taxes as employees and receive a Form W-2 from their church.

SOCIAL SECURITY SYSTEMS

FICA (Federal Insurance Contributions Act)	**SECA** (Self-Employment Contributions Act)
Non-minister employees of a church are all subject to FICA. Employee pays 7.65% Employer pays 7.65% 15.30%	All qualified ministers are subject to SECA (unless they have opted out of Social Security). Self-employed individuals pay the full 15.3%.
The 15.3% is paid on a wage base of up to $137,700 for 2020.	The 15.3% is paid on a wage base of up to $137,700 for 2020.
Medicare taxes still apply to wages in excess of $137,700.	Medicare taxes still apply to wages in excess of $137,700.

When FICA is inappropriately withheld (7.65%) from a minister's pay and matched (7.65%) by the employer, it subjects the minister and the employer to possible action by the IRS because of the following:

- The minister has often underpaid his or her income taxes. The 7.65% match that was paid by the church is really unreported compensation because it is not being reported in Box 1 of the Form W-2. Additionally, the minister is paying FICA instead of SECA, and the IRS can require that this be corrected retroactively.
- The employer is underreporting the employee's income by the 7.65% FICA match. Also, the employer is reporting FICA Social Security taxes when it should not. The IRS could require the employer to retroactively correct Forms 941 and W-2.

  Example: A church hires and pays a minister to perform ministerial services, subject to the church's control. Under the common-law rules (pages 15-16), the minister is an employee of the church while performing those services. The church reports the minister's wages on Form W-2 for income tax purposes, but no Social Security taxes are withheld. The minister is self-employed for Social Security purposes and must pay self-employment tax (SECA) on those wages, unless the minister requests and receives an exemption from self-employment tax. On Form W-2, Boxes 3 through 6 are left blank.

Many churches reimburse ministers for a portion or all of their SECA liability (see page 56-57). SECA reimbursements represent additional taxable compensation in the year paid to the minister for both income and Social Security tax purposes.

Because of the SECA deductions (see page 115), a full SECA reimbursement is effectively less than the gross 15.3% rate.

Example: A church provides a cash salary of $75,000 and provides a parsonage that has an annual fair rental value of $15,000. Even though a full reimbursement of the minister's SECA is slightly less than 15.3%, the church decides to reimburse at the 15.3% rate for simplicity. The church grosses up the monthly pay by $1,147.50 (15.3% times $90,000 divided by 12 months).

Computing the Self-Employment Tax

When computing the self-employment tax, net earnings include the gross income earned from performing qualified services minus the deductions related to that income.

This includes church compensation reported in Box 1 of Form W-2 (the designated housing allowance should not be shown in this box), the net profit or loss from Schedule C, any housing allowance excluded from Form W-2, Box 1 or the fair rental value of church-provided housing, and amounts that should have been included on Form W-2, Box 1, such as business expense reimbursements made under a nonaccountable plan, a self-employment Social Security tax reimbursement or allowance, love offerings, etc.

Key Issue

Unless a minister has opted out of Social Security, the net ministerial income plus the excluded housing allowance and the fair rental value of church-provided housing is subject to self-employment Social Security tax. This is true even if the minister is retired and receiving Social Security benefits. There is no age limit on paying Social Security tax.

The following tax rates apply to net earnings from self-employment of $400 or more each year:

	Tax Rate		Maximum Earnings Base	
Year	OASDI	Medicare	OASDI	Medicare
2018	12.4%	2.9%	$128,400	no limit
2019	12.4%	2.9%	132,900	no limit
2020	12.4%	2.9%	137,700	no limit
2021	12.4%	2.9%	141,900	no limit

OASDI = Old-age, survivors, and disability insurance, also known as Social Security

The minister may deduct unreimbursed business expenses for the SECA computation even though deductions are not claimed elsewhere on Form 1040.

Moving expenses do not qualify as business expenses. Therefore, they are also included on the W-2 if they are reimbursed or paid on behalf of the minister.

Example: A minister has the following ministerial income and expenses: church salary $80,000 (of which the housing allowance is $12,000); net Schedule C

Self-Employment Social Security Tax Worksheet

Inclusions:

Salary paid by church as reflected on Form W-2, Box 1	$ ________
Net profit or loss as reflected on Schedule C (includes speaking honoraria, offerings received for marriages, baptisms, funerals, and other fees)	________
Housing allowance excluded from salary on Form W-2, or	________
Fair rental value of church-provided housing (including paid utilities)	________
Nonaccountable business expense reimbursements (if not included on Form W-2)	________
Reimbursement of self-employment taxes (if not included on Form W-2)	________
Other amounts that should have been included on Form W-2, Box 1, such as love offerings	________

Deductions:

Unreimbursed ministerial business and professional expenses or reimbursed expenses paid under a nonaccountable plan not deducted on Schedule C	________
Net earnings from self-employment (to Schedule SE)	$ ________

Note 1: A minister's net earnings from self-employment are not affected by the foreign earned income exclusion or the foreign housing exclusion or deduction if the minister is a U.S. citizen or resident alien who is serving abroad and living in a foreign country.

Note 2: Amounts received as pension payments or annuity payments related to a church-sponsored tax-sheltered annuity by a retired minister are generally considered to be excluded from the Social Security calculation.

income related to special speaking engagements, weddings, funerals, etc., $1,350.

The minister's self-employment income is

Salary from church	$68,000
Church-designated housing allowance	12,000
Schedule C net earnings	1,350
Total	$81,350

Use the worksheet above to calculate net earnings from self-employment. Net earnings are transferred to Form SE, page 1, Line 2, to calculate the SECA tax.

Both Spouses Are Ministers

If a husband and wife who are both duly ordained, commissioned, or licensed ministers have an agreement with a church that each will perform specific services for which they will receive pay, jointly or separately, they must divide the compensation according to the agreement. Such a division of income would have no impact on their income tax if they filed a joint return. But each of them could obtain Social Security coverage by dividing the compensation and subjecting the compensation to Social Security (SECA) tax.

Caution

A minister's spouse who is not duly ordained, commissioned, or licensed as a minister of a church but who receives pay for performing services for the church should not include his or her earnings with the minister's self-employment income. The non-minister spouse is generally an employee of the church for federal income tax and Social Security (FICA) tax purposes.

If the agreement for services is with one spouse only and the other spouse receives no pay for any specific duties, amounts paid for services are included only in the income of the spouse having the agreement. Pay should never be split merely for the purpose of allowing a spouse to qualify for Social Security or to avoid exceeding the Social Security earnings limit for one spouse.

Self-Employment Tax Deductions

Ministers can take an income tax deduction equal to one-half of their self-employment tax liability. The deduction is claimed against gross income on Form 1040, Schedule 1, Line 14.

They may also deduct a portion of their self-employment tax liability in calculating their self-employment tax. This deduction is made on Schedule SE, Part I, Line 4a by multiplying self-employment income by .9235.

Idea

Because of the deductibility of the self-employment tax in both the income tax and self-employment tax computations, if the church desires to reimburse the minister's entire Social Security tax obligation, it is effectively less than the gross 15.3% FICA rate. See page 56 for the effective rate at various marginal income tax rates.

The purpose of these deductions is to equalize the Social Security taxes paid by (and for) employees and self-employed persons with equivalent income.

Use of Income Tax Withholding to Pay Social Security Taxes

Under a voluntary withholding agreement, a minister may ask the church to withhold a sufficient amount to cover federal income taxes *plus* enough for the self-employment taxes (SECA). The church must report all amounts withheld under such an arrangement as federal income taxes. The other option for the payment of income and Social Security taxes is to use the Form 1040-ES in paying quarterly estimated taxes.

Key Issue

Ministers may take advantage of an opportunity to enter into a voluntary withholding arrangement with their church to withhold enough federal income tax to cover both their federal income tax and self-employment Social Security tax obligation. Withholding the proper amount each payday is a very efficient way to pay taxes. This avoids the risk of filing Forms 1040-ES late and incurring underpayment penalties.

Example: A minister projected that he will owe $1,000 of federal income tax for 2020 and $3,000 of self-employment Social Security tax for a total tax obligation of $4,000. The minister and his spouse will not have withholding from non-church employment. They will not qualify for the earned income tax credit. The minister could enter into a voluntary withholding agreement whereby the church would withhold federal income tax from each paycheck so that by the end of 2020, $4,000 was withheld (this would be reported on Form W-2, Box 2). No FICA-type Social Security tax is withheld from the minister's pay since he is not subject to that type of Social Security. Alternatively, the minister could file Forms 1040-ES on April 15, 2021; June 15, 2021; September 15, 2021; and January 15, 2022, submitting payments of $1,000 per filing.

Opting Out of Social Security

Warning

Opting out of Social Security is relatively simple. Form 4361 must be filed by the due date of the minister's tax return for the second year with $400 or more of ministerial income, any portion of which comes from the exercise of ministry. But the simplicity of opting out should not be confused with the significant difficulty of complying with the requirements for opting out.

All ministers are automatically covered by Social Security (SECA) for services in the exercise of ministry, unless an exemption has been approved by the IRS after filing Form 4361. The minister must certify that he or she opposes the *acceptance* of any public insurance (with respect to services performed as a minister), either conscientiously or because of religious principles, including Social Security benefits. *Either reason for opposition must be based on religious belief.* This includes an opposition to insurance that helps pay for or provide services for medical care (such as Medicare) and Social Security benefits.

To claim the exemption from self-employment tax, the minister must:

- file Form 4361
- be conscientiously opposed to public insurance (which includes insurance systems established by the Social Security Act) because of the minister's individual religious considerations (not because of general conscience), or because of the principles of the minister's religious denomination
- file for other than economic reasons
- inform the ordaining, commissioning, or licensing body of the church or order that he or she is personally opposed to public insurance
- establish that the religious organization that ordained, commissioned, or licensed the minister or his or her religious order is a tax-exempt religious organization
- establish that the organization is a church or a convention or association of churches
- sign and return the statement sent by the IRS to verify that the requested exemption is based on the grounds listed on the statement

Tip

Even though a minister signs Form 4361 and certifies that he or she is opposed to accepting public insurance benefits which are based on earnings from services performed in his or her capacity as a minister, the minister can still purchase life insurance or participate in retirement programs administered by nongovernmental institutions.

Deadline for filing for an exemption

The application for exemption from self-employment tax must be filed by the date the tax return is due, including extensions, for the second year in which the minister had net ministerial income of $400 or more. These do not have to be consecutive tax years.

Example 1: A minister ordained in 2019 has net earnings of $400 in 2019 and $500 in 2020. An application for exemption must be filed no later than April 15, 2021, if no extension has been filed. If the minister does not receive the approved exemption by April 15, 2021, the self-employment tax for 2020 is due by that date.

Example 2: A minister has $300 in net clergy earnings in 2019 but earned $400 in both 2018 and 2020. An application for exemption must be filed by April 15, 2021, if no extension has been filed. If the minister does not receive the approved exemption by April 15, 2021, the self-employment tax for 2020 is due by that date.

Example 3: A minister, ordained in 2018, earned $700 net for that year. In 2019, ministerial compensation was $1,000 and related expenses were $1,000. Therefore, the 2019 net earnings were zero. Also in 2019, $7,000 in net self-employment earnings was received from non-ministerial sources. In 2020, net ministerial earnings were $1,500 and self-employment income of $12,000 was received from non-ministerial sources.

Because the minister had ministerial net earnings in 2018 and 2020 that were more than $400 each year, the application for exemption must be filed by April 15, 2021. If the minister does not receive the approved exemption by April 15, 2021, the self-employment tax for 2020 is due by that date.

Example 4: A minister was ordained in 2019 with $1,000 and $2,000 of net ministerial earnings for 2019 and 2020, respectively. The minister filed Form 4361 in 2020 (this was a timely filing since the last day to file without extensions is April 15, 2021) and the application was approved by the IRS. The minister had already paid self-employment Social Security tax on the $1,000 of net ministerial earnings for 2019 since the Form 4361 had not yet been filed. Based on the approval of Form 4361, the minister can file an amended income tax return for 2019 using Form 1040X (see pages 138-39) and receive a refund of the Social Security tax paid on the net ministerial earnings for that year.

Tip

If the exemption is approved, it does not apply to non-ministerial wages or to any other self-employment income. For example, a bi-vocational pastor who is employed part-time in a secular job is subject to FICA on the wages from the secular job. If a minister performs independent contractor services unrelated to his or her ministry, this net profit is subject to Social Security.

A minister must include with Form 4361 a statement that the minister has informed the ordaining body of the minister's church of his or her opposition to the coverage.

A second ordination with a second church generally does not provide a second opportunity for a minister to opt out by filing Form 4361.

Basis of filing for exemption

Neither economics nor any other non-religious reason is a valid basis for the exemption. Many ministers are improperly counseled to opt out of Social Security because it may not be a "good investment." The minister's view of the soundness of the Social Security program has absolutely no relationship to the application for exemption.

Caution

Sadly, opting out of Social Security is one of the most abused provisions of the tax law that applies to ministers. Too often ministers have opted out because they are concerned about long-term safety of the program or they feel they have a better way to invest the funds. These reasons do not provide a basis to sign Form 4361.

The first consideration is the minister's ability to sign Form 4361 with a clear conscience. Key words in qualifying for exemption from Social Security coverage on ministerial earnings are "religious principles" and "conscientiously opposed to the acceptance of any public insurance." Religious principles do not simply consist of the conviction that perhaps Social Security will not be there when retirement comes or that a better retirement plan can be purchased through an annuity or other retirement program. The belief must be an integral part of the minister's religious system of beliefs, his or her theology.

Further, this religious principle must be one that would prevent the minister from ever asking for the benefits from such a plan based on the church salary. No basis exists for an objection related to *paying* the taxes or to the level of the taxes to be paid.

If a minister opts out and does not have sufficient Social Security credits from prior employment or from future non-ministerial employment, neither the minister nor his or her dependents will be covered under Social Security benefits, survivors' benefits, or Medicare. If a minister opts out of Social Security, he or she should make alternate plans to provide for catastrophic illness, disability, or death, as well as for retirement.

This is not a decision to be taken lightly. First, the minister must act on religious convictions. Second, he or she must be prepared financially with alternatives to the benefits of Social Security coverage.

Although a minister may opt out of Social Security with respect to ministerial income, he or she may still receive Social Security benefits related to nonministerial wages.

The importance of the approved Form 4361

The timely filing of Form 4361 by a minister does not constitute exemption from Social Security tax. The exemption is not effective until it has been approved by an appropriate IRS officer.

Form 4361 must be filed in triplicate. The exemption is not effective until a minister receives one of the three copies of the form back from the IRS marked "Approved."

Form **4361** (Rev. January 2011) Department of the Treasury Internal Revenue Service

Application for Exemption From Self-Employment Tax for Use by Ministers, Members of Religious Orders and Christian Science Practitioners

OMB No. 1545-0074

File Original and Two Copies

File original and two copies and attach supporting documents. This exemption is granted only if the IRS returns a copy to you marked "approved."

Please type or print

1 Name of taxpayer applying for exemption (as shown on Form 1040): Harold T. Baldwin

Social security number: 603-42-8941

Number and street (including apt. no.): PO Box 183

Telephone number (optional):

City or town, state, and ZIP code: Milton, PA 17647

2 Check **one** box: ☐ Christian Science practitioner ☒ Ordained minister, priest, rabbi ☐ Member of religious order not under a vow of poverty ☐ Commissioned or licensed minister (see line 6)

3 Date ordained, licensed, etc. (Attach supporting document. See instructions.) 7/1/17

4 Legal name of ordaining, licensing, or commissioning body or religious order: Christian General Conference

Employer identification number: 48-9017682

Number, street, and room or suite no.: PO Box 5002

City or town, state, and ZIP code: Nashville, AR 71852

5 Enter the first 2 years after the date shown on line 3 that you had net self-employment earnings of $400 or more, any of which came from services as a minister, priest, rabbi, etc.; member of a religious order; or Christian Science practitioner . . . ▶ 2018 | 2019

6 If you apply for the exemption as a licensed or commissioned minister and your denomination also ordains ministers, please indicate how your ecclesiastical powers differ from those of an ordained minister of your denomination. Attach a copy of your denomination's bylaws relating to the powers of ordained, commissioned, and licensed ministers.

7 I certify that I am conscientiously opposed to, or because of my religious principles I am opposed to, the acceptance (for services I perform as a minister, member of a religious order not under a vow of poverty, or Christian Science practitioner) of any public insurance that makes payments in the event of death, disability, old age, or retirement; or that makes payments toward the cost of, or provides services for, medical care. (Public insurance includes insurance systems established by the Social Security Act.)

I certify that as a duly ordained, commissioned, or licensed minister of a church or a member of a religious order not under a vow of poverty, I have informed the ordaining, commissioning, or licensing body of my church or order that I am conscientiously opposed to, or because of religious principles I am opposed to, the acceptance (for services I perform as a minister or as a member of a religious order) of any public insurance that makes payments in the event of death, disability, old age, or retirement; or that makes payments toward the cost of, or provides services for, medical care, including the benefits of any insurance system established by the Social Security Act.

I certify that I have never filed Form 2031 to revoke a previous exemption from social security coverage on earnings as a minister, member of a religious order not under a vow of poverty, or Christian Science practitioner.

I request to be exempted from paying self-employment tax on my earnings from services as a minister, member of a religious order not under a vow of poverty, or Christian Science practitioner, under section 1402(e) of the Internal Revenue Code. I understand that the exemption, if granted, will apply only to these earnings. Under penalties of perjury, I declare that I have examined this application and to the best of my knowledge and belief, it is true and correct.

Signature ▶ Harold T. Baldwin Date ▶ 1/30/20

Caution: *Form 4361 is **not proof** of the right to an exemption from federal income tax withholding or social security tax, the right to a parsonage allowance exclusion (section 107 of the Internal Revenue Code), assignment by your religious superiors to a particular job, or the exemption or church status of the ordaining, licensing, or commissioning body, or religious order.*

For Internal Revenue Service Use

☐ Approved for exemption from self-employment tax on ministerial earnings

☐ Disapproved for exemption from self-employment tax on ministerial earnings

By ________________ (Director's signature) ________________ (Date)

General Instructions

Section references are to the Internal Revenue Code unless otherwise noted.

Purpose of form. File Form 4361 to apply for an exemption from self-employment tax if you have ministerial earnings (defined later) and are:

- An ordained, commissioned, or licensed minister of a church;
- A member of a religious order who has not taken a vow of poverty; or
- A Christian Science practitioner.

Note. If you are a commissioned or licensed minister of a religious denomination or church that ordains its ministers, you may be treated in the same manner as an ordained minister if you perform substantially all the religious functions within the scope of the tenets and practices of your religious denomination or church.

This application must be based on your religious or conscientious opposition to the acceptance (for services performed as a minister, member of a religious order not under a vow of poverty, or Christian Science practitioner) of any public insurance that makes payments for death, disability, old age, or retirement; or that makes payments for the cost of, or provides services for, medical care, including any insurance benefits established by the Social Security Act.

If you are a duly ordained, commissioned, or licensed minister of a church or a member of a religious order not under a vow of poverty, prior to filing this form you must inform the ordaining, commissioning, or licensing body of your church or order that, on religious or conscientious grounds, you are opposed to the acceptance of public insurance benefits based on ministerial service.

For Privacy Act and Paperwork Reduction Act Notice, see page 2 Cat. No. 41586H Form **4361** (Rev. 1-2011)

Caution: Very few ministers qualify to file Form 4361. The filing must be based on the minister's conscience or religious principles, not because of a preference to invest retirement funds elsewhere.

Even if a minister has been approved for an exemption from self-employment Social Security taxes, this exemption does not apply to Social Security taxes on earnings as an employee or independent contractor resulting from work that is *not* in the exercise of ministry.

Example: The IRS approved the self-employment Social Security tax exemption for Minister A. In addition to her church employment, she works part-time at a secular job. While the church employment is in the exercise of ministry, the part-time employment is not. Therefore, she is not subject to self-employment Social Security tax on her compensation from the church, but she is subject to FICA-type Social Security tax on the part-time employment.

Opting back into Social Security

There is currently no formal method available for ministers to opt back into Social Security, although legislation was introduced in Congress in 2020 to provide an opportunity to opt back in (see page 1). As of this printing, it has not been passed.

Working After Retirement

There is no retirement earnings test for persons who have attained full retirement age (FRA). But for individuals who have not attained FRA, there is a limit on earnings from current work. The earnings limit is a retirement test and is a separate issue from income taxes.

If the minister earns more than the exempt amount (see below), the benefits to the minister and family members that are based on work record will be reduced. If a family member earns more than the exempt amount, only that person's benefit is reduced.

If the minister is under FRA throughout 2020, he or she can earn $18,240. If the earnings exceed this, then $1 of benefits is withheld for every $2 earned above $18,240. If the earnings exceed this limit, some benefits may still be payable.

If the minister attains FRA in 2020, he or she can earn $48,600 in the period before the month in which FRA is attained with no reduction in benefits. If the minister's earnings exceed this, then $1 in benefits is withheld for every $3 earned above $48,600.

After retirement, ministers may receive special payments for work they did before they started getting Social Security benefits. Usually, these special payments will not affect their Social Security benefit if they are compensation for work done before retirement.

Examples of special payments include bonuses, accumulated vacation or sick pay, and severance pay.

Canada Pension Plan

Under an agreement between the United States and Canada, a minister is subject to the laws of the country in which the services are performed for the purposes of United States Social Security and the Canada Pension Plan, respectively. In other words, a Canadian citizen who moves to the United States to pastor a church generally must pay United States Social Security (SECA) tax.

There is one exception to the general rule if the minister is required by a Canadian employer to transfer to a related organization in the United States on a temporary basis for a period not exceeding 60 months, with the intention of returning to the employment with the Canadian employer at the end of the temporary assignment. In this case, the Canadian employer must complete Form CPT56, Certificate of Coverage Under the Canada Pension Plan Pursuant to Article V of the Agreement on Social Security Between Canada and the United States, which may be obtained at www.ccra-adrc.gc.ca.

Some ministers may work in both the United States and Canada (see Publication IC84-6 Canada-United States Social Security Agreement issued by the Canada Revenue Agency). Each country issues "certificates of coverage" to confirm a particular work is covered under the Social Security laws of that country.

- **Improperly opting out of Social Security.** The improper (actually, the word is "illegal," but it is such a harsh word) opting out of Social Security by ministers is a blight on the profession.

  Sadly, there are people who have promoted ministers opting out of Social Security for reasons that are inconsistent with federal law! Many ministers, in their naiveté, have accepted faulty advice.

  The issue not a matter of whether it makes good money-sense for a minister to pay into Social Security. It's simply the right thing to do. Ministers are required to pay Social Security unless they are one of the rare ministers who are opposed to receiving public insurance (including Social Security) based on conscientious opposition or religious principles.

  Opting out for reasons inconsistent with federal law is not only an ethical issue but is a decision that can cause great harm to the minister and his family in retirement.

- **Correctly calculating the Social Security tax.** Paying the self-employment Social Security tax is often a bitter pill to swallow for ministers—the Social Security tax usually dwarfs the amount of income tax. But calculating the correct amount of Social Security tax due is vital, although challenging.

Paying Taxes

In This Chapter

- Voluntary tax withholding
- Estimated tax
- Excess Social Security withheld (FICA)
- Earned income credit
- Extension of time to file
- Extension of time to pay
- Offers in compromise
- Filing an amended tax return

The federal income tax is a pay-as-you-go tax. Like all taxpayers, ministers must pay the tax as they receive or earn income during the year.

Lay employees are subject to income tax withholding. The pay of qualified ministers is *not* subject to federal income tax withholding. Ministers who are employees for income tax purposes may provide for the funding for any federal income tax as well as self-employment Social Security tax obligation by:

- entering into a voluntary withholding agreement with the church, where the church withholds and remits income tax for the minister,
- paying quarterly estimated taxes using Form 1040-ES, or
- apply federal withholding from spousal compensation.

Ministers who do not prepay their taxes through a voluntary withholding agreement, or using Form 1040-ES, or through additional spousal withholding may be subject to an underpayment penalty.

IRS Publication 505 provides additional information on tax withholding and estimated taxes.

Voluntary Tax Withholding

Federal income tax withheld from earnings as an employee should be reported to the minister on Form W-2. The total amount withheld from all sources should be entered on Line 25d, Form 1040, page 2.

Churches are not required to withhold income taxes from wages paid to ministers for services performed in the exercise of their ministry. On the other hand, this exemption does not apply to non-ministerial church employees such as a church secretary, groundskeeper, or custodian.

Idea

Though not required, churches should *offer* to withhold federal (and state and local, where applicable) income taxes (never FICA taxes!) from a minister's pay. Filing Forms 1040-ES often means having to save money for the 4/15, 6/15, 9/15, and 1/15 deadlines. Withholding the proper amount each week or payday is much more efficient.

A minister may have a voluntary withholding agreement with the employing church to cover income taxes. The amount may be set high enough to also cover the amount for self-employment Social Security tax liability. This agreement to withhold income taxes from wages should be in writing, although there is no required form. It may be as simple as a letter from the minister to the church requesting that a specified amount be withheld as federal income taxes. Or a minister may request voluntary withholding by submitting Form W-4 (Employee's Withholding Allowance Certificate) to the church. On this form, one can indicate any additional amount to be withheld in excess of the regular federal income tax withholding.

A voluntary withholding arrangement may be concluded at any time by the minister, the church, or mutually. Conversely, the minister may specify that the withholding agreement will cease on a certain date.

If a minister submits Form W-4 as the basis for a voluntary withholding arrangement, the church will withhold the federal income tax liability. This would *not* automatically provide any coverage of the SECA tax obligation. The SECA tax obligation could still be covered by indicating an additional amount of federal income tax to be withheld on Form W-4, Line 4(c).

If federal income taxes withheld are sufficient to cover both the minister's income and self-employment Social Security (SECA) taxes, it is very important that the amounts be reported as "federal income taxes withheld" when the church remits the taxes and completes quarterly Forms 941 and annual Forms W-2 and W-3. FICA Social Security taxes should never be withheld or remitted for qualified ministers.

For personal budgeting purposes, a minister may request the church to withhold amounts from compensation to assist the minister in setting aside funds for estimated tax payments. Coinciding with the Form 1040-ES due dates (April 15, June 15, September 15, and January 15, unless the due dates fall on a weekend or holiday), the church pays the withheld amounts directly to the minister and then the minister uses the funds to make the appropriate estimated tax payments to the IRS. This sort of withholding has no impact on Form W-2.

Example 1: A minister's cash compensation is $80,000 for 2020 (this is in addition to a housing allowance), and the anticipated income and self-employment Social Security tax obligation for 2020 is $15,000. The minister uses the estimated tax method to pay income and self-employment Social Security tax.

Based on an agreement with the minister, a church withholds $1,250 per month from the minister's compensation in relation to the minister's tax obligation, both federal and Social Security (SECA). The church pays the minister $3,750 on April 15, June 15, September 15, and January 15 to provide the amount the minister needs to submit with Form 1040-ES. The $15,000 withheld does not impact the reporting on Form W-2, *e.g.*, Box 1 of Form W-2 shows $80,000. The $15,000 is not included in Box 2 as Federal Income Tax Withheld because the church did not remit funds to the IRS by the church for payroll tax purposes.

Example 2: A minister's cash compensation is $80,000 for 2020 (this is in addition to a housing allowance), and the church and the minister enter into a voluntary withholding arrangement for federal income tax purposes.

Based on the agreement, the church withholds $1,250 of federal income taxes per month and remits the withheld amounts to the IRS through the payroll tax reporting process. The Form W-2 for 2020 shows compensation in Box 1 of $80,000 and Federal Income Tax Withheld in Box 2 of $15,000.

Estimated Tax

Estimated tax is the method used to prepay income and self-employment taxes for income that is not subject to withholding. The estimated tax is the expected tax for the year minus your expected withholding and credits.

If filing a declaration of estimated tax, the employee must complete the quarterly Forms 1040-ES. However, if the 2021 estimated taxes are $1,000 or less, no declaration of estimated tax is required.

Filing Tip

When using the estimated tax method of prepaying income and Social Security taxes to the IRS, pay at least as much as your previous year's total tax liability (before offsetting withholding, estimated tax payments, etc.). Spread the payments equally over the four Forms 1040-ES. This will generally avoid underpayment penalties.

Three Ways to Pay Your Taxes

1

Estimated Taxes

The minister pays federal income taxes and Social Security taxes (SECA) directly to the IRS in quarterly payments.

2

Voluntary Withholding

The church withholds federal income tax and pays quarterly to the IRS. Additional federal income tax may be withheld to cover the minister's Social Security tax (SECA) liability.

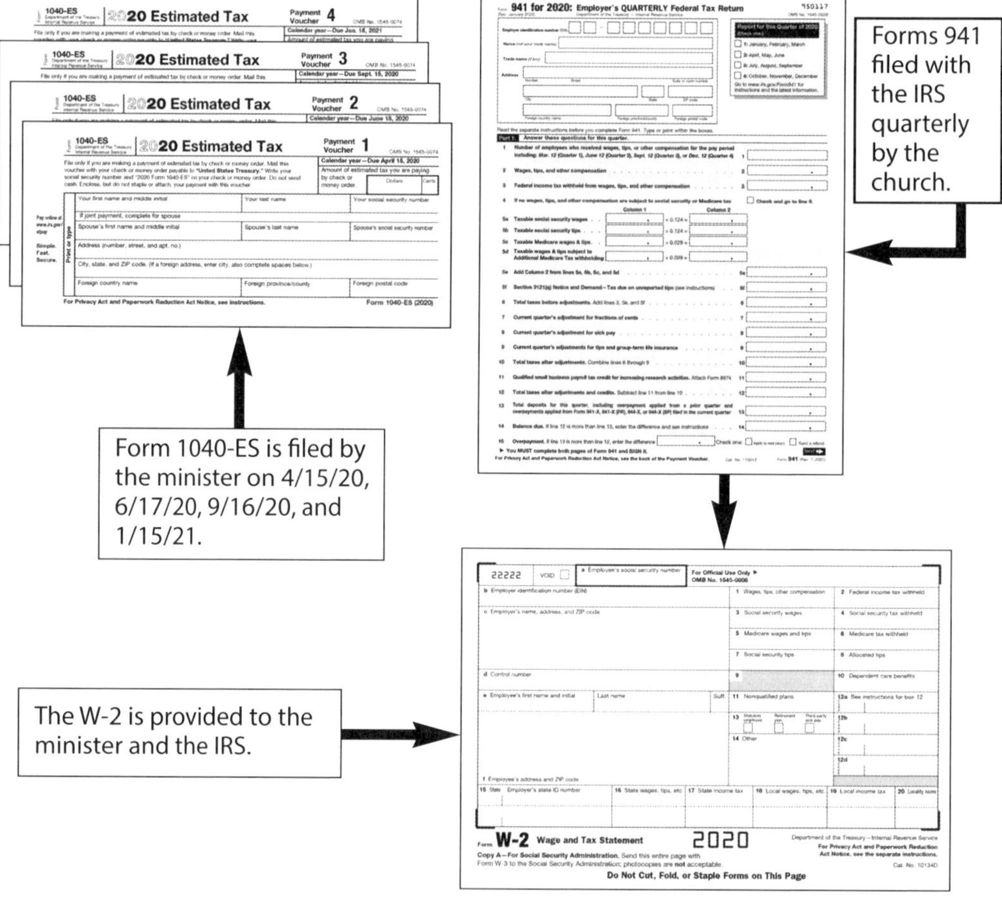

3

Payroll withholding from the minister's pay. The church does not remit the amounts withheld to the IRS. The amounts are paid directly to the minister on or before 4/15/21, 6/15/21, 9/15/21, and 1/15/22. The minister then files Form 1040-ES and remits the money to the IRS.

Calculate the Most Important Tax Planning Number for 2021 Taxes

It is only necessary to pay by December 31 (January 15 if paying estimates) the lowest of the "safe harbor" amounts. Use this worksheet to calculate them to know how much to withhold or pay in estimated taxes.

100% of your last year's (2020) tax liability (the number on Line 15 on your Form 1040): __________

90% of your estimated 2021 tax (federal income tax and self-employment Social Security tax) liability. Recalculate this number at least three times before October to update changes in your tax circumstances. (The October date gives you enough time to make changes in withholdings or your final estimated payment.)

Estimated 2021 tax liability: ______________ x 90% = __________

You can also avoid a penalty if you owe less than $1,000 on April 15 after considering withholdings. But be careful using this loophole—if you miscalculate just a little bit, you could be facing a penalty. So recalculate this at least three times a year as well.

Estimated 2021 tax liability: __________

Minus projected 2021 federal income tax withholdings: __________

Equals: (must be less than $1,000) __________

Fill in the lowest of these numbers: __________

You only have to pay this amount by the end of the year.

A special rule applies to individuals with adjusted gross income for the previous year in excess of $150,000.

If the estimated tax payments for 2021 equal 90% of the minister's 2021 tax liability, underpayment penalties will be avoided. An option is to make the 2021 estimated tax payments equal to 100% of the minister's 2020 federal and Social Security taxes (Form 1040, page 2, Line 16). This method generally avoids underpayment penalties and is easier to calculate.

Remember

April 15, the day taxes are due, is the same date the first estimated amounts are due for the next year.

Ministers with an adjusted gross income of over $150,000 ($75,000 for married individuals filing separately) may fall under special rules requiring larger estimated tax payments. At this income level, if the estimated tax payments for 2021 equal 110% of the 2020 tax liability, underpayment penalties will be avoided.

In estimating 2021 taxes, net earnings from self-employment should be reduced by 7.65% before calculating the self-employment tax of 15.3%. Since there is an income tax deduction for one-half of the self-employment tax (Form 1040, Schedule 1, Line 14).

The minister pays one-fourth of his or her total estimated taxes in installments as follows:

For the Period			2021 Due Date
January 1	-	March 31	April 15
April 1	-	May 31	June 15
June 1	-	August 31	September 15
September 1	-	December 31	January 15

Estimated tax payments are counted as paid when the IRS receives them. Thus, paying more later does not offset shortfalls from prior installments. Withheld tax is considered as paid evenly throughout the year. Therefore, increasing withholding late in a year offsets earlier underpayments.

Excess Social Security Withheld (FICA)

If a person worked for two or more employers during 2020 and together they paid him or her more than $137,700 in wages, too much FICA tax was likely withheld from the wages. The person can claim the extra amount as a credit on Line 10 of Form 1040, Schedule 3, to reduce the income tax when the return is filed. If the Social Security tax withholding shown in Box 4 of all the Forms W-2 exceeds $8,537.40 for 2020, the worker is entitled to a refund of the excess.

Of course, such a situation would occur for a person who was not employed as a qualified minister, because in such a case, FICA would not be withheld. A qualified minister would be in such a position only through other employment.

If filing a joint return, the worker cannot add any Social Security withheld from his or her spouse's income to the amount withheld from his or her income. The worker must figure the excess separately for both himself and his or her spouse to determine if either has excess withholding.

Earned Income Credit

Many ministers qualify for the earned income credit (EIC). The program furnishes a basic benefit for families even when there are no dependent children. There are three supplemental benefits to adjust for families with two or more children, those with a newborn child, and those that incur certain health insurance costs for their children.

Employees may be eligible for the maximum EIC, based on married filing jointly, if their 2020 taxable and nontaxable earned income was less than $21,710 if there is no qualifying child; less than $47,646 if there is one qualifying child; less than $53,330 if there are two or more children; and less than $56,844 if there are three or more qualifying children. Fees received from activities such as weddings and funerals are not includible in calculating earned income. The employee cannot claim the EIC unless the investment income is $3,500 or less.

Tip

For 2020, a qualifying child was, at the end of 2020, under age 19, or under age 24 and a student, or any age and permanently and totally disabled, and who lived with the taxpayer in the United States for more than half of 2020. If the child was married or meets the conditions to be a qualifying child of another person (other than your spouse if filing a joint return), special rules apply. See IRS Publication 596.

A child is a qualifying child if the child meets three tests: relationship, age, and residency.

➢ **Relationship.** The child must be either the son, daughter, adopted child, stepchild, eligible foster child of the employee, or any descendant of those.

➢ **Age.** The child must be under age 19 at the end of 2020, a full-time student under age 24 at the end of 2020, or permanently and totally disabled at any time during 2020, regardless of age.

➢ **Residency.** The child must have lived with the employee in the United States for more than half of 2020 (all of 2020 if an eligible foster child).

In the earned income calculation, the fair rental value of a parsonage provided by the church is *includible*. Plus, a housing allowance designated by the church related to either a parsonage or minister-provided housing counts as earned income. (Exception: If the minister has opted out of Social Security, neither the fair rental value of a parsonage nor housing allowances designated is includible.)

If claiming the EIC, the employee can either have the IRS calculate the amount of the credit, or the employee can calculate it (he or she must complete and attach Schedule EIC to the return if he or she has at least one qualifying child). If the employee calculates it, he or she must complete a worksheet found in the IRS instructions that determines whether the earned income credit is based on earned income or on modified adjusted gross income (generally equal to the adjusted gross income after disregarding certain losses). Then the employee must look up the amount of the credit in an IRS table.

Extension of Time to File

All ministers should file their 2020 tax returns with the IRS service center and make payment by April 15, 2021 to avoid penalties and interest.

If the minister has applied for an extension of time to file the return, remember that the final payment is still due by April 15, 2021, with the extension application. The extension of time to file is not an extension of the time to pay.

Six-month extension to file

To receive a six-month extension of time, the minister taxpayer should file Form 4868, Application for Automatic Extension of Time to File U.S. Individual Income Tax Return. The form must be filed by April 15, 2021.

As an alternative option to filing a paper Form 4868, he or she can electronically file Form 4868 using (1) a tax software package, (2) through a tax professional, or (3) through other service providers.

Service providers may charge a convenience fee based on the amount of the tax payment being made. Fees may vary among service providers. The taxpayer will be told what the fee is during the transaction and will have the option to continue or cancel the transaction. The convenience fee can also be determined by calling the providers' toll-free automated customer service numbers or visiting their websites. Do not add the convenience fee to the tax payment.

Remember

Obtaining a six-month extension is easy. No reason for late filing is needed. The IRS will automatically grant the extension. However, this is not an extension of time to pay—only an extension of time to file. If the amount owed on a minister's return will generate an underpayment penalty, filing 4868 will not help the minister.

Form **4868**
Department of the Treasury
Internal Revenue Service (99)

Application for Automatic Extension of Time To File U.S. Individual Income Tax Return

OMB No. 1545-0074
2020

For calendar year 2020, or other tax year beginning , 2020, and ending , 20 .

Part I Identification			**Part II** Individual Income Tax	
1 Your name(s) (see instructions)			4 Estimate of total tax liability for 2020 . .	$
			5 Total 2020 payments	
Address (see instructions)			6 **Balance due.** Subtract line 5 from line 4. See instructions	
			7 Amount you're paying (see instructions) . ▶	
City, town, or post office	State	ZIP code	8 Check here if you're "out of the country" and a U.S. citizen or resident. See instructions . . . . . . ▶	☐
2 Your social security number	3 Spouse's social security number		9 Check here if you file Form 1040-NR and didn't receive wages as an employee subject to U.S. income tax withholding . . . . ▶	☐

For Privacy Act and Paperwork Reduction Act Notice, see instructions later. Cat. No. 13141W Form **4868** (2020)

Penalties

An elaborate system of penalties exists to make sure that tax returns are filed correctly and tax liabilities are paid on time. In addition, interest is charged on many penalties, including the late filing penalty, substantial understatement penalty, overvaluation penalty, negligence penalty, and fraud penalty.

- **Failure to pay penalty.** Even if the IRS grants an extension of time to file, if 90% of the tax is not paid on time, the taxpayer will be subject to a penalty of one-half of 1% of the unpaid tax for each month or part of a month that the tax is not paid, to a maximum of 25% of the tax. The penalty can be avoided only if it can be shown that failure to pay is due to reasonable cause and not willful neglect.

- **Penalty computed by the IRS.** If the taxpayer does not want to figure the penalty, the IRS will figure it and send a bill. In certain situations the taxpayer must complete Form 2210 and attach it to the return.

- **Form 2210.** If the minister taxpayer wants to calculate the penalty, he or she must complete Part I and either Part II or Part III of Form 2210, Underpayment of Estimated Tax by Individuals and Fiduciaries.

Tip

Ask a professional to look over tax due notices from the IRS. It is not unusual for the IRS to send a penalty notice when no penalty is actually due. Demonstrating that a minister does not owe a penalty may be as simple as completing Form 2210.

Generally, a taxpayer *will not* have to pay a penalty in any of the following situations:

- ☐ If the total of the 2020 withholding and estimated tax payments was at least as much as the 2019 tax and all required estimated tax payments were on time, the taxpayer is not subject to the special rule limiting use of prior year's tax.

- ☐ The tax balance on the return is no more than 10% of the total 2020 tax, and all required estimated tax payments were on time.
- ☐ The total 2020 tax minus withholding is less than $1,000.
- ☐ The employee did not owe tax for 2020.

Interest

If a minister taxpayer has not paid the entire tax due by April 15, 2021, he or she must pay interest from then until the date the tax liability is paid. Receiving an automatic extension of time to file the tax return will not relieve the employee of the burden of interest.

State extensions

For states that have a state income tax, check the instruction forms that come with the return to determine how to file an extension. In some states, if no additional tax is owed, there is no need to file a separate state extension. Instead, the state will allow the same extensions that the IRS grants, and a copy of the federal extension should be attached to the state return for filing. Other states may require their own forms.

Extension of Time to Pay

It is important for a minister to file the return on time even if it is impossible to pay the tax. Filing on time will avoid late filing penalties which are one-half of 1% per month based on the balance of tax due, up to a maximum penalty of 25%. *Note:* Filing stops the penalties, but not the interest.

If a taxpayer can't pay the full amount due, he or she should pay as much as possible when filing the return. Generally, taxes should not be charged directly to a credit card unless it's a small amount that can be paid off quickly. While an employee might earn frequent flyer miles, he or she will pay interest charges to the credit card company, plus a credit card cost to the IRS of up to 3%, and none of that is deductible.

Tip

Ministers desiring to pay their taxes on an installment plan should ask for a six-month extension of time to pay or make the IRS an offer in compromise. Professional assistance should be sought on these very specialized forms.

Installment payments

The IRS may permit a taxpayer to pay the taxes on an installment plan. The request for an installment agreement cannot be turned down if the tax owed is not more than $10,000 and all three of the following are applicable:

- During the past five tax years, the individual has filed all income tax returns timely and paid any income tax due, and has not previously entered into an installment agreement for payment of income tax;
- The IRS determines that the individual cannot pay the tax owed in full when it is due and the IRS is given any information needed to make that determination; and
- The individual agrees to pay the full amount owed within three years and to comply with the tax laws while the agreement is in effect.

A minister can file Form 9465, Installment Agreement Request, or request an installment agreement online if the amount owed is not more than $50,000, but the IRS requires the payments to start within a month. If approved, generally the minister will still owe the IRS the late-payment penalty plus interest, including interest on the penalty. To limit interest and penalty charges, the minister should file the return on time and pay as much of the tax as possible with the return. The IRS charges an installment agreement user fee depending on whether payment is made online.

If the IRS approves the request, the taxpayer will be notified on how to pay the fee and how to make the first installment payment.

Six-month extension to pay

Even if a six-month extension of time is granted until October 15, 2021 to file the 2020 return by filing Form 4868 (see page 133), generally the taxes must be paid by April 15, 2021.

A taxpayer may be able to put off paying the taxes for six months until October 15, 2021, without a penalty by using Form 1127 (see page 136), Application for Extension of Time for Payment of Tax. Getting this extension is not easy. The employee will have to prove to the IRS that he or she does not have the money to pay the taxes, cannot borrow, and, if forced to pay at that time, the employee and family will suffer "undue hardship."

Hardship means more than inconvenience. Substantial financial loss must be shown if the tax is paid on the date it is due, such as a loss caused by selling property at a sacrifice price.

If the taxpayer files for this extension, he or she must include a complete statement of all his or her assets and liabilities and an itemized list of all money received and spent for three months prior to the request. Plus, the IRS may require security such as a notice of lien, mortgage, pledge, deed of trust of specific property, or personal surety.

Form **1127**
(Rev. December 2011)
Department of the Treasury
Internal Revenue Service

Application for Extension of Time for Payment of Tax Due to Undue Hardship

OMB No. 1545-2131

Before you begin: Use the chart on page 3 to see if you should file this form.

Name(s) shown on return | **Identifying number**

Number, street, and apt., room, or suite no. If you have a P.O. box, see instructions.

City, town, or post office, state, and ZIP code. If you have a foreign address, see instructions.

Part I **Request for Extension**

I request an extension from ____________, 20 ____, to ____________, 20 ____, to pay tax of $ ________.

This request is for (check only one box):

☐ The tax shown or required to be shown on Form ________.

☐ An amount determined as a deficiency on Form ________.

This request is for calendar year 20 ____, or fiscal year ending ____________, 20 ____.

Part II **Reason for Extension**

Undue hardship. Enter below a detailed explanation of the undue hardship that will result if your application is denied. (If more space is required, please attach a separate sheet.) To establish undue hardship, you must show that you would sustain a substantial financial loss if forced to pay a tax or deficiency on the due date. For a complete definition of "undue hardship," see the instructions on page 3 under *Who Should File.*

Part III **Supporting Documentation**

To support my application, I certify that I have attached (you must check both boxes or your application will not be accepted):

☐ A statement of my assets and liabilities at the end of last month (showing book and market values of assets and whether securities are listed or unlisted), and

☐ An itemized list of my income and expenses for each of the 3 months prior to the due date of the tax.

Signature and Verification

Under penalties of perjury, I declare that I have examined this application, including any accompanying schedules and statements, and to the best of my knowledge and belief, it is true, correct, and complete; and, if prepared by someone other than the taxpayer, that I am authorized to prepare this form.

Signature of taxpayer ▶ ________________ Date ▶ ________

Signature of spouse ▶ ________________ Date ▶ ________

Signature of preparer other than taxpayer ▶ ________________ Date ▶ ________

FOR IRS USE ONLY (Do not detach)

This application is ☐ Approved ☐ Denied ☐ Returned:

Reason(s): ________________

Signature of authorized official | Date

For Privacy Act and Paperwork Reduction Act Notice, see instructions. Cat. No. 17238O Form **1127** (Rev. 12-2011)

Offers in Compromise

An Offer in Compromise (OIC) allows a minister taxpayer to settle tax debt for less than the full amount owed. The IRS will consider the minister's unique set of facts and circumstances, including ability to pay, income, expense, and asset equity. The IRS will generally accept an OIC when it is unlikely that the tax liability can be collected in full and the amount offered reasonably reflects collection potential.

The IRS may legally compromise for one of the following reasons:

- **Doubt as to liability**—doubt exists that the assessed tax is correct.
- **Doubt as to collectibility**—doubt exists that the taxpayer could ever pay the full amount of tax owed. The IRS will generally consider a doubt as to collectibility offer when the taxpayer is unable to pay the taxes in full either by liquidating assets or through current installment agreement guidelines.
- **Effective tax administration**—there is no doubt the tax is correct and no doubt the amount owed could be collected, but an exceptional circumstance exists that allows the IRS to consider the offer. To be eligible for compromise on this basis, the taxpayer must demonstrate that collection of the tax would create an economic hardship or would be unfair and inequitable.

To work out an offer in compromise, the taxpayer must show that paying the whole tax would cause a severe or unusual economic hardship. Examples of economic hardship include:

- incapability of earning a living because of a long-term medical condition, or
- liquidation of assets would render the taxpayer unable to pay his or her basic living expenses.

The taxpayer should file Form 656, Offer in Compromise, with the IRS and choose one of the following options:

- **Lump sum cash.** Submit an initial payment of 20 percent of the total offer amount with the application. If the offer is accepted, the taxpayer will receive written confirmation. Any remaining balance due on the offer is paid in five or fewer payments.
- **Periodic payment.** Submit the initial payment with the application. Continue to pay the remaining balance in monthly installments while the IRS considers the offer. If accepted, monthly payments continue until paid in full.

Filing an Amended Tax Return

There may still be time to revise 2017, 2018, and 2019 income tax returns by filing Form 1040X (see page 139). Taxpayers may review these tax returns to determine if they missed out on any tax savings. Or, if they find more money is owed, they can pay before the IRS catches up with them and the interest due has increased. Interest or penalties should not be included on Form 1040X; the IRS will adjust them.

Tip

A minister may need to amend his or her tax return either to pay more taxes or to get a refund from the IRS. Tax returns can generally be amended if Form 1040X is filed within three years of the due date, plus extensions, of the year being amended.

Form 1040X should be filed only after the original return is filed. Generally, Form 1040X must be filed within three years, plus extensions, after the date the original return was filed or within two years after the date the tax was paid, whichever is later. If Form 1040 was filed early (before April 15), it is considered filed on the due date. If correcting wages or other employee compensation, attach a copy of all additional or corrected Forms W-2 received after filing the original return. A separate Form 1040X should be filed for each year being amended.

Employees must not forget to amend their state return, if appropriate. The IRS and the state tax authorities exchange information. If an amended federal return is filed without an amended state return when required to do so, the state may find out about the amended data from the IRS.

Form **1040-X** (Rev. January 2020)

Department of the Treasury—Internal Revenue Service

Amended U.S. Individual Income Tax Return

► Go to *www.irs.gov/Form1040X* for instructions and the latest information.

OMB No. 1545-0074

This return is for calendar year [X] 2019 ☐ 2018 ☐ 2017 ☐ 2016

Other year. Enter one: calendar year **or** fiscal year (month and year ended):

Your first name and middle initial	Last name	Your social security number
Milton L.	Brown	541 16 8194
If joint return, spouse's first name and middle initial	Last name	Spouse's social security number
Alessia S.	Brown	238 49 7209

Current home address (number and street). If you have a P.O. box, see instructions.	Apt. no.	Your phone number
418 Trenton Street		

City, town or post office, state, and ZIP code. If you have a foreign address, also complete spaces below. See instructions.

Springfield, OH 45504

Foreign country name	Foreign province/state/county	Foreign postal code

Amended return filing status. You **must** check one box even if you are not changing your filing status. **Caution:** In general, you can't change your filing status from a joint return to separate returns after the due date.

[X] **Full-year health care coverage (or, for amended 2018 returns only, exempt).** If amending a 2019 return, leave blank. See instructions.

☐ Single [X] Married filing jointly ☐ Married filing separately (MFS) ☐ Qualifying widow(er) (QW) ☐ Head of household (HOH)

If you checked the MFS box, enter the name of spouse. If you checked the HOH or QW box, enter the child's name if the qualifying person is a child but not your dependent. ►

Use Part III on the back to explain any changes		A. Original amount reported or as previously adjusted (see instructions)	B. Net change—amount of increase or (decrease)—explain in Part III	C. Correct amount
Income and Deductions				
1 Adjusted gross income. If a net operating loss (NOL) carryback is included, check here ► ☐	1	32,000	(3,000)	29,000
2 Itemized deductions or standard deduction	2	11,400	0	11,400
3 Subtract line 2 from line 1	3	20,600	(3,000)	17,600
4a Exemptions (amended 2017 or earlier returns only). **If changing,** complete Part I on page 2 and enter the amount from line 29	4a	10,950	0	10,950
b Qualified business income deduction (amended 2018 or later returns only)	4b			
5 Taxable income. Subtract line 4a or 4b from line 3. If the result is zero or less, enter -0-	5	9,650	(3,000)	6,650
Tax Liability				
6 Tax. Enter method(s) used to figure tax (see instructions):	6	965	(300)	665
7 Credits. If a general business credit carryback is included, check here ► ☐	7			
8 Subtract line 7 from line 6. If the result is zero or less, enter -0-	8	965	(300)	665
9 Health care: individual responsibility (amended 2018 or earlier returns only). See instructions	9			
10 Other taxes	10	5,500		5,500
11 Total tax. Add lines 8, 9, and 10	11	6,465	(300)	6,165
Payments				
12 Federal income tax withheld and excess social security and tier 1 RRTA tax withheld. (**If changing,** see instructions.)	12			
13 Estimated tax payments, including amount applied from prior year's return	13	7,000		7,000
14 Earned income credit (EIC)	14			
15 Refundable credits from: ☐ Schedule 8812 Form(s) ☐ 2439 ☐ 4136 ☐ 8863 ☐ 8885 ☐ 8962 or ☐ other (specify):	15			

16 Total amount paid with request for extension of time to file, tax paid with original return, and additional tax paid after return was filed	16	
17 Total payments. Add lines 12 through 15, column C, and line 16	17	7,000
Refund or Amount You Owe		
18 Overpayment, if any, as shown on original return or as previously adjusted by the IRS	18	535
19 Subtract line 18 from line 17. (If less than zero, see instructions.)	19	6,465
20 **Amount you owe.** If line 11, column C, is more than line 19, enter the difference	20	
21 If line 11, column C, is less than line 19, enter the difference. This is the amount **overpaid** on this return	21	300
22 Amount of line 21 you want **refunded to you**	22	300
23 Amount of line 21 you want **applied to your (enter year):** estimated tax	23	

Complete and sign this form on page 2.

For Paperwork Reduction Act Notice, see instructions. Cat. No. 11360L Form **1040-X** (Rev. 1-2020)

Amended returns must be filed within three years of the return due date plus approved extensions.

- **Filing income tax returns and paying the tax due.** Unfortunately, some ministers do not file their tax returns when they are due and/or do not pay the amount of tax due. Few things will bring more shame to a minister and the church.

  One of the few things worse than getting behind on filing tax returns and paying taxes is taking the position that it is not required to file tax returns—an approach taken by tax protesters. There is no validity to such a position.

- **Withholding of income tax by the church.** Ministers should take advantage of income tax withholding by the employing church. This is one of the most important decisions a minister can make to ensure timely payment of income tax (and additional income tax may be withheld to cover Social Security (SECA) tax).

  True, a church is not required to withhold federal (and state) income tax from the minister's pay—it's voluntary for both the church and the minister. But most churches will gladly handle the modest additional paperwork to assist the minister with tax withholding. If taxes are withheld in a timely manner, underpayment penalties can be eliminated, and the minister is more likely to file his or her return—and on time!

- **Properly calculating the earned income tax credit.** While it is sad that a minister would ever qualify for the earned income tax credit (confirming the minister is being paid below the poverty line) from the perspective of adequate compensation, there is no shame in claiming the credit.

  Care should be taken to compute the earned income tax credit based on accurate data. The fair rental value of a parsonage provided by the church plus a housing allowance (parsonage or minister-owned housing) is includible in the earned income calculation for this credit (unless the minister has opted out of Social Security).

Line-by-Line

Form 1040

The basic Form 1040 for 2020 consists of two half-pages. The first half-page includes basic taxpayer and dependent identification information and income and deductions, while the second page is where all tax reporting occurs. Many ministers may report information on several schedules, especially as it relates to self-employment taxes.

Reviewing the Form 1040 and Schedules 1–3 line-by-line may jog your memory about money received or spent in 2020.

- **Filing status. Married filing jointly:** If the minister's spouse died in 2020, he or she can still file jointly and take advantage of tax rates that would be lower than if the minister can file as a single person or as a head of household.

  Married filing separately: If the minister is married and lives in a separate-property state, compute the tax two ways—jointly and separately. Then, file the return resulting in the lower tax.

  Head of household: If the minister is single, he or she may qualify as head of household if he or she provided a home for someone else—such as a parent. Filing as head of household rather than as a single person can save a bundle on taxes.

  Qualifying widow(er): If the minister's spouse died in 2018 or 2019 and the minister has a dependent child, there is benefit from joint-return rates as a qualifying widow(er).

Filing Tip

All compensation from Form W-2 is reported on Line 1. Be sure the church has not included the housing allowance amount in Box 1 of Form W-2.

- **Dependents.** Remember to include a Social Security number for any dependents. If a child does not have one, obtain Form SS-5, "Application for a Social Security

Form 1040, page 1 (cont'd.)

Form **1040** Department of the Treasury—Internal Revenue Service (99) **U.S. Individual Income Tax Return** **2020** OMB No. 1545-0074 IRS Use Only—Do not write or staple in this space.

Filing Status Check only one box. ☐ Single ☐ Married filing jointly ☐ Married filing separately (MFS) ☐ Head of household (HOH) ☐ Qualifying widow(er) (QW)

If you checked the MFS box, enter the name of your spouse. If you checked the HOH or QW box, enter the child's name if the qualifying person is a child but not your dependent ▶

Your first name and middle initial	Last name			Your social security number
If joint return, spouse's first name and middle initial	Last name			Spouse's social security number
Home address (number and street). If you have a P.O. box, see instructions.			Apt. no.	**Presidential Election Campaign** Check here if you, or your spouse if filing jointly, want $3 to go to this fund. Checking a box below will not change your tax or refund. ☐ You ☐ Spouse
City, town, or post office. If you have a foreign address, also complete spaces below.		State	ZIP code	
Foreign country name	Foreign province/state/county		Foreign postal code	

At any time during 2020, did you receive, sell, send, exchange, or otherwise acquire any financial interest in any virtual currency? ☐ Yes ☐ No

Standard Deduction **Someone can claim:** ☐ You as a dependent ☐ Your spouse as a dependent ☐ Spouse itemizes on a separate return or you were a dual-status alien

Age/Blindness **You:** ☐ Were born before January 2, 1956 ☐ Are blind **Spouse:** ☐ Was born before January 2, 1956 ☐ Is blind

Dependents (see instructions): If more than four dependents, see instructions and check here ▶ ☐

(1) First name Last name	(2) Social security number	(3) Relationship to you	(4) ✔ if qualifies for (see instructions): Child tax credit	Credit for other dependents
			☐	☐
			☐	☐
			☐	☐
			☐	☐

Attach Sch. B if required.

Line					Line	
1	Wages, salaries, tips, etc. Attach Form(s) W-2				1	
2a	Tax-exempt interest	2a		b Taxable interest	2b	
3a	Qualified dividends	3a		b Ordinary dividends	3b	
4a	IRA distributions	4a		b Taxable amount	4b	
5a	Pensions and annuities	5a		b Taxable amount	5b	
6a	Social security benefits	6a		b Taxable amount	6b	
7	Capital gain or (loss). Attach Schedule D if required. If not required, check here ▶ ☐				7	
8	Other income from Schedule 1, line 9				8	
9	Add lines 1, 2b, 3b, 4b, 5b, 6b, 7, and 8. This is your **total income** ▶				9	
10	Adjustments to income:					
a	From Schedule 1, line 22	10a				
b	Charitable contributions if you take the standard deduction. See instructions	10b				
c	Add lines 10a and 10b. These are your **total adjustments to income** ▶				10c	
11	Subtract line 10c from line 9. This is your **adjusted gross income** ▶				11	
12	**Standard deduction or itemized deductions** (from Schedule A)				12	
13	Qualified business income deduction. Attach Form 8995 or Form 8995-A				13	
14	Add lines 12 and 13				14	
15	**Taxable income.** Subtract line 14 from line 11. If zero or less, enter -0-				15	

Standard Deduction for—
- Single or Married filing separately, $12,400
- Married filing jointly or Qualifying widow(er), $24,800
- Head of household, $18,650
- If you checked any box under *Standard Deduction*, see instructions.

For Disclosure, Privacy Act, and Paperwork Reduction Act Notice, see separate instructions. Cat. No. 11320B Form **1040** (2020)

Number." If unable to secure the Social Security number before the filing deadline, the minister may file for an extension of time to file.

- **Income and deductions (lines 1 to 15).**

  Line 1: If the minister is considered an employee for income tax purposes, he or she should receive Form W-2 from the church. The total amount of the taxable wages is shown in Box 1 of Form W-2; attach Copy B of the W-2 to your Form 1040. Include the data from other W-2s received for the minister or spouse on this line. If the church erroneously included the housing allowance in Box 1, Form W-2, the minister should ask the church to reissue a corrected Form W-2.

Form 1040, page 1 (cont'd.)

If the cash housing allowance designated and paid by the church exceeds the lowest of (1) the amount actually used to provide a home from current ministerial income, (2) the amount properly designated by the employer, or (3) the fair rental value of the home including utilities and furnishings, enter the difference on the dotted line next to Line 1.

Filing Tip

Form 1040, Page 1, Line 1. If the housing allowance designated by the employer exceeds the housing allowance exclusion to which the minister is entitled, he or she must include the difference on Line 1 with a description "Excess housing allowance."

Line 2a: Here's where to note any tax-exempt interest from municipal bonds or municipal bond funds. Don't worry—that income is not taxable. But Social Security recipients must count all their tax-exempt interest when computing how much of their Social Security benefits will be taxable.

Line 2b: Include as taxable-interest income the total amount of earnings on savings accounts, certificates of deposit, credit union accounts, corporate bonds and corporate bond mutual funds, U.S. treasuries and U.S. government mutual funds, and interest paid to the minister for a belated federal or state tax refund (whether or not a Form 1099-INT has been received). If the statements have not yet been received, call the issuer to get them. If more than $1,500 of taxable interest income was received in 2020, Schedule B must also be completed.

Line 3a and 3b: Enter as dividend income only ordinary dividends, not capital-gains dividends paid by mutual funds, which are reported on Schedule D. Form 1099-DIV statements show the amount and type of dividends received during 2020. If more than $1,500 in dividend income was received in 2020, Schedule B must be completed. Remember: earnings from a money-market mutual fund are considered dividend income, not interest income.

Line 4a: Report all distributions from IRAs.

Line 5a: Pensions and annuities on this line, including amounts that were rolled over tax-free in 2020 from one account into another.

Line 4b and 5b: Report the taxable portion of these distributions. If any distributions were received from a denominationally-sponsored plan, the minister may be eligible to exclude a portion or all of these payments as a housing allowance.

Line 6a: No more than 85% of Social Security benefits can be taxed for 2020 and none at all if the provisional income is below $32,000 on a joint return, $25,000 for

Form 1040, page 1 (cont'd.)

singles. If the income doesn't exceed the threshold, leave this line blank. If it does, use the worksheet on SSA-1099 to compute taxes on the benefits.

Line 6b: Report any taxable portion of Social Security benefits on this line.

Line 7: Enter capital-gains dividends if there were no other capital gains or losses in 2020.

Line 10b: for a taxpayer who does not itemize deductions, enter the cash contribution amount up to $300 that was given to charity.

Line 12: Claim the standard deduction only if the amount exceeds what could be written off in itemizing expenses on Schedule A. For 2020, the standard deduction is $24,800 married filing jointly, $18,650 head of household, $12,400 single, and $12,400 for married filing separately. The deduction amounts are higher if the minister or spouse is 65 or older or legally blind.

Line 13: Compute your qualified business income deduction on Form 8995/8995-A and reflect the amount on Line 13. Most ministers will qualify for this deduction because of Schedule C net income from fees for speaking, weddings, funerals, etc.

Form 1040 – Page 2

Form 1040 (2020) Page 2

	16	Tax (see instructions). Check if any from Form(s): 1 ☐ 8814 2 ☐ 4972 3 ☐		16	
	17	Amount from Schedule 2, line 3		17	
	18	Add lines 16 and 17		18	
	19	Child tax credit or credit for other dependents		19	
	20	Amount from Schedule 3, line 7		20	
	21	Add lines 19 and 20		21	
	22	Subtract line 21 from line 18. If zero or less, enter -0-		22	
	23	Other taxes, including self-employment tax, from Schedule 2, line 10		23	
	24	Add lines 22 and 23. This is your **total tax** ▶		24	
	25	Federal income tax withheld from:			
	a	Form(s) W-2	25a		
	b	Form(s) 1099	25b		
	c	Other forms (see instructions)	25c		
	d	Add lines 25a through 25c		25d	
• If you have a qualifying child, attach Sch. EIC. • If you have nontaxable combat pay, see instructions.	26	2020 estimated tax payments and amount applied from 2019 return		26	
	27	Earned income credit (EIC)	27		
	28	Additional child tax credit. Attach Schedule 8812	28		
	29	American opportunity credit from Form 8863, line 8	29		
	30	Recovery rebate credit. See instructions	30		
	31	Amount from Schedule 3, line 13	31		
	32	Add lines 27 through 31. These are your **total other payments and refundable credits** ▶		32	
	33	Add lines 25d, 26, and 32. These are your **total payments** ▶		33	
Refund	34	If line 33 is more than line 24, subtract line 24 from line 33. This is the amount you **overpaid**		34	
	35a	Amount of line 34 you want **refunded to you.** If Form 8888 is attached, check here ▶ ☐		35a	
Direct deposit? See instructions.	▶b	Routing number ▶c Type: ☐ Checking ☐ Savings			
	▶d	Account number			
	36	Amount of line 34 you want **applied to your 2021 estimated tax** ▶	36		
Amount You Owe For details on how to pay, see instructions.	37	Subtract line 33 from line 24. This is the **amount you owe now** ▶		37	
		Note: Schedule H and Schedule SE filers, line 37 may not represent all of the taxes you owe for 2020. See Schedule 3, line 12e, and its instructions for details.			
	38	Estimated tax penalty (see instructions) ▶	38		

Third Party Designee Do you want to allow another person to discuss this return with the IRS? See instructions ▶ ☐ **Yes.** Complete below. ☐ **No**

Designee's name ▶ Phone no. ▶ Personal identification number (PIN) ▶

Sign Here Under penalties of perjury, I declare that I have examined this return and accompanying schedules and statements, and to the best of my knowledge and belief, they are true, correct, and complete. Declaration of preparer (other than taxpayer) is based on all information of which preparer has any knowledge.

Joint return? See instructions. Keep a copy for your records.

Your signature	Date	Your occupation	If the IRS sent you an Identity Protection PIN, enter it here (see inst.) ▶
Spouse's signature. If a joint return, **both** must sign.	Date	Spouse's occupation	If the IRS sent your spouse an Identity Protection PIN, enter it here (see inst.) ▶
Phone no.	Email address		

Paid Preparer Use Only

Preparer's name	Preparer's signature	Date	PTIN	Check if: ☐ Self-employed
Firm's name ▶			Phone no.	
Firm's address ▶			Firm's EIN ▶	

Go to *www.irs.gov/Form1040* for instructions and the latest information. Form **1040** (2020)

- **Tax computation (lines 16 to 33). Line 19:** If the minister has a dependent child (a child under the age of 19 at the end of the tax year or a student and younger than 24), he or she should complete Schedule 8812 to claim up to a maximum credit of $2,000 per qualifying child. This credit can reduce the actual taxes owed dollar-for-dollar, but only $1,400 per child can be refundable beyond 2020.

  Line 25a-d: Then show the amount of federal income tax the church withheld (from the W-2, Box 2) along with other federal income tax withholding from other employment of the minister or the spouse here. Also include tax withheld on the other Forms 1099 and W-2. The amount withheld should be shown in Box 6 of Form 1099-SSA and Box 4 of other Forms 1099.

  Line 26: Enter the amount of estimated tax payments made during the year. Don't get confused. Even though the fourth quarter 2020 estimated tax payment was made in January 2021, it's counted on the 2020 return.

Form 1040, page 2 (cont'd.)

Line 28: Enter the amount of your child tax credit on this line based on the completion of Schedule 8812.

- **Refund or amount owed (Lines 34 to 38). Line 38:** The IRS assumes the taxpayer must pay the estimated tax penalty if he or she owes $1,000 or more than what has been paid through withholding or estimated tax and the amount due is more than 110% of the 2019 tax bill. The minister may qualify for one of several exceptions, however. Use Form 2210 to document an exception to an underpayment penalty.

Schedule 1 – Additional income and adjustments to income

SCHEDULE 1 (Form 1040)
Department of the Treasury Internal Revenue Service

Additional Income and Adjustments to Income

▶ Attach to Form 1040, 1040-SR, or 1040-NR.
▶ Go to *www.irs.gov/Form1040* for instructions and the latest information.

OMB No. 1545-0074
2020
Attachment Sequence No. **01**

Name(s) shown on Form 1040, 1040-SR, or 1040-NR | **Your social security number**

Part I Additional Income

1	Taxable refunds, credits, or offsets of state and local income taxes	1	
2a	Alimony received	2a	
b	Date of original divorce or separation agreement (see instructions) ▶		
3	Business income or (loss). Attach Schedule C	3	
4	Other gains or (losses). Attach Form 4797	4	
5	Rental real estate, royalties, partnerships, S corporations, trusts, etc. Attach Schedule E	5	
6	Farm income or (loss). Attach Schedule F	6	
7	Unemployment compensation	7	
8	Other income. List type and amount ▶	8	
9	Combine lines 1 through 8. Enter here and on Form 1040, 1040-SR, or 1040-NR, line 8	9	

Part II Adjustments to Income

10	Educator expenses	10	
11	Certain business expenses of reservists, performing artists, and fee-basis government officials. Attach Form 2106	11	
12	Health savings account deduction. Attach Form 8889	12	
13	Moving expenses for members of the Armed Forces. Attach Form 3903	13	
14	Deductible part of self-employment tax. Attach Schedule SE	14	
15	Self-employed SEP, SIMPLE, and qualified plans	15	
16	Self-employed health insurance deduction	16	
17	Penalty on early withdrawal of savings	17	
18a	Alimony paid	18a	
b	Recipient's SSN ▶		
c	Date of original divorce or separation agreement (see instructions) ▶		
19	IRA deduction	19	
20	Student loan interest deduction	20	
21	Tuition and fees deduction. Attach Form 8917	21	
22	Add lines 10 through 21. These are your **adjustments to income.** Enter here and on Form 1040, 1040-SR, or 1040-NR, line 10a	22	

For Paperwork Reduction Act Notice, see your tax return instructions. Cat. No. 71479F **Schedule 1 (Form 1040) 2020**

Schedule 1 (cont'd.)

Schedule 1, Line 1: If a state or local tax refund was received in 2020 that was deducted on Schedule A in a prior year, include the refund here.

Line 3: Ministers almost always receive some honoraria or fee income from speaking engagements, weddings, funerals, and so on. This income, less related expenses (see pages 175 and 186), should be reported on Schedule C and entered on this line. If the minister has multiple Schedule Cs, the amounts from all Schedule Cs should be combined on this line.

Filing Tip

Schedule 1, Line 3. The only ministerial income that should be reported on Line 3 is fees from weddings, funerals, speaking engagements, and similar income. Expenses related to this income should be deducted on Schedule C.

Line 10: If you or your spouse is an eligible educator, you can deduct up to $250 for unreimbursed teaching-related expenses on this line ($500 if you are both teachers and file jointly). Qualified expenses are amounts you actually paid or incurred for participation in professional development courses, books, supplies, computer equipment (including related software and services), other equipment, and supplementary materials that you use in the classroom. For courses in health or physical education, the expenses for supplies must be for athletic supplies.

Line 12: Contributions made by a taxpayer to a health savings account (HSA) up to $3,550 for an individual plan and $7,100 for a family plan are deductible on this line. Individuals who have reached age 55 by the end of the tax year are allowed to increase their annual contribution for years after 2020.

Line 14: One-half of the Social Security tax that is deductible for income tax purposes is reflected on this line. This number comes from Schedule SE, Part I, Line 13.

Line 15: If a minister is employed as a chaplain or any other minister of a non-religious organization, use the dotted space next to Line 22 for the deduction of 403(b) contributions that were sent directly to the plan.

Line 20: Interest paid on a qualifying student loan, on which you are legally obligated to pay the interest, may be deducted on this line. The maximum deductible amount of interest is $2,500, and it is phased out at high income levels. The deduction may not be claimed if you are filing married filing separately.

Line 21: Line 21 is used for the tuition and fees deduction for 2020 (since Congress extended it). The deduction is calculated on Form 8917.

Schedule 2 – Additional Taxes

SCHEDULE 2 (Form 1040)
Department of the Treasury Internal Revenue Service

Additional Taxes

▶ Attach to Form 1040, 1040-SR, or 1040-NR.
▶ Go to *www.irs.gov/Form1040* for instructions and the latest information.

OMB No. 1545-0074
2020
Attachment Sequence No. 02

Name(s) shown on Form 1040, 1040-SR, or 1040-NR | **Your social security number**

Part I Tax

1	Alternative minimum tax. Attach Form 6251	1	
2	Excess advance premium tax credit repayment. Attach Form 8962	2	
3	Add lines 1 and 2. Enter here and on Form 1040, 1040-SR, or 1040-NR, line 17	3	

Part II Other Taxes

4	Self-employment tax. Attach Schedule SE	4	
5	Unreported social security and Medicare tax from Form: a ☐ 4137 b ☐ 8919	5	
6	Additional tax on IRAs, other qualified retirement plans, and other tax-favored accounts. Attach Form 5329 if required	6	
7a	Household employment taxes. Attach Schedule H	7a	
b	Repayment of first-time homebuyer credit from Form 5405. Attach Form 5405 if required	7b	
8	Taxes from: a ☐ Form 8959 b ☐ Form 8960 c ☐ Instructions; enter code(s)	8	
9	Section 965 net tax liability installment from Form 965-A [9]		
10	Add lines 4 through 8. These are your **total other taxes.** Enter here and on Form 1040 or 1040-SR, line 23, or Form 1040-NR, line 23b	10	

For Paperwork Reduction Act Notice, see your tax return instructions. Cat. No. 71478U **Schedule 2 (Form 1040) 2020**

Line 1: Few ministers will have taxable income high enough to trigger the alternative minimum tax.

Line 2: If a minister had an excess advance payment of the premium tax credit, it would be calculated on Form 8962 with the amount carried over to Line 2.

Line 4: If the taxpayer is a qualified minister (see pages 14-19) and has not opted out of Social Security (see pages 117-122), he or she is self-employed for Social Security tax purposes. Social Security is not withheld and matched by the church but is calculated on Schedule SE if there were net earnings of $400 or more. Payment is sent with Form 1040. The tax is 15.3% of the first $137,700 of 2020 self-employment income. If the total wages and self-employment earnings were less than $137,700, time and headaches can probably be saved by filing the Short Schedule SE on the front of the SE form.

Line 5b: The minister will owe not only the tax on qualified plans but also the 10% penalty on any amount withdrawn from an IRA or another retirement plan if the minister was under 59½, unless certain exceptions are met.

Line 7b: Enter the first-time homebuyer credit you must repay if you bought the home in 2008.

Schedule 3 – Additional Credits and Payments

SCHEDULE 3 (Form 1040)
Department of the Treasury
Internal Revenue Service

Additional Credits and Payments

▶ Attach to Form 1040, 1040-SR, or 1040-NR.
▶ Go to *www.irs.gov/Form1040* for instructions and the latest information.

OMB No. 1545-0074
2020
Attachment Sequence No. **03**

Name(s) shown on Form 1040, 1040-SR, or 1040-NR | **Your social security number**

Part I Nonrefundable Credits

1	Foreign tax credit. Attach Form 1116 if required	1	
2	Credit for child and dependent care expenses. Attach Form 2441	2	
3	Education credits from Form 8863, line 19	3	
4	Retirement savings contributions credit. Attach Form 8880	4	
5	Residential energy credits. Attach Form 5695	5	
6	Other credits from Form: **a** ☐ 3800 **b** ☐ 8801 **c** ☐	6	
7	Add lines 1 through 6. Enter here and on Form 1040, 1040-SR, or 1040-NR, line 20	7	

Part II Other Payments and Refundable Credits

8	Net premium tax credit. Attach Form 8962			8	
9	Amount paid with request for extension to file (see instructions)			9	
10	Excess social security and tier 1 RRTA tax withheld			10	
11	Credit for federal tax on fuels. Attach Form 4136			11	
12	Other payments or refundable credits:				
a	Form 2439	12a			
b	Qualified sick and family leave credits from Schedule(s) H and Form(s) 7202	12b			
c	Health coverage tax credit from Form 8885	12c			
d	Other:	12d			
e	Deferral for certain Schedule H or SE filers (see instructions)	12e			
f	Add lines 12a through 12e			12f	
13	Add lines 8 through 12f. Enter here and on Form 1040, 1040-SR, or 1040-NR, line 31			13	

For Paperwork Reduction Act Notice, see your tax return instructions. Cat. No. 71480G **Schedule 3 (Form 1040) 2020**

Line 1: If you paid income tax to a foreign country or U.S. possession, you may be able to take this credit. Generally, you must complete and attach Form 1116 to do so. However, if all of your foreign-source gross income was from interest and dividends; and all of that income and the foreign tax paid on it was reported to you on Form 1099-INT, Form 1099-DIV, or Schedule K; and the total of your foreign taxes wasn't more than $600 if married filing jointly, then you generally do not have to complete Form 1116.

Line 2: You may be able to take this credit if you paid someone to care for: (1) your qualifying child under age 13 whom you claim as your dependent, (2) your disabled spouse or any other disabled person who couldn't care for himself or herself, or (3) your child whom you couldn't claim as a dependent because of the rules for children of divorced or separated parents.

Schedule 3 (cont'd.)

Line 3: If you (or your dependent) paid qualified expenses in 2020 for yourself or your spouse, or your dependent to enroll in or attend an eligible educational institution, you may be able to take an education credit. See Form 8863 for details.

Line 4: Taxpayers with adjusted gross income of $65,000 or less may claim a credit on this line equal to a certain percentage of the employee contributions made to a retirement account or IRA (must complete Form 8880).

Filing Tip

Schedule 3, Line 4. If contributions were made to a 403(b) or 401(k) plan, and the adjusted gross income was $50,000 or less, the minister may be eligible for the retirement savings contributions credit. The credit is also available for contributions to either a traditional or a Roth IRA. The excluded portion of minister's housing does not reduce this credit.

Schedule A – Itemized Deductions

If the minister lives in church-provided housing, he or she often cannot itemize. But run down Schedule A just to see whether there might be more write-offs than the standard deduction will permit.

- **Medical and dental expenses (Lines 1 to 4).** Don't overlook the cost of getting to and from the doctor or pharmacist. Write off 17 cents per mile plus the cost of parking. If the taxpayer didn't drive, deduct any bus, train, air, or taxi fares. The cost of trips to see out-of-town specialists and as much as $50 per night ($100 for parent and child) for the cost of lodging when out of town to get medical care count toward the 10% limit of adjusted gross income. Include all health insurance premiums, as well as Medicare Part B premiums for 2020.

- **Taxes you paid (Lines 5 to 7).** Even though real estate taxes are a housing expense excludable under the housing allowance, they may still be deducted (even for multiple properties if not deducted elsewhere on the return) on Line 5b as an itemized deduction—one of the few "double benefits" allowed in the tax law.

  The deduction for state and local taxes is limited to $10,000 ($5,000 if married filing married separately). State and local taxes are the taxes that you include on Lines 5a, 5b, and 5c.

- **Interest you paid (Lines 8 to 10).** The rules for deducting interest vary, depending on whether the loan proceeds are used for business, personal, or investment activities. See Publication 535 for more information about deducting business interest expenses. See Publication 550 for more information about deducting investment interest expenses. You can't deduct personal interest. However you can deduct qualified home

Schedule A (cont'd.)

mortgage interest (on your Schedule A) and interest on certain student loans (on Form 1040, Schedule 1, Line 20), as explained in Publications 936 and 970.

If you use the proceeds of a loan for more than one purpose (for example, personal and business), you must allocate the interest on the loan to each use. Allocate interest on a loan in the same way as the loan is allocated, by tracing disbursements of the debt proceeds to specific uses.

Line 8a: If the minister bought a house during 2020, review all escrow or settlement papers for any mortgage interest paid that was not shown on the lender's year-end statement. If interest was paid on a second mortgage or line of credit secured by the minister's home, include the interest expense here.

It is possible to deduct mortgage interest as an itemized deduction even if the interest is included in housing expenses subject to a housing allowance.

Interest on a home equity loan or line of credit is not deductible on Schedule A unless the loan proceeds were used to buy, build, or substantially improve the minister's home that secures the loan.

Filing Tip

Schedule A, Lines 8a-c. These lines relate to the most significant tax break available to ministers who own their own homes. Even though real estate taxes, mortgage interest, and points are excludable under the housing allowance, subject to certain limits, the same amounts are deductible as itemized deductions.

Likewise, the only mortgage interest properly includible as a housing expense under a housing allowance is when the loan proceeds were used to provide housing. For example, interest on a second mortgage used to finance a child's college education is not deductible on Schedule A and does not qualify as a housing expense for housing allowance purposes.

Don't overlook points paid to get the mortgage. All of the points are generally deductible as interest here. Points paid for a refinancing must be amortized over the life of the loan. But it is permissible to deduct on the 2020 return the portion of all points paid that correspond with the percentage of refinancing used for home improvements.

- **Gifts to charity (Lines 11 to 14). Line 11:** For gifts you made in 2020, there must be written acknowledgments from the charity of any single gifts of $250 or more and for all gifts of cash.

Schedule A (cont'd.)

The following amounts are *not* deductible as charitable contributions:

- An amount paid to or for the benefit of a college or university in exchange for the right to purchase tickets to an athletic event in the college or university's stadium.
- Travel expenses (including meals and lodging) while away from home performing donated services, unless there was no significant element of personal pleasure, recreation, or vacation in the travel.
- Political contributions
- Dues, fees, or bills paid to country clubs, lodges, fraternal orders, or similar groups.
- Value of your time or services.
- Value of blood given to a blood bank.
- The transfer of a future interest in tangible personal property. Generally no deduction is allowed until the entire interest has been transferred.
- Gifts to individuals and groups that are operated for personal profit.
- Gifts to foreign organizations.
- Gifts to civic leagues, social and sports clubs, labor unions, and chambers of commerce.
- Cost of tuition.

Line 12: Deduct charitable mileage for any volunteer work at the rate of 14 cents a mile.

Filing Tip

Schedule C. Only business expenses related to the income reported on Schedule C may be reported on the form. A minister's housing expenses are not deducted on this form (or generally any other form). Unreimbursed expenses related to employee compensation are not deductible as a result of tax reform.

Schedule C – Profit or Loss from Business

While a minister should receive Form W-2 for employment compensation and report the amount in Box 1 of Form W-2 on Form 1040, Line 1, most ministers have some income from honoraria or fees related to weddings or funerals. Additionally, a minister may have speaking fees unrelated to the employer, or product royalties, or other self-employment income reportable on Schedule C.

Schedule C (cont'd.)

Only expenses related to the income reported on Schedule C may be deducted on the form. For example, if a minister received honoraria of $500 for speaking at a church other than where employed, the $500 is reported on Schedule C and the travel and other expenses related to the speaking engagement are deductible on the form. Expenses related to a minister's primary employment (compensation that was reported on Form W-2) is no longer deductible. This highlights the importance of churches adopting an accountable expense reimbursement policy.

Schedule SE – Self-Employment Tax

Most ministers will need to file Schedule SE to report income subject to self-employment taxes.

When computing the self-employment tax, net earnings include the gross income earned from performing qualified services minus the deductions related to that income. See Self-Employment Social Security Tax Worksheet on page 115.

Form 2441 – Child and Dependent Care Expenses

If the minister paid someone to care for his or her child or other qualifying person so he or she (and spouse, if filing a joint return) could work or look for work in 2020, the minister may be able to take the credit for child and dependent care expenses.

- **Qualifying person (Line 2[a]).** A qualifying person is any child under age 13 who can be claimed as a dependent. If the child turned 13 during the year, the child is a qualifying person for the part of the year he or she was under age 13.
- **Qualified expenses (Line 2[c]).** These include amounts paid for household services and care of the qualifying person while the taxpayer worked or looked for work. Child support payments are not qualified expenses. Household services include the services of a cook, maid, babysitter, housekeeper, or cleaning person if the services were partly for the care of the qualifying person.

Form 8863 – Education Credits

Education credits may be taken if the minister, spouse, or a dependent claimed on the taxpayer's return was a student enrolled at or attending an eligible educational institution.

Form 8863 (cont'd.)

- **American Opportunity Credit (Part I).** The minister may be able to take a credit of up to $2,500 for qualified expenses paid in 2020 for each student who qualifies for the credit (see instructions for Form 8863).

Tip

It does not matter whether the education expenses were paid in cash, by check, by credit card, or with borrowed funds.

- **Lifetime learning credit (Part II).** The maximum lifetime learning credit for 2020 is $2,000, regardless of the number of students. The lifetime learning credit cannot be taken for any student for whom the American Opportunity Credit is being taken.

- **Qualified expenses (worksheet in form instructions).** Generally, qualified expenses are amounts paid in 2020 for tuition and fees required for the student's enrollment or attendance at an eligible educational institution. Qualified expenses do not include amounts paid for room and board, insurance, medical expenses, transportation, or course-related books, supplies, and equipment.

Form 8880 – Credit for Qualified Retirement Savings Contributions

You may be able to take a tax credit for making eligible contributions to your IRA or employer-sponsored retirement plan. And if you're the designated beneficiary you may be eligible for a credit for contributions to your Achieving a Better Life Experience (ABLE) account.

You are eligible for the credit if you are

1. age 18 or older;
2. not a full-time student; and
3. not claimed as a dependent on another person's return.

The amount of the credit is 50%, 20%, or 10% of your retirement plan or IRA or ABLE account contributions, depending on your adjusted gross income (reported on your Form 1040 series return). The maximum contribution amount that may qualify for the credit is $2,000 ($4,000 if married filing jointly), making the maximum credit $1,000 ($2,000 if married filing jointly). Use the chart on the next page to calculate your credit.

The Saver's Credit can be taken for contributions to a traditional or Roth IRA; your 401(k), SIMPLE IRA, SARSEP, 403(b), 501(c)(18), or government 457(b) plan; and your voluntary after-tax employee contributions to your qualified retirement and 403(b) plans.

Form 8880 (cont'd.)

Credit Rate	Married Filing Jointly	Head of Household	All Other Filers*
50% of your contribution	AGI not more than $39,000	AGI not more than $29,250	AGI not more than $19,500
20% of your contribution	$39,001 – $42,500	$29,251 – $31,875	$19,501 – $21,250
20% of your contribution	$42,501 – $65,000	$31,876 – $48,750	$21,251 – $32,500
0% of your contribution	more than $65,000	more than $48,750	more than $32,500

Rollover contributions (money that you moved from another retirement plan or IRA) aren't eligible for the Saver's Credit. Also, your eligible contributions may be reduced by any recent distributions you received from a retirement plan or IRA.

The Saver's Credit can be taken for your contributions to an ABLE account if you're the designated beneficiary.

Form 8889 – Health Savings Account

The minister may be required to file Form 8889 if he or she participated in a Health Savings Account (HSA) in 2020.

- **HSA distributions (Line 14).** Amounts withdrawn from the HSA in 2020 are reflected on this line. There is generally no tax impact of HSA withdrawals unless they exceed unreimbursed medical expenses.
- **Unreimbursed medical expenses (Line 15).** Medical expenses that were not reimbursed by your medical insurance may generally be included on this line.

Tip

There is no requirement to file Form 8889 if HSA withdrawals for the year do not exceed unreimbursed medical expenses.

Form 8962 – Premium Tax Credit

The premium tax credit is for those that were enrolled in health insurance through a state marketplace. The credit provides financial assistance to pay the premiums. This form reconciles whether there is a refund owed to a taxpayer or whether the taxpayer owes additional taxes related to an advance payment of the premium tax credit.

Form 8962 (cont'd.)

- **Part I.** This section determines the annual contribution amount one is required to pay out of pocket.
- **Part II.** This section reconciles how much one has paid based on Form 1095-A and how much should be paid based on actual income as determined in Part I.
- **Part III.** This section is used to determine any necessary repayment of excess advance payment of a premium tax credit.
- **Parts IV & V.** Use these parts to make allocations as it may relate to divorces, married filing separately, marriages, or where a policy is shared between two tax families. See the Instructions to 8962 for further details.

Form 8995 – Qualified Business Income Deduction Simplified Computation

A minister may deduct up to the lesser of 20% of qualified business income (QBI) from the taxable income reported on Schedule C (and certain other income) or 20% of the minister's taxable income, calculated before the QBI deduction, minus net capital gain. Enter the amount from Schedule C, Line 31 on Form 8995, Line 1. Enter the amount from Line 15 of Form 8995 on Form 1040, page 1, Line 10.

Schedule A

SCHEDULE A (Form 1040)
Department of the Treasury
Internal Revenue Service (99)

Itemized Deductions

▶ Go to *www.irs.gov/ScheduleA* for instructions and the latest information.
▶ Attach to Form 1040 or 1040-SR.
Caution: If you are claiming a net qualified disaster loss on Form 4684, see the instructions for line 16.

OMB No. 1545-0074
2020
Attachment Sequence No. 07

Name(s) shown on Form 1040 or 1040-SR | **Your social security number**

Section	Line	Description	Box	Total
Medical and Dental Expenses		**Caution:** Do not include expenses reimbursed or paid by others.		
	1	Medical and dental expenses (see instructions)	1	
	2	Enter amount from Form 1040 or 1040-SR, line 11 [2]		
	3	Multiply line 2 by 7.5% (0.075)	3	
	4	Subtract line 3 from line 1. If line 3 is more than line 1, enter -0-		4
Taxes You Paid	5	State and local taxes.		
	a	State and local income taxes or general sales taxes. You may include either income taxes or general sales taxes on line 5a, but not both. If you elect to include general sales taxes instead of income taxes, check this box ▶ ☐	5a	
	b	State and local real estate taxes (see instructions)	5b	
	c	State and local personal property taxes	5c	
	d	Add lines 5a through 5c	5d	
	e	Enter the smaller of line 5d or $10,000 ($5,000 if married filing separately)	5e	
	6	Other taxes. List type and amount ▶	6	
	7	Add lines 5e and 6		7
Interest You Paid *Caution: Your mortgage interest deduction may be limited (see instructions).*	8	Home mortgage interest and points. If you didn't use all of your home mortgage loan(s) to buy, build, or improve your home, see instructions and check this box ▶ ☐		
	a	Home mortgage interest and points reported to you on Form 1098. See instructions if limited	8a	
	b	Home mortgage interest not reported to you on Form 1098. See instructions if limited. If paid to the person from whom you bought the home, see instructions and show that person's name, identifying no., and address ▶	8b	
	c	Points not reported to you on Form 1098. See instructions for special rules	8c	
	d	Mortgage insurance premiums (see instructions)	8d	
	e	Add lines 8a through 8d	8e	
	9	Investment interest. Attach Form 4952 if required. See instructions	9	
	10	Add lines 8e and 9		10
Gifts to Charity *Caution: If you made a gift and got a benefit for it, see instructions.*	11	Gifts by cash or check. If you made any gift of $250 or more, see instructions	11	
	12	Other than by cash or check. If you made any gift of $250 or more, see instructions. You **must** attach Form 8283 if over $500	12	
	13	Carryover from prior year	13	
	14	Add lines 11 through 13		14
Casualty and Theft Losses	15	Casualty and theft loss(es) from a federally declared disaster (other than net qualified disaster losses). Attach Form 4684 and enter the amount from line 18 of that form. See instructions		15
Other Itemized Deductions	16	Other—from list in instructions. List type and amount ▶		16
Total Itemized Deductions	17	Add the amounts in the far right column for lines 4 through 16. Also, enter this amount on Form 1040 or 1040-SR, line 12		17
	18	If you elect to itemize deductions even though they are less than your standard deduction, check this box ▶ ☐		

For Paperwork Reduction Act Notice, see the Instructions for Forms 1040 and 1040-SR. Cat. No. 17145C **Schedule A (Form 1040) 2020**

Medical. Taxes will be minimized if the employer pays for health insurance. Minimize medical expenses using a health reimbursement arrangement.

Taxes. Real estate taxes may be deducted here even if excluded from income under a housing allowance.

Interest. Mortgage interest may be deducted here even if excluded from income under a housing allowance.

Contributions. Be sure to include gifts-in-kind on Line 12.

Schedule C

SCHEDULE C (Form 1040)
Department of the Treasury Internal Revenue Service (99)

Profit or Loss From Business
(Sole Proprietorship)
▶ Go to *www.irs.gov/ScheduleC* for instructions and the latest information.
▶ Attach to Form 1040, 1040-SR, 1040-NR, or 1041; partnerships generally must file Form 1065.

OMB No. 1545-0074
2020
Attachment Sequence No. **09**

Name of proprietor | **Social security number (SSN)**

A Principal business or profession, including product or service (see instructions) | **B Enter code from instructions** ▶

C Business name. If no separate business name, leave blank. | **D Employer ID number (EIN)** (see instr.)

E Business address (including suite or room no.) ▶
City, town or post office, state, and ZIP code

F Accounting method: **(1)** ☐ Cash **(2)** ☐ Accrual **(3)** ☐ Other (specify) ▶

G Did you "materially participate" in the operation of this business during 2020? If "No," see instructions for limit on losses . ☐ Yes ☐ No

H If you started or acquired this business during 2020, check here . . . ▶ ☐

I Did you make any payments in 2020 that would require you to file Form(s) 1099? See instructions . . . ☐ Yes ☐ No

J If "Yes," did you or will you file required Form(s) 1099? . . . ☐ Yes ☐ No

Part I Income

1	Gross receipts or sales. See instructions for line 1 and check the box if this income was reported to you on Form W-2 and the "Statutory employee" box on that form was checked . . . ▶ ☐	1	
2	Returns and allowances . . .	2	
3	Subtract line 2 from line 1 . . .	3	
4	Cost of goods sold (from line 42) . . .	4	
5	**Gross profit.** Subtract line 4 from line 3 . . .	5	
6	Other income, including federal and state gasoline or fuel tax credit or refund (see instructions) . . .	6	
7	**Gross income.** Add lines 5 and 6 . . . ▶	7	

Part II Expenses. Enter expenses for business use of your home **only** on line 30.

8	Advertising . . .	8		18	Office expense (see instructions)	18	
9	Car and truck expenses (see instructions) . . .	9		19	Pension and profit-sharing plans .	19	
				20	Rent or lease (see instructions):		
10	Commissions and fees .	10		a	Vehicles, machinery, and equipment	20a	
11	Contract labor (see instructions)	11		b	Other business property . . .	20b	
12	Depletion . . .	12		21	Repairs and maintenance . . .	21	
13	Depreciation and section 179 expense deduction (not included in Part III) (see instructions) . . .	13		22	Supplies (not included in Part III) .	22	
				23	Taxes and licenses . . .	23	
				24	Travel and meals:		
14	Employee benefit programs (other than on line 19) . .	14		a	Travel . . .	24a	
				b	Deductible meals (see instructions) . . .	24b	
15	Insurance (other than health)	15		25	Utilities . . .	25	
16	Interest (see instructions):			26	Wages (less employment credits) .	26	
a	Mortgage (paid to banks, etc.)	16a		27a	Other expenses (from line 48) . .	27a	
b	Other . . .	16b		b	**Reserved for future use** . . .	27b	
17	Legal and professional services	17					

28	**Total expenses** before expenses for business use of home. Add lines 8 through 27a . . . ▶	28	
29	Tentative profit or (loss). Subtract line 28 from line 7 . . .	29	
30	Expenses for business use of your home. Do not report these expenses elsewhere. Attach Form 8829 unless using the simplified method. See instructions. **Simplified method filers only:** Enter the total square footage of (a) your home: ______ and (b) the part of your home used for business: ______ . Use the Simplified Method Worksheet in the instructions to figure the amount to enter on line 30 . . .	30	
31	**Net profit or (loss).** Subtract line 30 from line 29. • If a profit, enter on both **Schedule 1 (Form 1040), line 3,** and on **Schedule SE, line 2.** (If you checked the box on line 1, see instructions). Estates and trusts, enter on **Form 1041, line 3.** • If a loss, you **must** go to line 32.	31	
32	If you have a loss, check the box that describes your investment in this activity. See instructions. • If you checked 32a, enter the loss on both **Schedule 1 (Form 1040), line 3,** and on **Schedule SE, line 2.** (If you checked the box on line 1, see the line 31 instructions). Estates and trusts, enter on **Form 1041, line 3.** • If you checked 32b, you **must** attach **Form 6198.** Your loss may be limited.		**32a** ☐ All investment is at risk. **32b** ☐ Some investment is not at risk.

For Paperwork Reduction Act Notice, see the separate instructions. Cat. No. 11334P **Schedule C (Form 1040) 2020**

Income. Include honoraria and fee income.

Expenses. Only include expenses related to income on Line 1.

Net Profit. Include in income on page 1 and on Schedule SE.

Schedule SE

SCHEDULE SE (Form 1040)

Department of the Treasury Internal Revenue Service (99)

Self-Employment Tax

▶ Go to *www.irs.gov/ScheduleSE* for instructions and the latest information.

▶ Attach to Form 1040, 1040-SR, or 1040-NR.

OMB No. 1545-0074

2020

Attachment Sequence No. **17**

Name of person with self-employment income (as shown on Form 1040, 1040-SR, or 1040-NR) | Social security number of person with **self-employment** income ▶

Part I Self-Employment Tax

Note: If your only income subject to self-employment tax is **church employee income,** see instructions for how to report your income and the definition of church employee income.

A If you are a minister, member of a religious order, or Christian Science practitioner **and** you filed Form 4361, but you had $400 or more of **other** net earnings from self-employment, check here and continue with Part I . . . . ▶ ☐

Skip lines 1a and 1b if you use the farm optional method in Part II. See instructions.

Line	Description	Box	Amount
1a	Net farm profit or (loss) from Schedule F, line 34, and farm partnerships, Schedule K-1 (Form 1065), box 14, code A	1a	
b	If you received social security retirement or disability benefits, enter the amount of Conservation Reserve Program payments included on Schedule F, line 4b, or listed on Schedule K-1 (Form 1065), box 20, code AH	1b	( )
	Skip line 2 if you use the nonfarm optional method in Part II. See instructions.		
2	Net profit or (loss) from Schedule C, line 31; and Schedule K-1 (Form 1065), box 14, code A (other than farming). See instructions for other income to report or if you are a minister or member of a religious order	2	
3	Combine lines 1a, 1b, and 2	3	
4a	If line 3 is more than zero, multiply line 3 by 92.35% (0.9235). Otherwise, enter amount from line 3	4a	
	Note: If line 4a is less than $400 due to Conservation Reserve Program payments on line 1b, see instructions.		
b	If you elect one or both of the optional methods, enter the total of lines 15 and 17 here	4b	
c	Combine lines 4a and 4b. If less than $400, **stop;** you don't owe self-employment tax. **Exception:** If less than $400 and you had **church employee income,** enter -0- and continue ▶	4c	
5a	Enter your **church employee income** from Form W-2. See instructions for definition of church employee income	5a	
b	Multiply line 5a by 92.35% (0.9235). If less than $100, enter -0-	5b	
6	Add lines 4c and 5b	6	
7	Maximum amount of combined wages and self-employment earnings subject to social security tax or the 6.2% portion of the 7.65% railroad retirement (tier 1) tax for 2020	7	137,700
8a	Total social security wages and tips (total of boxes 3 and 7 on Form(s) W-2) and railroad retirement (tier 1) compensation. If $137,700 or more, skip lines 8b through 10, and go to line 11	8a	
b	Unreported tips subject to social security tax from Form 4137, line 10	8b	
c	Wages subject to social security tax from Form 8919, line 10	8c	
d	Add lines 8a, 8b, and 8c	8d	
9	Subtract line 8d from line 7. If zero or less, enter -0- here and on line 10 and go to line 11 ▶	9	
10	Multiply the **smaller** of line 6 or line 9 by 12.4% (0.124)	10	
11	Multiply line 6 by 2.9% (0.029)	11	
12	**Self-employment tax.** Add lines 10 and 11. Enter here and on **Schedule 2 (Form 1040), line 4**	12	
13	**Deduction for one-half of self-employment tax.** Multiply line 12 by 50% (0.50). Enter here and on **Schedule 1 (Form 1040), line 14**	13	

Part II Optional Methods To Figure Net Earnings (see instructions)

Farm Optional Method. You may use this method **only** if **(a)** your gross farm income[1] wasn't more than $8,460, **or (b)** your net farm profits[2] were less than $6,107.

Line	Description	Box	Amount
14	Maximum income for optional methods	14	5,640
15	Enter the **smaller** of: two-thirds (2/3) of gross farm income[1] (not less than zero) **or** $5,640. Also, include this amount on line 4b above	15	

Nonfarm Optional Method. You may use this method **only** if **(a)** your net nonfarm profits[3] were less than $6,107 and also less than 72.189% of your gross nonfarm income,[4] **and (b)** you had net earnings from self-employment of at least $400 in 2 of the prior 3 years. **Caution:** You may use this method no more than five times.

Line	Description	Box	Amount
16	Subtract line 15 from line 14	16	
17	Enter the **smaller** of: two-thirds (2/3) of gross nonfarm income[4] (not less than zero) **or** the amount on line 16. Also, include this amount on line 4b above	17	

[1] From Sch. F, line 9; and Sch. K-1 (Form 1065), box 14, code B.

[2] From Sch. F, line 34; and Sch. K-1 (Form 1065), box 14, code A—minus the amount you would have entered on line 1b had you not used the optional method.

[3] From Sch. C, line 31; and Sch. K-1 (Form 1065), box 14, code A.

[4] From Sch. C, line 7; and Sch. K-1 (Form 1065), box 14, code C.

For Paperwork Reduction Act Notice, see your tax return instructions. Cat. No. 11358Z **Schedule SE (Form 1040) 2020**

Net earnings from self-employment (see worksheet on page 115)

Self-employment tax on Form 1040, Schedule 2, Line 4

Deductible portion of Schedule SE on Form 1040, Schedule 1, Line 14

Form 2441

Form **2441** — **Child and Dependent Care Expenses**

▶ Attach to Form 1040, 1040-SR, or 1040-NR.

▶ Go to *www.irs.gov/Form2441* for instructions and the latest information.

Department of the Treasury Internal Revenue Service (99)

OMB No. 1545-0074 — **2020** — Attachment Sequence No. **21**

Name(s) shown on return | **Your social security number**

You cannot claim a credit for child and dependent care expenses if your filing status is married filing separately unless you meet the requirements listed in the instructions under "Married Persons Filing Separately." If you meet these requirements, check this box. ☐

Part I **Persons or Organizations Who Provided the Care**—You **must** complete this part. (If you have more than two care providers, see the instructions.)

1 (a) Care provider's name	(b) Address (number, street, apt. no., city, state, and ZIP code)	(c) Identifying number (SSN or EIN)	(d) Amount paid (see instructions)

Did you receive **dependent care benefits?** — **No** ▶ Complete only Part II below. — **Yes** ▶ Complete Part III on the back next.

Caution: If the care was provided in your home, you may owe employment taxes. For details, see the instructions for Schedule 2 (Form 1040), line 7a.

Part II **Credit for Child and Dependent Care Expenses**

2 Information about your **qualifying person(s).** If you have more than two qualifying persons, see the instructions.

(a) Qualifying person's name — First	Last	(b) Qualifying person's social security number	(c) **Qualified expenses** you incurred and paid in 2020 for the person listed in column (a)

3 Add the amounts in column (c) of line 2. **Don't** enter more than $3,000 for one qualifying person or $6,000 for two or more persons. If you completed Part III, enter the amount from line 31 . . **3**

4 Enter your **earned income.** See instructions . . . **4**

5 If married filing jointly, enter your spouse's earned income (if you or your spouse was a student or was disabled, see the instructions); **all others,** enter the amount from line 4 . . . **5**

6 Enter the **smallest** of line 3, 4, or 5 . . . **6**

7 Enter the amount from Form 1040, 1040-SR, or 1040-NR, line 11 . **7**

8 Enter on line 8 the decimal amount shown below that applies to the amount on line 7.

If line 7 is: Over	But not over	Decimal amount is	If line 7 is: Over	But not over	Decimal amount is
$0	15,000	.35	$29,000	31,000	.27
15,000	17,000	.34	31,000	33,000	.26
17,000	19,000	.33	33,000	35,000	.25
19,000	21,000	.32	35,000	37,000	.24
21,000	23,000	.31	37,000	39,000	.23
23,000	25,000	.30	39,000	41,000	.22
25,000	27,000	.29	41,000	43,000	.21
27,000	29,000	.28	43,000	No limit	.20

8 X .

9 Multiply line 6 by the decimal amount on line 8. If you paid 2019 expenses in 2020, see the instructions . . . **9**

10 Tax liability limit. Enter the amount from the Credit Limit Worksheet in the instructions . . . **10**

11 **Credit for child and dependent care expenses.** Enter the **smaller** of line 9 or line 10 here and on Schedule 3 (Form 1040), line 2 . . . **11**

For Paperwork Reduction Act Notice, see your tax return instructions. Cat. No. 11862M Form **2441** (2020)

Care provider. If the care provider is an individual, the Social Security number must be provided. Otherwise, insert the employer identification number.

Qualifying persons. Only children under age 13, a disabled spouse, or disabled dependents may be listed here.

Form 8863

Form **8863**
Department of the Treasury
Internal Revenue Service (99)

Education Credits
(American Opportunity and Lifetime Learning Credits)
► Attach to Form 1040 or 1040-SR.
► Go to *www.irs.gov/Form8863* for instructions and the latest information.

OMB No. 1545-0074
2020
Attachment Sequence No. **50**

Name(s) shown on return | Your social security number

CAUTION *Complete a separate Part III on page 2 for each student for whom you're claiming either credit before you complete Parts I and II.*

Part I Refundable American Opportunity Credit

1 After completing Part III for each student, enter the total of all amounts from all Parts III, line 30 . . . **1**

2 Enter: $180,000 if married filing jointly; $90,000 if single, head of household, or qualifying widow(er) . . . **2**

3 Enter the amount from Form 1040 or 1040-SR, line 11. If you're filing Form 2555 or 4563, or you're excluding income from Puerto Rico, see Pub. 970 for the amount to enter . . . **3**

4 Subtract line 3 from line 2. If zero or less, **stop**; you can't take any education credit . . . **4**

5 Enter: $20,000 if married filing jointly; $10,000 if single, head of household, or qualifying widow(er) . . . **5**

6 If line 4 is:
- Equal to or more than line 5, enter 1.000 on line 6 . . .
- Less than line 5, divide line 4 by line 5. Enter the result as a decimal (rounded to at least three places) . . . **6**

7 Multiply line 1 by line 6. **Caution:** If you were under age 24 at the end of the year **and** meet the conditions described in the instructions, you **can't** take the refundable American opportunity credit; skip line 8, enter the amount from line 7 on line 9, and check this box . . . ► ☐ **7**

8 **Refundable American opportunity credit.** Multiply line 7 by 40% (0.40). Enter the amount here and on Form 1040 or 1040-SR, line 29. Then go to line 9 below. . . . **8**

Part II Nonrefundable Education Credits

9 Subtract line 8 from line 7. Enter here and on line 2 of the Credit Limit Worksheet (see instructions) . **9**

10 After completing Part III for each student, enter the total of all amounts from all Parts III, line 31. If zero, skip lines 11 through 17, enter -0- on line 18, and go to line 19 . . . **10**

11 Enter the smaller of line 10 or $10,000 . . . **11**

12 Multiply line 11 by 20% (0.20) . . . **12**

13 Enter: $138,000 if married filing jointly; $69,000 if single, head of household, or qualifying widow(er) . . . **13**

Qualified expenses. Only tuition and fees required for enrollment or attendance at an eligible educational institution are includible here.

Form 8863 (2020) Page **2**

Name(s) shown on return | Your social security number

CAUTION ***Complete Part III for each student for whom you're claiming either the American opportunity credit or lifetime learning credit. Use additional copies of page 2 as needed for each student.***

Part III Student and Educational Institution Information. See instructions.

20 Student name (as shown on page 1 of your tax return)	21 Student social security number (as shown on page 1 of your tax return)
22 Educational institution information (see instructions)	
a. Name of first educational institution	**b.** Name of second educational institution (if any)
(1) Address. Number and street (or P.O. box). City, town or post office, state, and ZIP code. If a foreign address, see instructions.	**(1)** Address. Number and street (or P.O. box). City, town or post office, state, and ZIP code. If a foreign address, see instructions.
(2) Did the student receive Form 1098-T from this institution for 2020? ☐ Yes ☐ No	**(2)** Did the student receive Form 1098-T from this institution for 2020? ☐ Yes ☐ No
(3) Did the student receive Form 1098-T from this institution for 2019 with box 7 checked? ☐ Yes ☐ No	**(3)** Did the student receive Form 1098-T from this institution for 2019 with box 7 checked? ☐ Yes ☐ No
(4) Enter the institution's employer identification number (EIN) if you're claiming the American opportunity credit or if you checked "Yes" in **(2)** or **(3)**. You can get the EIN from Form 1098-T or from the institution. __ __ - __ __ __ __ __ __ __	**(4)** Enter the institution's employer identification number (EIN) if you're claiming the American opportunity credit or if you checked "Yes" in **(2)** or **(3)**. You can get the EIN from Form 1098-T or from the institution. __ __ - __ __ __ __ __ __ __

23 Has the Hope Scholarship Credit or American opportunity credit been claimed for this student for any 4 tax years before 2020? ☐ Yes — **Stop!** Go to line 31 for this student. ☐ No — Go to line 24.

24 Was the student enrolled at least half-time for at least one academic period that began or is treated as having begun in 2020 at an eligible educational institution in a program leading towards a postsecondary degree, certificate, or other recognized postsecondary educational credential? See instructions. ☐ Yes — Go to line 25. ☐ No — **Stop!** Go to line 31 for this student.

25 Did the student complete the first 4 years of postsecondary education before 2020? See instructions. ☐ Yes — **Stop!** Go to line 31 for this student. ☐ No — Go to line 26.

Eligible educational institution. An eligible institution is generally any accredited public, nonprofit, or private college, university, vocational school, or other postsecondary institution.

Form 8880

Form **8880** — Department of the Treasury, Internal Revenue Service

Credit for Qualified Retirement Savings Contributions

► Attach to Form 1040, 1040-SR, or 1040-NR.
► Go to *www.irs.gov/Form8880* for the latest information.

OMB No. 1545-0074 — **2020** — Attachment Sequence No. **54**

Name(s) shown on return | **Your social security number**

CAUTION

*You **cannot** take this credit if **either** of the following applies.*

- *The amount on Form 1040, 1040-SR, or 1040-NR, line 11, is more than $32,500 ($48,750 if head of household; $65,000 if married filing jointly).*
- *The person(s) who made the qualified contribution or elective deferral **(a)** was born after January 1, 2003; **(b)** is claimed as a dependent on someone else's 2020 tax return; or **(c)** was a **student** (see instructions).*

			(a) You	(b) Your spouse
1	Traditional and Roth IRA contributions, and ABLE account contributions by the designated beneficiary for 2020. **Do not** include rollover contributions	1		
2	Elective deferrals to a 401(k) or other qualified employer plan, voluntary employee contributions, and 501(c)(18)(D) plan contributions for 2020 (see instructions)	2		
3	Add lines 1 and 2	3		
4	Certain distributions received **after** 2017 and **before** the due date (including extensions) of your 2020 tax return (see instructions). If married filing jointly, include **both** spouses' amounts in **both** columns. See instructions for an exception	4		
5	Subtract line 4 from line 3. If zero or less, enter -0-	5		
6	In each column, enter the **smaller** of line 5 or $2,000	6		

7 Add the amounts on line 6. If zero, **stop;** you can't take this credit . . . 7

8 Enter the amount from Form 1040, 1040-SR, or 1040-NR, line 11* . . . 8

9 Enter the applicable decimal amount from the table below.

If line 8 is—		And your filing status is—		
Over—	But not over—	Married filing jointly	Head of household	Single, Married filing separately, or Qualifying widow(er)
		Enter on line 9—		
---	$19,500	0.5	0.5	0.5
$19,500	$21,250	0.5	0.5	0.2
$21,250	$29,250	0.5	0.5	0.1
$29,250	$31,875	0.5	0.2	0.1
$31,875	$32,500	0.5	0.1	0.1
$32,500	$39,000	0.5	0.1	0.0
$39,000	$42,500	0.2	0.1	0.0
$42,500	$48,750	0.1	0.1	0.0
$48,750	$65,000	0.1	0.0	0.0
$65,000	---	0.0	0.0	0.0

9 x 0.

Note: If line 9 is zero, **stop;** you can't take this credit.

10 Multiply line 7 by line 9 . . . 10

11 Limitation based on tax liability. Enter the amount from the Credit Limit Worksheet in the instructions 11

12 **Credit for qualified retirement savings contributions.** Enter the **smaller** of line 10 or line 11 here and on Schedule 3 (Form 1040), line 4 . . . 12

* See Pub. 590-A for the amount to enter if you claim any exclusion or deduction for foreign earned income, foreign housing, or income from Puerto Rico or for bona fide residents of American Samoa.

For Paperwork Reduction Act Notice, see your tax return instructions. Cat. No. 33394D Form **8880** (2020)

Elective deferrals. Elective deferrals to a 401(k) or 403(b) plan. These amounts may be shown in Box 12 of your Form W-2 for 2019.

Form 8995

Form **8995**

Department of the Treasury
Internal Revenue Service

Qualified Business Income Deduction Simplified Computation

► Attach to your tax return.
► Go to *www.irs.gov/Form8995* for instructions and the latest information.

OMB No. 1545-0123

2020

Attachment Sequence No. 55

Name(s) shown on return | **Your taxpayer identification number**

Note. *You can claim the qualified business income deduction **only** if you have qualified business income from a qualified trade or business, real estate investment trust dividends, publicly traded partnership income, or a domestic production activities deduction passed through from an agricultural or horticultural cooperative. See instructions.*
Use this form if your taxable income, before your qualified business income deduction, is at or below $163,300 ($326,600 if married filing jointly), and you aren't a patron of an agricultural or horticultural cooperative.

1	(a) Trade, business, or aggregation name	(b) Taxpayer identification number	(c) Qualified business income or (loss)
i			
ii			
iii			
iv			
v			

2	Total qualified business income or (loss). Combine lines 1i through 1v, column (c)	2			
3	Qualified business net (loss) carryforward from the prior year	3	( )		
4	Total qualified business income. Combine lines 2 and 3. If zero or less, enter -0-	4			
5	Qualified business income component. Multiply line 4 by 20% (0.20)			5	
6	Qualified REIT dividends and publicly traded partnership (PTP) income or (loss) (see instructions)	6			
7	Qualified REIT dividends and qualified PTP (loss) carryforward from the prior year	7	( )		
8	Total qualified REIT dividends and PTP income. Combine lines 6 and 7. If zero or less, enter -0-	8			
9	REIT and PTP component. Multiply line 8 by 20% (0.20)			9	
10	Qualified business income deduction before the income limitation. Add lines 5 and 9			10	
11	Taxable income before qualified business income deduction	11			
12	Net capital gain (see instructions)	12			
13	Subtract line 12 from line 11. If zero or less, enter -0-	13			
14	Income limitation. Multiply line 13 by 20% (0.20)			14	
15	Qualified business income deduction. Enter the lesser of line 10 or line 14. Also enter this amount on the applicable line of your return ►			15	
16	Total qualified business (loss) carryforward. Combine lines 2 and 3. If greater than zero, enter -0-			16	( )
17	Total qualified REIT dividends and PTP (loss) carryforward. Combine lines 6 and 7. If greater than zero, enter -0-			17	( )

For Privacy Act and Paperwork Reduction Act Notice, see instructions. Cat. No. 37806C Form **8995** (2020)

Schedule C net income. Net income from speaking fees, wedding and funeral honoraria, etc.

Sample Return No. 1 – Active Minister

FACTS

Minister considered to be an employee for income tax purposes with an accountable business expense plan.

The Browns live in a home they are personally purchasing. Pastor Brown has entered into a voluntary withholding agreement with the church, and $15,000 of federal income taxes are withheld.

Income, Benefits, and Reimbursements:

Church salary	$74,850
Christmas and other special-occasion gifts paid by the church based on designated member-gifts to the church	750
Honoraria for performing weddings, funerals, and baptisms	650
Honorarium for speaking as an evangelist at another church	1,000
Interest income:	
Taxable	325
Self-employment tax allowance	12,000

Business Expenses, Itemized Deductions, Housing, and Other Data:

The church reimbursed 100% of church-related expenses (including 9,412 business miles) paid personally under an accountable reimbursement plan, based on timely substantiation of the expenses.

Expenses related to honoraria income:	
Parking	$ 50
Travel – 958 x 57.5¢ per mile	551
Potential itemized deductions:	
Unreimbursed doctors, dentists, and drugs	1,500
State and local income taxes: withheld from 2020 salary	1,600
Real estate taxes on home	2,000
Home mortgage interest	14,850
Cash charitable contributions	8,200
Noncash charitable contributions – household furniture/fair market value	480
Student loan interest	1,906
Housing data:	
Designation	26,000
Actual expenses	25,625
Fair rental value plus furnishings including utilities	25,000
403(b) pre-tax contributions for Pastor Brown:	
Voluntary employee contributions made under a salary reduction agreement	500
Nonvoluntary employer contributions	2,000

Form **1040** Department of the Treasury—Internal Revenue Service (99)
U.S. Individual Income Tax Return **2020** OMB No. 1545-0074 IRS Use Only—Do not write or staple in this space.

Filing Status Check only one box. ☐ Single ☒ Married filing jointly ☐ Married filing separately (MFS) ☐ Head of household (HOH) ☐ Qualifying widow(er) (QW)
If you checked the MFS box, enter the name of your spouse. If you checked the HOH or QW box, enter the child's name if the qualifying person is a child but not your dependent ▶

Your first name and middle initial	Last name	Your social security number
Milton L.	Brown	541 16 8194
If joint return, spouse's first name and middle initial	**Last name**	**Spouse's social security number**
Alessia S.	Brown	238 49 7249

Home address (number and street). If you have a P.O. box, see instructions. 418 Trenton Street — Apt. no.
City, town, or post office. If you have a foreign address, also complete spaces below. Springfield, OH 45504 — State — ZIP code
Foreign country name — Foreign province/state/county — Foreign postal code

Presidential Election Campaign Check here if you, or your spouse if filing jointly, want $3 to go to this fund. Checking a box below will not change your tax or refund. ☒ You ☐ Spouse

At any time during 2020, did you receive, sell, send, exchange, or otherwise acquire any financial interest in any virtual currency? ☐ Yes ☒ No

Standard Deduction **Someone can claim:** ☐ You as a dependent ☐ Your spouse as a dependent
☐ Spouse itemizes on a separate return or you were a dual-status alien

Age/Blindness **You:** ☐ Were born before January 2, 1956 ☐ Are blind **Spouse:** ☐ Was born before January 2, 1956 ☐ Is blind

Dependents (see instructions): If more than four dependents, see instructions and check here ▶ ☐

(1) First name	Last name	(2) Social security number	(3) Relationship to you	(4) ✔ if qualifies for (see instructions): Child tax credit	Credit for other dependents
Charles	Brown	514 43 9196	Son	☒	☐
				☐	☐
				☐	☐
				☐	☐

Attach Sch. B if required.

1	Wages, salaries, tips, etc. Attach Form(s) W-2 . . . Excess Housing Allowance $1,000 .			1	68,850
2a	Tax-exempt interest . . .	2a	b Taxable interest	2b	325
3a	Qualified dividends . . .	3a	b Ordinary dividends	3b	
4a	IRA distributions . . .	4a	b Taxable amount	4b	
5a	Pensions and annuities . .	5a	b Taxable amount	5b	
6a	Social security benefits . .	6a	b Taxable amount	6b	
7	Capital gain or (loss). Attach Schedule D if required. If not required, check here ▶ ☐			7	
8	Other income from Schedule 1, line 9			8	1,205
9	Add lines 1, 2b, 3b, 4b, 5b, 6b, 7, and 8. This is your **total income** ▶			9	70,380
10	Adjustments to income:				
a	From Schedule 1, line 22	10a	8,611		
b	Charitable contributions if you take the standard deduction. See instructions	10b			
c	Add lines 10a and 10b. These are your **total adjustments to income** ▶			10c	8,611
11	Subtract line 10c from line 9. This is your **adjusted gross income** ▶			11	61,769
12	**Standard deduction or itemized deductions** (from Schedule A)			12	27,130
13	Qualified business income deduction. Attach Form 8995 or Form 8995-A			13	224
14	Add lines 12 and 13			14	27,354
15	**Taxable income.** Subtract line 14 from line 11. If zero or less, enter -0-			15	34,415

Standard Deduction for—
- Single or Married filing separately, $12,400
- Married filing jointly or Qualifying widow(er), $24,800
- Head of household, $18,650
- If you checked any box under *Standard Deduction*, see instructions.

For Disclosure, Privacy Act, and Paperwork Reduction Act Notice, see separate instructions. Cat. No. 11320B Form **1040** (2020)

Line 1 – See page 176 for calculation of the excess housing allowance.

Form 1040 (2020) Page **2**

Line	Description	Box	Amount
16	**Tax** (see instructions). Check if any from Form(s): 1 ☐ 8814 2 ☐ 4972 3 ☐	16	3,736
17	Amount from Schedule 2, line 3	17	
18	Add lines 16 and 17	18	3,736
19	Child tax credit or credit for other dependents	19	2,000
20	Amount from Schedule 3, line 7	20	50
21	Add lines 19 and 20	21	2,050
22	Subtract line 21 from line 18. If zero or less, enter -0-	22	1,686
23	Other taxes, including self-employment tax, from Schedule 2, line 10	23	13,409
24	Add lines 22 and 23. This is your **total tax** ▶	24	15,095
25	Federal income tax withheld from:		
a	Form(s) W-2	25a	
b	Form(s) 1099	25b	
c	Other forms (see instructions)	25c	
d	Add lines 25a through 25c	25d	15,000
26	2020 estimated tax payments and amount applied from 2019 return	26	
27	Earned income credit (EIC)	27	
28	Additional child tax credit. Attach Schedule 8812	28	
29	American opportunity credit from Form 8863, line 8	29	
30	Recovery rebate credit. See instructions	30	
31	Amount from Schedule 3, line 13	31	
32	Add lines 27 through 31. These are your **total other payments and refundable credits** ▶	32	0
33	Add lines 25d, 26, and 32. These are your **total payments** ▶	33	15,000

• If you have a qualifying child, attach Sch. EIC.
• If you have nontaxable combat pay, see instructions.

Refund

Line	Description	Box	Amount
34	If line 33 is more than line 24, subtract line 24 from line 33. This is the amount you **overpaid**	34	
35a	Amount of line 34 you want **refunded to you.** If Form 8888 is attached, check here ▶ ☐	35a	
▶ b	Routing number ▶ c Type: ☐ Checking ☐ Savings		
▶ d	Account number		
36	Amount of line 34 you want **applied to your 2021 estimated tax** ▶	36	

Direct deposit? See instructions.

Amount You Owe

For details on how to pay, see instructions.

Line	Description	Box	Amount
37	Subtract line 33 from line 24. This is the **amount you owe now** ▶	37	95
	Note: Schedule H and Schedule SE filers, line 37 may not represent all of the taxes you owe for 2020. See Schedule 3, line 12e, and its instructions for details.		
38	Estimated tax penalty (see instructions) ▶	38	

Third Party Designee

Do you want to allow another person to discuss this return with the IRS? See instructions ▶ ☐ **Yes.** Complete below. ☐ **No**

Designee's name ▶ Phone no. ▶ Personal identification number (PIN) ▶

Sign Here

Under penalties of perjury, I declare that I have examined this return and accompanying schedules and statements, and to the best of my knowledge and belief, they are true, correct, and complete. Declaration of preparer (other than taxpayer) is based on all information of which preparer has any knowledge.

Joint return? See instructions. Keep a copy for your records.

Your signature	Date	Your occupation	If the IRS sent you an Identity Protection PIN, enter it here (see inst.) ▶
Milton L. Brown	4/15/21	Minister	
Spouse's signature. If a joint return, both must sign.	**Date**	**Spouse's occupation**	**If the IRS sent your spouse an Identity Protection PIN, enter it here (see inst.) ▶**
Alessia S. Brown	4/15/21	Homemaker	

Phone no. Email address

Paid Preparer Use Only

Preparer's name	Preparer's signature	Date	PTIN	Check if: ☐ Self-employed

Firm's name ▶ Phone no.

Firm's address ▶ Firm's EIN ▶

Go to *www.irs.gov/Form1040* for instructions and the latest information. Form **1040** (2020)

SCHEDULE 1 (Form 1040)
Department of the Treasury Internal Revenue Service

Additional Income and Adjustments to Income

▶ Attach to Form 1040, 1040-SR, or 1040-NR.
▶ Go to *www.irs.gov/Form1040* for instructions and the latest information.

OMB No. 1545-0074
2020
Attachment Sequence No. 01

Name(s) shown on Form 1040, 1040-SR, or 1040-NR: Milton L. Brown
Your social security number: 541-16-8194

Part I Additional Income

1	Taxable refunds, credits, or offsets of state and local income taxes	1	
2a	Alimony received	2a	
b	Date of original divorce or separation agreement (see instructions) ▶		
3	Business income or (loss). Attach Schedule C	3	1,205
4	Other gains or (losses). Attach Form 4797	4	
5	Rental real estate, royalties, partnerships, S corporations, trusts, etc. Attach Schedule E	5	
6	Farm income or (loss). Attach Schedule F	6	
7	Unemployment compensation	7	
8	Other income. List type and amount ▶	8	
9	Combine lines 1 through 8. Enter here and on Form 1040, 1040-SR, or 1040-NR, line 8	9	1,205

Part II Adjustments to Income

10	Educator expenses	10	
11	Certain business expenses of reservists, performing artists, and fee-basis government officials. Attach Form 2106	11	
12	Health savings account deduction. Attach Form 8889	12	
13	Moving expenses for members of the Armed Forces. Attach Form 3903	13	
14	Deductible part of self-employment tax. Attach Schedule SE	14	6,705
15	Self-employed SEP, SIMPLE, and qualified plans	15	
16	Self-employed health insurance deduction	16	
17	Penalty on early withdrawal of savings	17	
18a	Alimony paid	18a	
b	Recipient's SSN ▶		
c	Date of original divorce or separation agreement (see instructions) ▶		
19	IRA deduction	19	
20	Student loan interest deduction	20	1,906
21	Tuition and fees deduction. Attach Form 8917	21	
22	Add lines 10 through 21. These are your **adjustments to income.** Enter here and on Form 1040, 1040-SR, or 1040-NR, line 10a	22	8,611

For Paperwork Reduction Act Notice, see your tax return instructions. Cat. No. 71479F **Schedule 1 (Form 1040) 2020**

Schedule 1, Line 14 – See page 112-14 for explanation of the self-employment tax deduction.

SCHEDULE 2
(Form 1040)

Department of the Treasury
Internal Revenue Service

Additional Taxes

▶ **Attach to Form 1040, 1040-SR, or 1040-NR.**
▶ **Go to *www.irs.gov/Form1040* for instructions and the latest information.**

OMB No. 1545-0074
2020
Attachment Sequence No. **02**

Name(s) shown on Form 1040, 1040-SR, or 1040-NR	**Your social security number**
Milton L. Brown	541-16-8194

Part I Tax

1	Alternative minimum tax. Attach Form 6251	1	
2	Excess advance premium tax credit repayment. Attach Form 8962	2	
3	Add lines 1 and 2. Enter here and on Form 1040, 1040-SR, or 1040-NR, line 17 . .	3	

Part II Other Taxes

4	Self-employment tax. Attach Schedule SE	4	13,409
5	Unreported social security and Medicare tax from Form: **a** ☐ 4137 **b** ☐ 8919 .	5	
6	Additional tax on IRAs, other qualified retirement plans, and other tax-favored accounts. Attach Form 5329 if required	6	
7a	Household employment taxes. Attach Schedule H	7a	
b	Repayment of first-time homebuyer credit from Form 5405. Attach Form 5405 if required	7b	
8	Taxes from: **a** ☐ Form 8959 **b** ☐ Form 8960 **c** ☐ Instructions; enter code(s) ______	8	
9	Section 965 net tax liability installment from Form 965-A . . . **9** ______		
10	Add lines 4 through 8. These are your **total other taxes.** Enter here and on Form 1040 or 1040-SR, line 23, or Form 1040-NR, line 23b	10	13,409

For Paperwork Reduction Act Notice, see your tax return instructions. Cat. No. 71478U **Schedule 2 (Form 1040) 2020**

SCHEDULE 3 (Form 1040)
Department of the Treasury
Internal Revenue Service

Additional Credits and Payments

▶ Attach to Form 1040, 1040-SR, or 1040-NR.
▶ Go to *www.irs.gov/Form1040* for instructions and the latest information.

OMB No. 1545-0074
2020
Attachment Sequence No. 03

Name(s) shown on Form 1040, 1040-SR, or 1040-NR: Milton L. Brown
Your social security number: 541-16-8194

Part I Nonrefundable Credits

1	Foreign tax credit. Attach Form 1116 if required	1	
2	Credit for child and dependent care expenses. Attach Form 2441	2	
3	Education credits from Form 8863, line 19	3	
4	Retirement savings contributions credit. Attach Form 8880	4	50
5	Residential energy credits. Attach Form 5695	5	
6	Other credits from Form: a ☐ 3800 b ☐ 8801 c ☐	6	
7	Add lines 1 through 6. Enter here and on Form 1040, 1040-SR, or 1040-NR, line 20	7	50

Part II Other Payments and Refundable Credits

8	Net premium tax credit. Attach Form 8962	8	
9	Amount paid with request for extension to file (see instructions)	9	
10	Excess social security and tier 1 RRTA tax withheld	10	
11	Credit for federal tax on fuels. Attach Form 4136	11	
12	Other payments or refundable credits:		
a	Form 2439	12a	
b	Qualified sick and family leave credits from Schedule(s) H and Form(s) 7202	12b	
c	Health coverage tax credit from Form 8885	12c	
d	Other:	12d	
e	Deferral for certain Schedule H or SE filers (see instructions)	12e	
f	Add lines 12a through 12e	12f	
13	Add lines 8 through 12f. Enter here and on Form 1040, 1040-SR, or 1040-NR, line 31	13	

For Paperwork Reduction Act Notice, see your tax return instructions. Cat. No. 71480G Schedule 3 (Form 1040) 2020

Lines 12e – Schedule SE filers may be allowed to defer payment of a portion of the minister's 2020 self-employment taxes if the minister was affected by the coronavirus.

SCHEDULE A (Form 1040)

Department of the Treasury Internal Revenue Service (99)

Itemized Deductions

▶ Go to *www.irs.gov/ScheduleA* for instructions and the latest information.
▶ Attach to Form 1040 or 1040-SR.

Caution: If you are claiming a net qualified disaster loss on Form 4684, see the instructions for line 16.

OMB No. 1545-0074 | **2020** | Attachment Sequence No. **07**

Name(s) shown on Form 1040 or 1040-SR: Milton L. Brown | Your social security number: 541-16-8194

Section	Line	Description	Box	Amount	Line	Total
Medical and Dental Expenses		**Caution:** Do not include expenses reimbursed or paid by others.				
	1	Medical and dental expenses (see instructions)	1	1,500		
	2	Enter amount from Form 1040 or 1040-SR, line 11 | 2 | 61,769				
	3	Multiply line 2 by 7.5% (0.075)	3	4,633		
	4	Subtract line 3 from line 1. If line 3 is more than line 1, enter -0-			4	0
Taxes You Paid	5	State and local taxes.				
	a	State and local income taxes or general sales taxes. You may include either income taxes or general sales taxes on line 5a, but not both. If you elect to include general sales taxes instead of income taxes, check this box ▶ ☐	5a	1,600		
	b	State and local real estate taxes (see instructions)	5b	2,000		
	c	State and local personal property taxes	5c			
	d	Add lines 5a through 5c	5d	3,600		
	e	Enter the smaller of line 5d or $10,000 ($5,000 if married filing separately)	5e	3,600		
	6	Other taxes. List type and amount ▶	6			
	7	Add lines 5e and 6			7	3,600
Interest You Paid Caution: Your mortgage interest deduction may be limited (see instructions).	8	Home mortgage interest and points. If you didn't use all of your home mortgage loan(s) to buy, build, or improve your home, see instructions and check this box ▶ ☐				
	a	Home mortgage interest and points reported to you on Form 1098. See instructions if limited	8a	14,850		
	b	Home mortgage interest not reported to you on Form 1098. See instructions if limited. If paid to the person from whom you bought the home, see instructions and show that person's name, identifying no., and address ▶	8b			
	c	Points not reported to you on Form 1098. See instructions for special rules	8c			
	d	Mortgage insurance premiums (see instructions)	8d			
	e	Add lines 8a through 8d	8e	14,850		
	9	Investment interest. Attach Form 4952 if required. See instructions	9			
	10	Add lines 8e and 9			10	14,850
Gifts to Charity Caution: If you made a gift and got a benefit for it, see instructions.	11	Gifts by cash or check. If you made any gift of $250 or more, see instructions	11	8,200		
	12	Other than by cash or check. If you made any gift of $250 or more, see instructions. You **must** attach Form 8283 if over $500	12	480		
	13	Carryover from prior year	13			
	14	Add lines 11 through 13			14	8,680
Casualty and Theft Losses	15	Casualty and theft loss(es) from a federally declared disaster (other than net qualified disaster losses). Attach Form 4684 and enter the amount from line 18 of that form. See instructions			15	
Other Itemized Deductions	16	Other—from list in instructions. List type and amount ▶			16	
Total Itemized Deductions	17	Add the amounts in the far right column for lines 4 through 16. Also, enter this amount on Form 1040 or 1040-SR, line 12			17	27,130
	18	If you elect to itemize deductions even though they are less than your standard deduction, check this box ▶ ☐				

For Paperwork Reduction Act Notice, see the Instructions for Forms 1040 and 1040-SR. Cat. No. 17145C **Schedule A (Form 1040) 2020**

Lines 5b and 8a – The real estate taxes and home mortgage interest are deducted on this form plus excluded from income on Line 1, Form 1040, page 1 as a housing allowance.

SCHEDULE C (Form 1040)

Department of the Treasury Internal Revenue Service (99)

Profit or Loss From Business

(Sole Proprietorship)

▶ Go to *www.irs.gov/ScheduleC* for instructions and the latest information.

▶ Attach to Form 1040, 1040-SR, 1040-NR, or 1041; partnerships generally must file Form 1065.

OMB No. 1545-0074

2020

Attachment Sequence No. **09**

Name of proprietor: Milton L. Brown

Social security number (SSN): 541-16-8194

A Principal business or profession, including product or service (see instructions): Minister

B Enter code from instructions ▶ 8 1 3 0 0 0

C Business name. If no separate business name, leave blank.

D Employer ID number (EIN) (see instr.)

E Business address (including suite or room no.) ▶ 418 Trenton Street

City, town or post office, state, and ZIP code: Springfield, OH 45504

F Accounting method: (1) [X] Cash (2) [ ] Accrual (3) [ ] Other (specify) ▶

G Did you "materially participate" in the operation of this business during 2020? If "No," see instructions for limit on losses . . . [X] Yes [ ] No

H If you started or acquired this business during 2020, check here . . . ▶ [ ]

I Did you make any payments in 2020 that would require you to file Form(s) 1099? See instructions . . . [ ] Yes [X] No

J If "Yes," did you or will you file required Form(s) 1099? . . . [ ] Yes [ ] No

Part I Income

		Line	Amount
1	Gross receipts or sales. See instructions for line 1 and check the box if this income was reported to you on Form W-2 and the "Statutory employee" box on that form was checked . . . ▶ [ ]	1	1,650
2	Returns and allowances . . .	2	
3	Subtract line 2 from line 1 . . .	3	1,650
4	Cost of goods sold (from line 42) . . .	4	
5	**Gross profit.** Subtract line 4 from line 3 . . .	5	1,650
6	Other income, including federal and state gasoline or fuel tax credit or refund (see instructions) . . .	6	
7	**Gross income.** Add lines 5 and 6 . . . ▶	7	1,650

Part II Expenses. Enter expenses for business use of your home only on line 30.

		Line	Amount			Line	Amount
8	Advertising . . .	8		18	Office expense (see instructions)	18	
9	Car and truck expenses (see instructions) . . .	9	445	19	Pension and profit-sharing plans .	19	
10	Commissions and fees .	10		20	Rent or lease (see instructions):		
11	Contract labor (see instructions)	11		a	Vehicles, machinery, and equipment	20a	
12	Depletion . . .	12		b	Other business property . . .	20b	
13	Depreciation and section 179 expense deduction (not included in Part III) (see instructions) . . .	13		21	Repairs and maintenance . . .	21	
				22	Supplies (not included in Part III) .	22	
				23	Taxes and licenses . . .	23	
				24	Travel and meals:		
14	Employee benefit programs (other than on line 19) . .	14		a	Travel . . .	24a	
15	Insurance (other than health)	15		b	Deductible meals (see instructions) . . .	24b	
16	Interest (see instructions):			25	Utilities . . .	25	
a	Mortgage (paid to banks, etc.)	16a		26	Wages (less employment credits) .	26	
b	Other . . .	16b		27a	Other expenses (from line 48) . .	27a	
17	Legal and professional services	17		b	**Reserved for future use** . . .	27b	

		Line	Amount
28	**Total expenses** before expenses for business use of home. Add lines 8 through 27a . . . ▶	28	445
29	Tentative profit or (loss). Subtract line 28 from line 7 . . .	29	1,205
30	Expenses for business use of your home. Do not report these expenses elsewhere. Attach Form 8829 unless using the simplified method. See instructions. **Simplified method filers only:** Enter the total square footage of (a) your home: ____ and (b) the part of your home used for business: ____ . Use the Simplified Method Worksheet in the instructions to figure the amount to enter on line 30 . . .	30	
31	**Net profit or (loss).** Subtract line 30 from line 29. • If a profit, enter on both **Schedule 1 (Form 1040), line 3,** and on **Schedule SE, line 2.** (If you checked the box on line 1, see instructions). Estates and trusts, enter on **Form 1041, line 3.** • If a loss, you **must** go to line 32.	31	1,205

32 If you have a loss, check the box that describes your investment in this activity. See instructions.

• If you checked 32a, enter the loss on both **Schedule 1 (Form 1040), line 3,** and on **Schedule SE, line 2.** (If you checked the box on line 1, see the line 31 instructions). Estates and trusts, enter on **Form 1041, line 3.**

• If you checked 32b, you **must** attach **Form 6198.** Your loss may be limited.

32a [ ] All investment is at risk.
32b [ ] Some investment is not at risk.

For Paperwork Reduction Act Notice, see the separate instructions. Cat. No. 11334P **Schedule C (Form 1040) 2020**

Gross receipts:

Honoraria (weddings, etc.)	$650
Speaking honorarium	1,000
	$1,650

Expenses:

See Attachment 1 on page 162.

Note: Page 2 of Schedule C is not displayed in this sample return, but it should be completed to reflect the vehicle information.

SCHEDULE SE (Form 1040)

Department of the Treasury Internal Revenue Service (99)

Self-Employment Tax

▶ Go to *www.irs.gov/ScheduleSE* for instructions and the latest information.
▶ Attach to Form 1040, 1040-SR, or 1040-NR.

OMB No. 1545-0074
2020
Attachment Sequence No. **17**

Name of person with self-employment income (as shown on Form 1040, 1040-SR, or 1040-NR): Milton L. Brown

Social security number of person with **self-employment** income ▶ 541-16-8194

Part I Self-Employment Tax

Note: If your only income subject to self-employment tax is **church employee income,** see instructions for how to report your income and the definition of church employee income.

A If you are a minister, member of a religious order, or Christian Science practitioner **and** you filed Form 4361, but you had $400 or more of **other** net earnings from self-employment, check here and continue with Part I . . . . ▶ ☐

Skip lines 1a and 1b if you use the farm optional method in Part II. See instructions.

1a	Net farm profit or (loss) from Schedule F, line 34, and farm partnerships, Schedule K-1 (Form 1065), box 14, code A			1a	
b	If you received social security retirement or disability benefits, enter the amount of Conservation Reserve Program payments included on Schedule F, line 4b, or listed on Schedule K-1 (Form 1065), box 20, code AH			1b	( )
	Skip line 2 if you use the nonfarm optional method in Part II. See instructions.				
2	Net profit or (loss) from Schedule C, line 31; and Schedule K-1 (Form 1065), box 14, code A (other than farming). See instructions for other income to report or if you are a minister or member of a religious order			2	94,899
3	Combine lines 1a, 1b, and 2			3	94,899
4a	If line 3 is more than zero, multiply line 3 by 92.35% (0.9235). Otherwise, enter amount from line 3			4a	87,639
	Note: If line 4a is less than $400 due to Conservation Reserve Program payments on line 1b, see instructions.				
b	If you elect one or both of the optional methods, enter the total of lines 15 and 17 here			4b	
c	Combine lines 4a and 4b. If less than $400, **stop;** you don't owe self-employment tax. **Exception:** If less than $400 and you had **church employee income,** enter -0- and continue ▶			4c	87,639
5a	Enter your **church employee income** from Form W-2. See instructions for definition of church employee income	5a			
b	Multiply line 5a by 92.35% (0.9235). If less than $100, enter -0-			5b	
6	Add lines 4c and 5b			6	87,639
7	Maximum amount of combined wages and self-employment earnings subject to social security tax or the 6.2% portion of the 7.65% railroad retirement (tier 1) tax for 2020			7	137,700
8a	Total social security wages and tips (total of boxes 3 and 7 on Form(s) W-2) and railroad retirement (tier 1) compensation. If $137,700 or more, skip lines 8b through 10, and go to line 11	8a			
b	Unreported tips subject to social security tax from Form 4137, line 10	8b			
c	Wages subject to social security tax from Form 8919, line 10	8c			
d	Add lines 8a, 8b, and 8c			8d	
9	Subtract line 8d from line 7. If zero or less, enter -0- here and on line 10 and go to line 11 ▶			9	137,700
10	Multiply the **smaller** of line 6 or line 9 by 12.4% (0.124)			10	10,867
11	Multiply line 6 by 2.9% (0.029)			11	2,542
12	**Self-employment tax.** Add lines 10 and 11. Enter here and on **Schedule 2 (Form 1040), line 4**			12	13,409
13	**Deduction for one-half of self-employment tax.** Multiply line 12 by 50% (0.50). Enter here and on **Schedule 1 (Form 1040), line 14**	13	6,705		

Part II Optional Methods To Figure Net Earnings (see instructions)

Farm Optional Method. You may use this method **only** if **(a)** your gross farm income[1] wasn't more than $8,460, **or (b)** your net farm profits[2] were less than $6,107.

14	Maximum income for optional methods	14	5,640
15	Enter the **smaller** of: two-thirds (2/3) of gross farm income[1] (not less than zero) **or** $5,640. Also, include this amount on line 4b above	15	

Nonfarm Optional Method. You may use this method **only** if **(a)** your net nonfarm profits[3] were less than $6,107 and also less than 72.189% of your gross nonfarm income,[4] **and (b)** you had net earnings from self-employment of at least $400 in 2 of the prior 3 years. **Caution:** You may use this method no more than five times.

16	Subtract line 15 from line 14	16	
17	Enter the **smaller** of: two-thirds (2/3) of gross nonfarm income[4] (not less than zero) **or** the amount on line 16. Also, include this amount on line 4b above	17	

[1] From Sch. F, line 9; and Sch. K-1 (Form 1065), box 14, code B.
[2] From Sch. F, line 34; and Sch. K-1 (Form 1065), box 14, code A—minus the amount you would have entered on line 1b had you not used the optional method.
[3] From Sch. C, line 31; and Sch. K-1 (Form 1065), box 14, code A.
[4] From Sch. C, line 7; and Sch. K-1 (Form 1065), box 14, code C.

For Paperwork Reduction Act Notice, see your tax return instructions. Cat. No. 11358Z **Schedule SE (Form 1040) 2020**

Line 2 – See Attachment 2 on page 176.
Line 13 – This line results in the deduction of a portion of the self-employment tax liability.

Form **8880** Department of the Treasury Internal Revenue Service

Credit for Qualified Retirement Savings Contributions

▶ Attach to Form 1040, 1040-SR, or 1040-NR.
▶ Go to *www.irs.gov/Form8880* for the latest information.

OMB No. 1545-0074
2020
Attachment Sequence No. **54**

Name(s) shown on return	Your social security number
Milton L. Brown	541-16-8194

*You **cannot** take this credit if **either** of the following applies.*

- *The amount on Form 1040, 1040-SR, or 1040-NR, line 11, is more than $32,500 ($48,750 if head of household; $65,000 if married filing jointly).*
- *The person(s) who made the qualified contribution or elective deferral **(a)** was born after January 1, 2003; **(b)** is claimed as a dependent on someone else's 2020 tax return; or **(c)** was a **student** (see instructions).*

			(a) You	(b) Your spouse
1	Traditional and Roth IRA contributions, and ABLE account contributions by the designated beneficiary for 2020. **Do not** include rollover contributions	1		
2	Elective deferrals to a 401(k) or other qualified employer plan, voluntary employee contributions, and 501(c)(18)(D) plan contributions for 2020 (see instructions)	2	500	
3	Add lines 1 and 2	3	500	
4	Certain distributions received **after** 2017 and **before** the due date (including extensions) of your 2020 tax return (see instructions). If married filing jointly, include **both** spouses' amounts in **both** columns. See instructions for an exception	4	0	
5	Subtract line 4 from line 3. If zero or less, enter -0-	5	500	
6	In each column, enter the **smaller** of line 5 or $2,000	6	500	

7	Add the amounts on line 6. If zero, **stop;** you can't take this credit	7	500
8	Enter the amount from Form 1040, 1040-SR, or 1040-NR, line 11* — **8** 61,769		
9	Enter the applicable decimal amount from the table below.	9	x 0.1

If line 8 is—		And your filing status is—		
Over—	But not over—	Married filing jointly	Head of household	Single, Married filing separately, or Qualifying widow(er)
		Enter on line 9—		
---	$19,500	0.5	0.5	0.5
$19,500	$21,250	0.5	0.5	0.2
$21,250	$29,250	0.5	0.5	0.1
$29,250	$31,875	0.5	0.2	0.1
$31,875	$32,500	0.5	0.1	0.1
$32,500	$39,000	0.5	0.1	0.0
$39,000	$42,500	0.2	0.1	0.0
$42,500	$48,750	0.1	0.1	0.0
$48,750	$65,000	0.1	0.0	0.0
$65,000	---	0.0	0.0	0.0

Note: If line 9 is zero, **stop;** you can't take this credit.

10	Multiply line 7 by line 9	10	50
11	Limitation based on tax liability. Enter the amount from the Credit Limit Worksheet in the instructions	11	3,736
12	**Credit for qualified retirement savings contributions.** Enter the **smaller** of line 10 or line 11 here and on Schedule 3 (Form 1040), line 4	12	50

* See Pub. 590-A for the amount to enter if you claim any exclusion or deduction for foreign earned income, foreign housing, or income from Puerto Rico or for bona fide residents of American Samoa.

For Paperwork Reduction Act Notice, see your tax return instructions. Cat. No. 33394D Form **8880** (2020)

Form **8995**

Department of the Treasury
Internal Revenue Service

Qualified Business Income Deduction Simplified Computation

► Attach to your tax return.
► Go to *www.irs.gov/Form8995* for instructions and the latest information.

OMB No. 1545-0123

2020

Attachment Sequence No. 55

Name(s) shown on return	Your taxpayer identification number
Milton L. Brown	541-16-8194

Note. *You can claim the qualified business income deduction **only** if you have qualified business income from a qualified trade or business, real estate investment trust dividends, publicly traded partnership income, or a domestic production activities deduction passed through from an agricultural or horticultural cooperative. See instructions.*

Use this form if your taxable income, before your qualified business income deduction, is at or below $163,300 ($326,600 if married filing jointly), and you aren't a patron of an agricultural or horticultural cooperative.

1	(a) Trade, business, or aggregation name	(b) Taxpayer identification number	(c) Qualified business income or (loss)
	Minister	541-16-8194	1,120
i			
ii			
iii			
iv		(1)	
v			

2	Total qualified business income or (loss). Combine lines 1i through 1v, column (c)	2	1,120		
3	Qualified business net (loss) carryforward from the prior year	3	(0)		
4	Total qualified business income. Combine lines 2 and 3. If zero or less, enter -0-	4	1,120		
5	Qualified business income component. Multiply line 4 by 20% (0.20)			5	224
6	Qualified REIT dividends and publicly traded partnership (PTP) income or (loss) (see instructions)	6			
7	Qualified REIT dividends and qualified PTP (loss) carryforward from the prior year	7	( )		
8	Total qualified REIT dividends and PTP income. Combine lines 6 and 7. If zero or less, enter -0-	8			
9	REIT and PTP component. Multiply line 8 by 20% (0.20)			9	0
10	Qualified business income deduction before the income limitation. Add lines 5 and 9			10	224
11	Taxable income before qualified business income deduction	11	34,639		
12	Net capital gain (see instructions)	12	0		
13	Subtract line 12 from line 11. If zero or less, enter -0-	13	34,639		
14	Income limitation. Multiply line 13 by 20% (0.20)			14	6,928
15	Qualified business income deduction. Enter the lesser of line 10 or line 14. Also enter this amount on the applicable line of your return ►			15	224
16	Total qualified business (loss) carryforward. Combine lines 2 and 3. If greater than zero, enter -0-			16	(0)
17	Total qualified REIT dividends and PTP (loss) carryforward. Combine lines 6 and 7. If greater than zero, enter -0-			17	(0)

For Privacy Act and Paperwork Reduction Act Notice, see instructions. Cat. No. 37806C Form **8995** (2020)

(1) Schedule C net profit (page 172)			$1,205
Less: Social Security tax deduction associated with the net profit:			
$1,205 x .9235	=	$1,112	
x 15.3%	=	170	
x 50%	=	85	85
Qualified business income			$1,120

Attachment 1.

Computation of expenses, allocable to tax-free ministerial income, that are nondeductible.

		Taxable	Tax-Free	Total
Salary as a minister		$ 67,850		$ 67,850
Housing allowance:				
Amount designated and paid by church	$ 26,000			
Actual expenses	25,625			
Fair rental value of home (including furnishings and utilities)	25,000			
Taxable portion of allowance (excess of amount designated and paid over lesser of actual expenses or fair rental value)	$ 1,000	1,000		1,000
Tax-free portion of allowance (lesser of amount designated, actual expenses, or fair rental value)			25,000	25,000
Gross income from weddings, baptisms, and honoraria		1,650		1,650
Ministerial Income		$ 70,500	$ 25,000	$ 95,500

% of nondeductible expenses: $25,000/$95,500 = 26%

Schedule C Deduction Computation

Parking and tolls	$ 50
Mileage (958 miles x 57.5 cents per mile)	551
Unadjusted Schedule C expenses	601
Minus:	
Nondeductible part of Schedule C expenses (26% x $601)	156
Schedule C deductions (Line 28) (See page 172)	$ 445

Attachment 2.

Net earnings from self-employment (attachment to Schedule SE, Form 1040)

Church wages	$ 67,850
Housing allowance	26,000
Net profit from Schedule C	1,205
	95,055
Less:	
Schedule C expenses allocable to tax-free income	(156)
Net Self-Employed Income	
Schedule SE, Line 2 (See page 173)	$ 94,899

Housing Allowance Worksheet
Minister Living in Home
Minister Owns or Is Buying

Minister's name: Milton L. Brown

For the period January 1, 2020 to December 31, 2020

Date designation approved December 20, 2019

Allowable Housing Expenses *(expenses paid by minister from current income)*

	Estimated Expenses	Actual
Down payment on purchase of housing	$	$
Housing loan principal and interest payments	18,117	17,875
Real estate commission, escrow fees		
Real property taxes	900	2,000
Personal property taxes on contents		
Homeowner's insurance	500	550
Personal property insurance on contents	150	200
Umbrella liability insurance	100	
Structural maintenance and repair		550
Landscaping, gardening, and pest control		200
Furnishings *(purchase, repair, replacement)*		400
Decoration and redecoration		
Utilities *(gas, electricity, water)* and trash collection	3,500	3,500
Local telephone expense *(base charge)*	150	150
Homeowner's association dues/condominium fees	219	200
Subtotal	23,636	
10% allowance for unexpected expenses	2,364	
TOTAL	$ 26,000	$ 25,625 (A)
Properly designated housing allowance		$ 26,000 (B)
Fair rental value of home, including furnishings, plus utilities		$ 25,000 (C)

Note: The amount excludable from income for federal income tax purposes is the lowest of A, B, or C.

The $1,000 difference between the designation ($26,000) and the fair rental value ($25,000) is reported as additional income on Form 1040, page 1, Line 1.

22222 | VOID ☐ | a Employee's social security number: 541-16-8194 | For Official Use Only ▶ OMB No. 1545-0008

b Employer identification number (EIN): 38-9417217	1 Wages, tips, other compensation: 67850.00	2 Federal income tax withheld: 15000.00
c Employer's name, address, and ZIP code: Magnolia Springs Church, 4805 Douglas Road, Springfield, OH 45504	3 Social security wages	4 Social security tax withheld
	5 Medicare wages and tips	6 Medicare tax withheld
	7 Social security tips	8 Allocated tips
d Control number	9	10 Dependent care benefits
e Employee's first name and initial: Milton L. / Last name: Brown / Suff.	11 Nonqualified plans	12a See instructions for box 12: Code E, 500
418 Trenton Street, Springfield, OH 45504	13 Statutory employee ☐ Retirement plan ☒ Third-party sick pay ☐	12b
	14 Other: Housing Allowance 26000	12c
f Employee's address and ZIP code		12d

15 State	Employer's state ID number	16 State wages, tips, etc.	17 State income tax	18 Local wages, tips, etc.	19 Local income tax	20 Locality name
OH	677803	67850.00	1600.00			

Form **W-2** **Wage and Tax Statement** 2020

Department of the Treasury—Internal Revenue Service

For Privacy Act and Paperwork Reduction Act Notice, see the separate instructions.

Copy A—For Social Security Administration. Send this entire page with Form W-3 to the Social Security Administration; photocopies are **not** acceptable.

Cat. No. 10134D

Do Not Cut, Fold, or Staple Forms on This Page

Explanation of compensation reported on Form W-2, Box 1:

Salary ($74,850 less $26,000 housing allowance and $500 403[b] contributions)	$48,350
Special occasion gifts	750
Reimbursement of self-employment tax	12,000
Moving expense reimbursement	6,750
	$67,850

Pastor Brown received reimbursements of $7,593 under an accountable expense reimbursement plan. The reimbursements are not included on Form W-2 or deductible on Form 1040. There is no requirement to add the reimbursements to taxable income for Social Security purposes on Schedule SE.

Sample Return No. 2 – Retired Minister

FACTS

Minister was an employee for income tax purposes and has since retired. The Halls live in a home they own.

Income, Benefits, and Reimbursements:

Denominational annuity distribution	$19,500
Honoraria for performing weddings, funerals, baptisms, and outside speaking engagements	3,200
Interest income (taxable)	750
Social Security benefit	31,500
Expenses related to honoraria income:	
Travel – 2,316 x 57.5¢ per mile	1,332
Meals	175
Housing data:	
Designation	19,500
Actual expenses	20,500
Fair rental value, plus furnishings, including utilities	25,000

Form **1040** Department of the Treasury—Internal Revenue Service (99) **U.S. Individual Income Tax Return** **2020** OMB No. 1545-0074 IRS Use Only—Do not write or staple in this space.

Filing Status Check only one box. ☐ Single ☐ Married filing jointly ☐ Married filing separately (MFS) ☐ Head of household (HOH) ☐ Qualifying widow(er) (QW)

If you checked the MFS box, enter the name of your spouse. If you checked the HOH or QW box, enter the child's name if the qualifying person is a child but not your dependent ▶

Your first name and middle initial	Last name	Your social security number
Donald L.	Hall	482 11 6043
If joint return, spouse's first name and middle initial	Last name	Spouse's social security number
Julie M.	Hall	720 92 1327

Home address (number and street). If you have a P.O. box, see instructions.	Apt. no.
804 Linden Avenue	

City, town, or post office. If you have a foreign address, also complete spaces below.	State	ZIP code
Pensacola	FL	32502

Foreign country name	Foreign province/state/county	Foreign postal code

Presidential Election Campaign Check here if you, or your spouse if filing jointly, want $3 to go to this fund. Checking a box below will not change your tax or refund. ☐ You ☐ Spouse

At any time during 2020, did you receive, sell, send, exchange, or otherwise acquire any financial interest in any virtual currency? ☐ Yes ☒ No

Standard Deduction **Someone can claim:** ☐ You as a dependent ☐ Your spouse as a dependent
☐ Spouse itemizes on a separate return or you were a dual-status alien

Age/Blindness **You:** ☒ Were born before January 2, 1956 ☐ Are blind **Spouse:** ☒ Was born before January 2, 1956 ☐ Is blind

Dependents (see instructions): If more than four dependents, see instructions and check here ▶ ☐

(1) First name Last name	(2) Social security number	(3) Relationship to you	(4) ✔ if qualifies for (see instructions): Child tax credit	Credit for other dependents
			☐	☐
			☐	☐
			☐	☐
			☐	☐

Attach Sch. B if required.

1	Wages, salaries, tips, etc. Attach Form(s) W-2			1	
2a	Tax-exempt interest	2a		2b	750
	b Taxable interest				
3a	Qualified dividends	3a		3b	
	b Ordinary dividends				
4a	IRA distributions	4a		4b	
	b Taxable amount				
5a	Pensions and annuities	5a	19,500	5b	0
	b Taxable amount				
6a	Social security benefits	6a	31,500	6b	0
	b Taxable amount				
7	Capital gain or (loss). Attach Schedule D if required. If not required, check here ▶ ☐			7	
8	Other income from Schedule 1, line 9			8	3,001
9	Add lines 1, 2b, 3b, 4b, 5b, 6b, 7, and 8. This is your **total income** ▶			9	3,751
10	Adjustments to income:				
a	From Schedule 1, line 22	10a	126		
b	Charitable contributions if you take the standard deduction. See instructions	10b			
c	Add lines 10a and 10b. These are your **total adjustments to income** ▶			10c	126
11	Subtract line 10c from line 9. This is your **adjusted gross income** ▶			11	3,625
12	**Standard deduction or itemized deductions** (from Schedule A)			12	27,400
13	Qualified business income deduction. Attach Form 8995 or Form 8995-A			13	
14	Add lines 12 and 13			14	27,400
15	**Taxable income.** Subtract line 14 from line 11. If zero or less, enter -0-			15	0

Standard Deduction for—
- Single or Married filing separately, $12,400
- Married filing jointly or Qualifying widow(er), $24,800
- Head of household, $18,650
- If you checked any box under *Standard Deduction,* see instructions.

For Disclosure, Privacy Act, and Paperwork Reduction Act Notice, see separate instructions. Cat. No. 11320B Form **1040** (2020)

Line 13 – Since taxable income (see Line 15) was zero, the minister did not qualify for the qualified business income deduction based on Schedule C net profit.

Line 14 – This reflects the standard deduction for married filing jointly in 2020, plus an additional $1,300 for each taxpayer since they were over age 65 on December 31, 2020.

Form 1040 (2020) Page 2

Line	Description			Line	Amount
16	**Tax** (see instructions). Check if any from Form(s): 1 ☐ 8814 2 ☐ 4972 3 ☐ ______			16	0
17	Amount from Schedule 2, line 3			17	
18	Add lines 16 and 17			18	0
19	Child tax credit or credit for other dependents			19	
20	Amount from Schedule 3, line 7			20	
21	Add lines 19 and 20			21	0
22	Subtract line 21 from line 18. If zero or less, enter -0-			22	
23	Other taxes, including self-employment tax, from Schedule 2, line 10			23	252
24	Add lines 22 and 23. This is your **total tax** ▶			24	252
25	Federal income tax withheld from:				
a	Form(s) W-2	25a			
b	Form(s) 1099	25b			
c	Other forms (see instructions)	25c			
d	Add lines 25a through 25c			25d	
26	2020 estimated tax payments and amount applied from 2019 return			26	
27	Earned income credit (EIC)	27			
28	Additional child tax credit. Attach Schedule 8812	28			
29	American opportunity credit from Form 8863, line 8	29			
30	Recovery rebate credit. See instructions	30			
31	Amount from Schedule 3, line 13	31			
32	Add lines 27 through 31. These are your **total other payments and refundable credits** ▶			32	0
33	Add lines 25d, 26, and 32. These are your **total payments** ▶			33	

• If you have a qualifying child, attach Sch. EIC.
• If you have nontaxable combat pay, see instructions.

Refund

Line	Description			Line	Amount
34	If line 33 is more than line 24, subtract line 24 from line 33. This is the amount you **overpaid**			34	
35a	Amount of line 34 you want **refunded to you.** If Form 8888 is attached, check here ▶ ☐			35a	
▶ b	Routing number	▶ c Type: ☐ Checking ☐ Savings			
▶ d	Account number				
36	Amount of line 34 you want **applied to your 2021 estimated tax** ▶	36			

Direct deposit? See instructions.

Amount You Owe

For details on how to pay, see instructions.

Line	Description			Line	Amount
37	Subtract line 33 from line 24. This is the **amount you owe now** ▶			37	252
	Note: Schedule H and Schedule SE filers, line 37 may not represent all of the taxes you owe for 2020. See Schedule 3, line 12e, and its instructions for details.				
38	Estimated tax penalty (see instructions) ▶	38			

Third Party Designee

Do you want to allow another person to discuss this return with the IRS? See instructions ▶ ☐ **Yes.** Complete below. ☒ **No**

Designee's name ▶ Phone no. ▶ Personal identification number (PIN) ▶

Sign Here

Under penalties of perjury, I declare that I have examined this return and accompanying schedules and statements, and to the best of my knowledge and belief, they are true, correct, and complete. Declaration of preparer (other than taxpayer) is based on all information of which preparer has any knowledge.

Joint return? See instructions. Keep a copy for your records.

Your signature	Date	Your occupation	If the IRS sent you an Identity Protection PIN, enter it here (see inst.) ▶
Ronald L. Hall	4/15/21	Retired Minister	
Spouse's signature. If a joint return, both must sign.	**Date**	**Spouse's occupation**	**If the IRS sent your spouse an Identity Protection PIN, enter it here (see inst.) ▶**
Julie M. Hall	4/15/21	Retired	
Phone no.	Email address		

Paid Preparer Use Only

Preparer's name	Preparer's signature	Date	PTIN	Check if: ☐ Self-employed
Firm's name ▶			Phone no.	
Firm's address ▶			Firm's EIN ▶	

Go to *www.irs.gov/Form1040* for instructions and the latest information. Form **1040** (2020)

SCHEDULE 1 (Form 1040)
Department of the Treasury Internal Revenue Service

Additional Income and Adjustments to Income

▶ Attach to Form 1040, 1040-SR, or 1040-NR.
▶ Go to *www.irs.gov/Form1040* for instructions and the latest information.

OMB No. 1545-0074
2020
Attachment Sequence No. **01**

Name(s) shown on Form 1040, 1040-SR, or 1040-NR	Your social security number
Donald L. Hall	482-11-6043

Part I Additional Income

1	Taxable refunds, credits, or offsets of state and local income taxes	1	
2a	Alimony received	2a	
b	Date of original divorce or separation agreement (see instructions) ▶		
3	Business income or (loss). Attach Schedule C	3	3,001
4	Other gains or (losses). Attach Form 4797	4	
5	Rental real estate, royalties, partnerships, S corporations, trusts, etc. Attach Schedule E	5	
6	Farm income or (loss). Attach Schedule F	6	
7	Unemployment compensation	7	
8	Other income. List type and amount ▶	8	
9	Combine lines 1 through 8. Enter here and on Form 1040, 1040-SR, or 1040-NR, line 8	9	3,001

Part II Adjustments to Income

10	Educator expenses	10	
11	Certain business expenses of reservists, performing artists, and fee-basis government officials. Attach Form 2106	11	
12	Health savings account deduction. Attach Form 8889	12	
13	Moving expenses for members of the Armed Forces. Attach Form 3903	13	
14	Deductible part of self-employment tax. Attach Schedule SE	14	126
15	Self-employed SEP, SIMPLE, and qualified plans	15	
16	Self-employed health insurance deduction	16	
17	Penalty on early withdrawal of savings	17	
18a	Alimony paid	18a	
b	Recipient's SSN ▶		
c	Date of original divorce or separation agreement (see instructions) ▶		
19	IRA deduction	19	
20	Student loan interest deduction	20	
21	Tuition and fees deduction. Attach Form 8917	21	
22	Add lines 10 through 21. These are your **adjustments to income.** Enter here and on Form 1040, 1040-SR, or 1040-NR, line 10a	22	126

For Paperwork Reduction Act Notice, see your tax return instructions. Cat. No. 71479F **Schedule 1 (Form 1040) 2020**

Schedule 1, Line 14 – See page 112-14 for explanation of the self-employment tax deduction.

SCHEDULE 2 (Form 1040)

Department of the Treasury Internal Revenue Service

Additional Taxes

▶ Attach to Form 1040, 1040-SR, or 1040-NR.
▶ Go to *www.irs.gov/Form1040* for instructions and the latest information.

OMB No. 1545-0074

2020

Attachment Sequence No. **02**

Name(s) shown on Form 1040, 1040-SR, or 1040-NR	Your social security number
Donald L. Hall	482-11-6043

Part I Tax

1	Alternative minimum tax. Attach Form 6251	1	
2	Excess advance premium tax credit repayment. Attach Form 8962	2	
3	Add lines 1 and 2. Enter here and on Form 1040, 1040-SR, or 1040-NR, line 17	3	

Part II Other Taxes

4	Self-employment tax. Attach Schedule SE	4	252
5	Unreported social security and Medicare tax from Form: **a** ☐ 4137 **b** ☐ 8919	5	
6	Additional tax on IRAs, other qualified retirement plans, and other tax-favored accounts. Attach Form 5329 if required	6	
7a	Household employment taxes. Attach Schedule H	7a	
b	Repayment of first-time homebuyer credit from Form 5405. Attach Form 5405 if required	7b	
8	Taxes from: **a** ☐ Form 8959 **b** ☐ Form 8960 **c** ☐ Instructions; enter code(s)	8	
9	Section 965 net tax liability installment from Form 965-A . . . 9		
10	Add lines 4 through 8. These are your **total other taxes.** Enter here and on Form 1040 or 1040-SR, line 23, or Form 1040-NR, line 23b	10	252

For Paperwork Reduction Act Notice, see your tax return instructions. Cat. No. 71478U **Schedule 2 (Form 1040) 2020**

SCHEDULE C (Form 1040)

Department of the Treasury Internal Revenue Service (99)

Profit or Loss From Business

(Sole Proprietorship)

▶ Go to *www.irs.gov/ScheduleC* for instructions and the latest information.

▶ Attach to Form 1040, 1040-SR, 1040-NR, or 1041; partnerships generally must file Form 1065.

OMB No. 1545-0074

2020

Attachment Sequence No. 09

Name of proprietor	Social security number (SSN)
Donald L. Hall	482-11-6043

A	Principal business or profession, including product or service (see instructions) Minister	B Enter code from instructions ▶ 8 1 3 0 0 0
C	Business name. If no separate business name, leave blank.	D Employer ID number (EIN) (see instr.)
E	Business address (including suite or room no.) ▶ 804 Linden Avenue	
	City, town or post office, state, and ZIP code Pensacola, FL 32502	
F	Accounting method: (1) [X] Cash (2) [ ] Accrual (3) [ ] Other (specify) ▶	
G	Did you "materially participate" in the operation of this business during 2020? If "No," see instructions for limit on losses	[X] Yes [ ] No
H	If you started or acquired this business during 2020, check here ▶	[ ]
I	Did you make any payments in 2020 that would require you to file Form(s) 1099? See instructions	[ ] Yes [X] No
J	If "Yes," did you or will you file required Form(s) 1099?	[ ] Yes [ ] No

Part I Income

1	Gross receipts or sales. See instructions for line 1 and check the box if this income was reported to you on Form W-2 and the "Statutory employee" box on that form was checked ▶ [ ]	1	3,200
2	Returns and allowances	2	
3	Subtract line 2 from line 1	3	3,200
4	Cost of goods sold (from line 42)	4	
5	**Gross profit.** Subtract line 4 from line 3	5	3,200
6	Other income, including federal and state gasoline or fuel tax credit or refund (see instructions)	6	
7	**Gross income.** Add lines 5 and 6 ▶	7	3,200

Part II Expenses. Enter expenses for business use of your home **only** on line 30.

8	Advertising	8		18	Office expense (see instructions)	18	
9	Car and truck expenses (see instructions)	9	187	19	Pension and profit-sharing plans	19	
				20	Rent or lease (see instructions):		
10	Commissions and fees	10		a	Vehicles, machinery, and equipment	20a	
11	Contract labor (see instructions)	11		b	Other business property	20b	
12	Depletion	12		21	Repairs and maintenance	21	
13	Depreciation and section 179 expense deduction (not included in Part III) (see instructions)	13		22	Supplies (not included in Part III)	22	
				23	Taxes and licenses	23	
				24	Travel and meals:		
14	Employee benefit programs (other than on line 19)	14		a	Travel	24a	
15	Insurance (other than health)	15		b	Deductible meals (see instructions)	24b	12
16	Interest (see instructions):			25	Utilities	25	
a	Mortgage (paid to banks, etc.)	16a		26	Wages (less employment credits)	26	
b	Other	16b		27a	Other expenses (from line 48)	27a	
17	Legal and professional services	17		b	**Reserved for future use**	27b	

28	**Total expenses** before expenses for business use of home. Add lines 8 through 27a ▶	28	199
29	Tentative profit or (loss). Subtract line 28 from line 7	29	3,001
30	Expenses for business use of your home. Do not report these expenses elsewhere. Attach Form 8829 unless using the simplified method. See instructions. **Simplified method filers only:** Enter the total square footage of (a) your home: ______ and (b) the part of your home used for business: ______. Use the Simplified Method Worksheet in the instructions to figure the amount to enter on line 30	30	
31	**Net profit or (loss).** Subtract line 30 from line 29. • If a profit, enter on both **Schedule 1 (Form 1040), line 3,** and on **Schedule SE, line 2.** (If you checked the box on line 1, see instructions). Estates and trusts, enter on **Form 1041, line 3.** • If a loss, you **must** go to line 32.	31	3,001
32	If you have a loss, check the box that describes your investment in this activity. See instructions. • If you checked 32a, enter the loss on both **Schedule 1 (Form 1040), line 3,** and on **Schedule SE, line 2.** (If you checked the box on line 1, see the line 31 instructions). Estates and trusts, enter on **Form 1041, line 3.** • If you checked 32b, you **must** attach **Form 6198.** Your loss may be limited.	32a [ ] All investment is at risk. 32b [ ] Some investment is not at risk.	

For Paperwork Reduction Act Notice, see the separate instructions. Cat. No. 11334P **Schedule C (Form 1040) 2020**

(1) Expenses have been reduced by 86% as allocable to tax-free income. Nearly every minister has honoraria and fee income and related expenses that are reportable on Schedule C.

Note: Page 2 of Schedule C is not displayed in this sample return, but it should be completed to reflect the vehicle information.

SCHEDULE SE (Form 1040)
Department of the Treasury Internal Revenue Service (99)

Self-Employment Tax

▶ Go to *www.irs.gov/ScheduleSE* for instructions and the latest information.
▶ Attach to Form 1040, 1040-SR, or 1040-NR.

OMB No. 1545-0074
2020
Attachment Sequence No. **17**

Name of person with self-employment income (as shown on Form 1040, 1040-SR, or 1040-NR): Donald L. Hall
Social security number of person with **self-employment** income ▶ 482-11-6043

Part I Self-Employment Tax

Note: If your only income subject to self-employment tax is **church employee income,** see instructions for how to report your income and the definition of church employee income.

A If you are a minister, member of a religious order, or Christian Science practitioner **and** you filed Form 4361, but you had $400 or more of **other** net earnings from self-employment, check here and continue with Part I . . . . ▶ ☐

Skip lines 1a and 1b if you use the farm optional method in Part II. See instructions.

Line	Description	Box	Amount
1a	Net farm profit or (loss) from Schedule F, line 34, and farm partnerships, Schedule K-1 (Form 1065), box 14, code A	1a	
b	If you received social security retirement or disability benefits, enter the amount of Conservation Reserve Program payments included on Schedule F, line 4b, or listed on Schedule K-1 (Form 1065), box 20, code AH	1b	( )

Skip line 2 if you use the nonfarm optional method in Part II. See instructions.

Line	Description	Box	Amount
2	Net profit or (loss) from Schedule C, line 31; and Schedule K-1 (Form 1065), box 14, code A (other than farming). See instructions for other income to report or if you are a minister or member of a religious order	2	1,780
3	Combine lines 1a, 1b, and 2	3	1,780
4a	If line 3 is more than zero, multiply line 3 by 92.35% (0.9235). Otherwise, enter amount from line 3. **Note:** If line 4a is less than $400 due to Conservation Reserve Program payments on line 1b, see instructions.	4a	1,644
b	If you elect one or both of the optional methods, enter the total of lines 15 and 17 here	4b	
c	Combine lines 4a and 4b. If less than $400, **stop;** you don't owe self-employment tax. **Exception:** If less than $400 and you had **church employee income,** enter -0- and continue ▶	4c	1,644
5a	Enter your **church employee income** from Form W-2. See instructions for definition of church employee income	5a	
b	Multiply line 5a by 92.35% (0.9235). If less than $100, enter -0-	5b	
6	Add lines 4c and 5b	6	1,644
7	Maximum amount of combined wages and self-employment earnings subject to social security tax or the 6.2% portion of the 7.65% railroad retirement (tier 1) tax for 2020	7	137,700
8a	Total social security wages and tips (total of boxes 3 and 7 on Form(s) W-2) and railroad retirement (tier 1) compensation. If $137,700 or more, skip lines 8b through 10, and go to line 11	8a	
b	Unreported tips subject to social security tax from Form 4137, line 10	8b	
c	Wages subject to social security tax from Form 8919, line 10	8c	
d	Add lines 8a, 8b, and 8c	8d	
9	Subtract line 8d from line 7. If zero or less, enter -0- here and on line 10 and go to line 11 ▶	9	137,700
10	Multiply the **smaller** of line 6 or line 9 by 12.4% (0.124)	10	204
11	Multiply line 6 by 2.9% (0.029)	11	48
12	**Self-employment tax.** Add lines 10 and 11. Enter here and on **Schedule 2 (Form 1040), line 4**	12	252
13	**Deduction for one-half of self-employment tax.** Multiply line 12 by 50% (0.50). Enter here and on **Schedule 1 (Form 1040), line 14**	13	126

Part II Optional Methods To Figure Net Earnings (see instructions)

Farm Optional Method. You may use this method **only** if **(a)** your gross farm income[1] wasn't more than $8,460, **or (b)** your net farm profits[2] were less than $6,107.

Line	Description	Box	Amount
14	Maximum income for optional methods	14	5,640
15	Enter the **smaller** of: two-thirds (2/3) of gross farm income[1] (not less than zero) **or** $5,640. Also, include this amount on line 4b above	15	

Nonfarm Optional Method. You may use this method **only** if **(a)** your net nonfarm profits[3] were less than $6,107 and also less than 72.189% of your gross nonfarm income,[4] **and (b)** you had net earnings from self-employment of at least $400 in 2 of the prior 3 years. **Caution:** You may use this method no more than five times 126

Line	Description	Box	Amount
16	Subtract line 15 from line 14	16	
17	Enter the **smaller** of: two-thirds (2/3) of gross nonfarm income[4] (not less than zero) **or** the amount on line 16. Also, include this amount on line 4b above	17	

[1] From Sch. F, line 9; and Sch. K-1 (Form 1065), box 14, code B.
[2] From Sch. F, line 34; and Sch. K-1 (Form 1065), box 14, code A—minus the amount you would have entered on line 1b had you not used the optional method.
[3] From Sch. C, line 31; and Sch. K-1 (Form 1065), box 14, code A.
[4] From Sch. C, line 7; and Sch. K-1 (Form 1065), box 14, code C.

For Paperwork Reduction Act Notice, see your tax return instructions. Cat. No. 11358Z **Schedule SE (Form 1040) 2020**

Line 2 – See Attachment 1 on page 186 for the calculation of this amount.

Line 6 – This line results in the deduction of a portion of the self-employment tax liability.

Attachment 1.
Computation of expenses, allocable to tax-free ministerial income, that are nondeductible.

		Taxable	Tax-Free	Total
% of nondeductible expenses				
Parsonage allowance:				
Ministerial retirement benefits designated as housing allowance	$ 19,500			
Actual expenses	20,500			
Fair rental value of home (including furnishings and utilities)	25,000			
Taxable portion of allowance	0			
Tax-free portion of allowance (lesser of amount designated, actual expenses, or fair rental value)			19,500	19,500
Gross income from occasional guest preaching engagements		3,200		3,200
Ministerial Income		$ 3,200	$ 19,500	$ 22,700

% of nondeductible expenses: $19,500/$22,700 = 86%

Schedule C Deduction Computation

	Total	Deductible 14%	Nondeductible 86%
Mileage (2,316 miles x 57.5 cents per mile)	$ 1,332	$ 187	$ 1,145
Meal expenses ($175 less 50% reduction)	88	12	76
Unadjusted Schedule C expenses	1,420	199	1,221

Attachment 2.
Computation for Schedule SE (Form 1040)

Gross income from Schedule C	$ 3,200
Less:	
Unadjusted Schedule C expenses	(1,420)
Net Self-Employed Income – Schedule SE, Line 2 (See page 185)	$ 1,780

Housing Allowance Worksheet
Minister Living in a Home Minister Owns or Is Buying

Minister's name: Donald L. Hall

For the period January 1, 20 20 to December 31, 20 20

Date designation approved December 20, 2019

Allowable Housing Expenses *(expenses paid by minister from current income)*

	Actual
Utilities *(gas, electricity, water)* and trash collection	$ 6,500
Local telephone expense *(base charge)*	
Decoration and redecoration	3,000
Structural maintenance and repair	7,600
Landscaping, gardening, and pest control	
Furnishings *(purchase, repair, replacement)*	3,000
Personal property insurance on minister-owned contents	100
Personal property taxes on contents	200
Umbrella liability insurance	100
TOTAL	$ 20,500 (A)
Properly designated housing allowance	$ 19,500 (B)
Fair rental value of home, including furnishings, plus utilities	$ 25,000 (C)

The amount excludable from income for federal income tax purposes is the lowest of A, B, or C.

9898 ☐ VOID ☐ CORRECTED

PAYER'S name, street address, city or town, state or province, country, ZIP or foreign postal code, and phone no.		1 Gross distribution	OMB No. 1545-0119	Distributions From Pensions, Annuities, Retirement or Profit-Sharing Plans, IRAs, Insurance Contracts, etc.
XYZ Retirement Fund 2055 Castle Street Indianapolis, IN 46950		$ 19500	2020	
		2a Taxable amount $	Form 1099-R	
		2b Taxable amount not determined ☒	Total distribution ☐	Copy A For Internal Revenue Service Center
PAYER'S TIN 79-0179214	RECIPIENT'S TIN 482-11-6043	3 Capital gain (included in box 2a) $	4 Federal income tax withheld $	File with Form 1096.
RECIPIENT'S name Daniel L. Hall		5 Employee contributions/ Designated Roth contributions or insurance premiums $	6 Net unrealized appreciation in employer's securities $	For Privacy Act and Paperwork Reduction Act Notice, see the **2020 General Instructions for Certain Information Returns.**
Street address (including apt. no.) 804 Linden Avenue		7 Distribution code(s) 7	IRA/ SEP/ SIMPLE ☐	8 Other $ %	
City or town, state or province, country, and ZIP or foreign postal code Pensacola, FL 32502		9a Your percentage of total distribution %	9b Total employee contributions $	

10 Amount allocable to IRR within 5 years	11 1st year of desig. Roth contrib.	12 FATCA filing requirement	14 State tax withheld	15 State/Payer's state no.	16 State distribution
$		☐	$ $		$ $
Account number (see instructions)		13 Date of payment	17 Local tax withheld $ $	18 Name of locality	19 Local distribution $ $

Form **1099-R** Cat. No. 14436Q www.irs.gov/Form1099R Department of the Treasury - Internal Revenue Service

Do Not Cut or Separate Forms on This Page — Do Not Cut or Separate Forms on This Page

Index

Projected 2021 Filing Dates

January

15 Quarterly Estimated Taxes (last payment for prior tax period)

February

15 W-4 (if claimed an exemption, to continue same exemption in current year)

April

15 Personal tax returns due (unless automatic extension, see October 15)

15 Quarterly Estimated Taxes, if not paid with return (first payment for current tax year)

June

15 Quarterly Estimated Taxes (2nd payment for current tax year)

September

15 Quarterly Estimated Taxes (3rd payment for current tax year)

October

15 Personal tax returns due (if automatic extension)

Biggest Tax Mistakes Made by Ministers

1. Filing as self-employed for income tax purposes on the church salary, using tax benefits only available to employees, and becoming vulnerable to reclassification by the IRS to employee status. (Chapter 1)

2. Failure to have unreimbursed medical expenses covered under a properly documented plan. (Chapter 3)

3. Failing to have at least a modest housing allowance designated when living in a church-provided parsonage. (Chapter 4)

4. Failure to understand the implications of the fair rental value test associated with the housing exclusion. (Chapter 4)

5. Failure of ministers to use an accountable reimbursement plan. (Chapter 5)

6. Not documenting reimbursable business expenses to reflect business purpose, business relationship, cost, time, and place. (Chapter 5)

7. Failing to keep a log of reimbursable miles driven when using personal vehicles for church purposes. (Chapter 5)

8. Insisting that the church deduct FICA-type Social Security from ministerial compensation. (Chapter 6)

9. Improperly opting out of Social Security because of the belief that it is not a good investment. (Chapter 6)

10. Failure to avoid tax underpayment penalties. (Chapter 7)

Tax and Finance Questions Most Frequently Asked by Ministers

1. **Social Security filing status.** Should I have FICA-type Social Security tax withheld from my pay or pay self-employment Social Security tax calculated on Schedule SE and pay it with my income tax return? (Chapter 1)

2. **Income tax filing status.** Should I file as an employee (receiving a Form W-2 from my employer) or as an independent contractor (receiving a Form 1099-NEC) for income tax purposes? (Chapter 1)

3. **Unreimbursed medical expenses.** Which of the three approved plans should I use to get tax-free treatment for my unreimbursed medical expenses: health savings account (HSA), health reimbursement arrangement (HRA), or health care flexible spending account (FSA)? (Chapter 3)

4. **Structuring the pay package.** How should my pay package be structured to achieve the best tax benefit for me? (Chapter 3)

5. **Fringe benefit planning.** How do I determine which of the fringe benefits I receive are tax-free, tax-deferred, or taxable? (Chapter 3)

6. **Housing allowance exclusion.** How much can I exclude as a housing allowance for income tax purposes? (Chapter 4)

7. **Accountable expense reimbursements.** Do the payments I am receiving from the church or ministry for expenses qualify as tax-free reimbursements? (Chapter 5)

8. **Social Security allowance.** Is the Social Security allowance I received taxable for income and Social Security tax purposes? (Chapter 6)

9. **Opting out of Social Security.** Under what conditions is it appropriate for me to opt out of Social Security? (Chapter 6)

10. **Paying income and Social Security taxes.** Should I have enough income tax withheld from my salary to cover my income and Social Security tax obligation, or should I pay quarterly estimated taxes? (Chapter 6)

The **Church Knowledge Center** contains hundreds of documents on church finance, governance, stewardship, and more. In addition, check out the ECFA website for special church webinars, newsletters, and other practical learning opportunities.

ECFA-certified churches have full access to these resources as a membership benefit, while ECFA friends are invited to access a basic level of Knowledge Center resources at no cost.

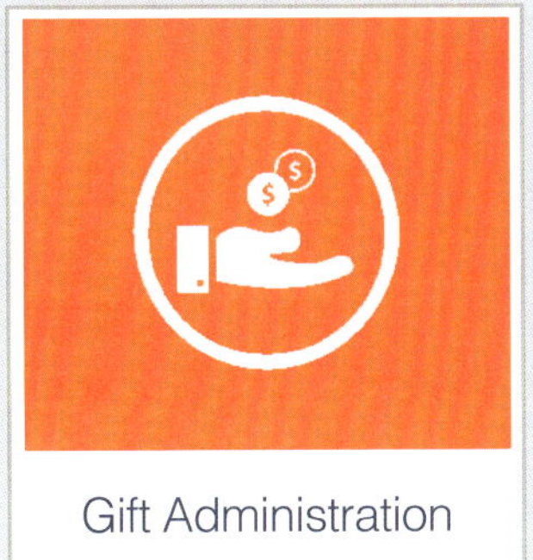

ECFA.org/KnowledgeCenter

ECFA.church/KnowledgeCenter